THE HITCH-HIKER'S GUIDE TO HEAVEN

John Blanchard

EP BOOKS
Faverdale North
Darlington
DL3 0PH, England

web: http://www.epbooks.org

e-mail: sales@epbooks.org

EP Books are distributed in the USA by:
JPL Distribution
3741 Linden Avenue Southeast
Grand Rapids, MI 49548
E-mail: orders@jpldistribution.com
Tel: 877.683.6935

First published 2013

British Library Cataloguing in Publication Data available

ISBN: 978-0-85234-938-0

John Blanchard has written a full book. Full of Christ. Full of Scripture. Full of wisdom. Full of comfort. Full of hope. Full of interest. If you have longed for a book that answers your questions about heaven, makes you eager to go there and tells you how to get there, you have found it in this full book. Read it, heed it and travel happily to heaven through the saving work of the Lord Jesus Christ.

Roger Ellsworth, Pastor, Parkview Baptist Church, Jackson, Tennessee.

Unlike some others, John Blanchard makes no claim to have been to heaven yet— not even briefly. But the truth is that in *The Hitch Hiker's Guide to Heaven* he provides us with something far better than speculations or personal experiences— a crystal clear, vibrant, biblical, Christ-centered, and at times quite beautiful, explanation of what heaven is and how to get there. Instead of personal speculation and experiences we are pointed to the revelation God has given to all his people. The result is a deep sense of reliability and a joyful satisfaction in the anticipation of both heaven and the promised resurrection.

Manageable in size, easy but elegant in style, *The Hitch-Hiker's Guide to Heaven* is a book of quiet but evident and joyful assurance because it points the reader to the (alas too often ignored or neglected) heart of heaven: being with Christ. Readers of Dr Blanchard's books have come to expect this focus from him. Far from disappointing us he has given us another 'must read'.

Sinclair Ferguson, theologian and author, Dundee, Scotland

Typically, John Blanchard has dug deep into his subject. This will make you long for the time when the invisible becomes visible, the unknowable knowable, and the unimaginable a reality. But, again typically, we are not allowed only to hope and long—there are some serious implications and John challenges us to face up to them.

Brian Edwards, preacher and author, Surbiton, England

The Bible commands us to set our minds and hearts on things above. Without hope our hearts grow sick. We are so earthbound that we need help to meditate on heaven. Yet so much said today about it is based on speculation or claims to personal revelation. John Blanchard avoids these pitfalls and grounds his teaching on heaven on the solid ground of the Bible. One need not agree with everything he says for this book to enlighten your mind and renew your hope. He helps pilgrims on earth to peer at the Celestial City through the telescope of Holy Scripture. What we see ravishes the heart!

Dr Joel R. Beeke, President of Puritan Reformed Theological Seminary, Grand Rapids, Michigan

Comprehensive, informative, thorough and reassuring, full of illustrations and great quotations. Easy to read, this will replace any wishful thinking about the future, with informed confidence based on timeless Scripture.

Charles Price, Senior Pastor, The Peoples Church, Toronto, Canada.

In the Introduction John Blanchard writes, 'I have for some time sensed the need for a ... book setting out basic biblical teaching on the subject (of heaven) arranged in such an accessible way that it will stimulate those whose "citizenship is in heaven" (Philippians 3:20) to look forward with growing enthusiasm to going home. Such a book should also encourage them to live in a way that reflects their destination and encourages others to join them. The pages that follow are my attempt to meet that need.' In *The Hitch-Hiker's Guide to Heaven* John Blanchard has more than succeeded in achieving these two goals. The volume is saturated with Scripture, studded with apt quotations, and is written with the simplicity, clarity, and authority we have come to associate with his preaching and writing. As a pastor I am regularly and intimately involved with people who are facing death or who have lost a loved one and I am staggered by the fuzzy, unbiblical thinking about death and heaven. I can't wait to put this volume in their hands, and to use some of what John has written in my preaching.

Leigh Robinson, Senior Pastor Rosebank Union Church, Johannesburg, South Africa.

This book, filled with real life stories and illustrations, brings the sublime realities of eternity and heaven into sharp focus. It is convicting to realise that we spend so little time thinking about the one place for which life on earth is but a brief period of preparation. Read this book, and let John Blanchard lead you by the hand and give you a panoramic view of what John Bunyan called the Celestial City so that you really long for heaven!

Conrad Mbewe, Pastor, Lusaka Baptist Church, Zambia.

Contents

Foreword

Shortly before his death from cancer on 4 April 2013, Roger Ebert, the celebrated *Chicago Sun-Times* film critic, expressed the increasingly widespread notion that death ends everything: 'Many readers have informed me that it is a tragic and dreary business to go into death without faith. I don't feel that way. I have no desire to live forever. The concept frightens me.'[1] He went on to say that as far as his plans for life after death were concerned he could say with the American poet, essayist and journalist Walt Whitman,

'I bequeath myself to the dirt to grow from the grass I love.
If you want me again, look for me under your boot-soles.'[2]

Ebert had no fear of Dante's Inferno and no hope of Milton's Paradise. Heaven was apparently nowhere in his thinking—and he was not alone. In an earlier era the Methodist preacher W. E.

Sangster bemoaned the fact that 'preaching is in the shadows, the world does not believe in it.'

We might say the same today of heaven. The prospect of a new life *then* is increasingly obscured by a preoccupation with our best life *now*. The pulpit is largely to blame. The American preacher A. W. Tozer once observed that the twentieth-century church was the best disguised set of pilgrims the world had ever seen. I wonder what he would make of us now? Confusion or disinterest in the pew is traceable to fogginess or silence in our pulpits. We would do well to take a leaf from the seventeenth-century British preacher Richard Baxter, who worked hard to ensure his church members understood that death is not the end of the pilgrimage, but merely the end of the beginning. He filled their minds and hearts with the 'age to come' (the *then*) so that they might live godly lives in 'the present age' (the *now*).

Jesus prayed, 'Father, I want those you have given me to be with me where I am' (John 17:24, NIV). As then, so now, our confidence in prospect of this reality does not lie in our ability to visualize it but in the total reliability of the one who promised it! When we trust him wholly, we find him wholly true. When we take a walk through the portrait gallery of saints of old we are reminded that, 'These all died in faith, not having received the things promised, but having seen them and greeted them from afar, and having acknowledged that they were strangers and exiles on the earth' (Hebrews 11: 13).

An up to date example of such faith is contained in this excerpt from the worship bulletin of a funeral service. These are the words of the deceased, who had penned them in prospect of his death.

'As I have walked through the valley of the shadow of death, I have walked hand in hand with Jesus, the one who has already walked through that valley and come out the other side, alive, raised from the dead. And as I hold his hand and trust him, I too am raised with him ... For most of my Christian life I have wanted to see Jesus face to face, to join in with the heavenly chorus in his presence around his royal throne and declare his praise in new ways. Something else has grown through the years: an abiding sense that this is not for me alone ... I have often thought of coming to heaven as Jesus standing at the finish line of a race awaiting those looking for him, trusting in him, pursuing him ...'[3]

These words are an apt introduction to this book by John Blanchard because he writes in such a manner that it is impossible not to hear the call of the evangelist. Refusing to be side-tracked by focusing on debatable details, he focuses on what is main and plain. He sets before us the biblical picture of 'a great multitude that no one could number, from every nation, from all tribes and peoples and languages, standing before the throne and before the Lamb' (Revelation 7:9).

Yet John Blanchard is also concerned to build up believers in their faith, and in *The Hitch-hiker's Guide to Heaven* he not only helps us to understand why the apostle Paul told the Philippians that to be with Christ is 'far better', he also stirs within us a longing to see others added to the company. In the meantime, as we run the race marked out for us, we affirm these words from Richard Baxter:

My knowledge of this life is small,
The eye of faith is dim.

It is enough that Christ knows all
And I shall be with Him.[4]

Alistair Begg
Parkside Church
Cleveland
Ohio

Preface

The title of this book was triggered off by *The Hitch-hiker's Guide to the Galaxy*, the zany science fiction comedy series created by the English dramatist Douglas Adams (1952–2001). Sometimes abbreviated to 'H2G2', it eventually spawned six novels, several stage shows, three series of comic book adaptions, a Hollywood film and a computer game.

Douglas Adams was firmly convinced that God did not exist. He called himself not merely an atheist, but a 'radical atheist', one who was absolutely sure that his position was valid. The well-known atheist Richard Dawkins dedicated his 2006 anti-God diatribe *The God Delusion* to Adams, describing him as 'my cleverest, funniest, wittiest, tallest *and possibly only* convert'.[5] The idea of two leading atheists pointing me towards the title for a book that glories in the reality of a God who is 'from everlasting to everlasting' (Psalm 90:2), who tells us that 'heaven is my throne' (Isaiah 66:1) and who promises that those who trust him will 'dwell in the house of the LORD for ever' (Psalm 23:6) was more than I could resist—so *The Hitch-hiker's Guide to Heaven* it is.

In the Preface to *The God Delusion* Richard Dawkins says, 'If this book works as I intend, religious readers who open it will be atheists when they put it down.'[6] There may well have been such cases, but it has been delightful to read of those who have made the reverse journey, beginning to read *The God Delusion* as atheists, agnostics or sceptics but becoming believers in God by the time they had come to an end of its puerile attempts to write him off. While *The Hitch-hiker's Guide to Heaven* has been written for Christians, I have set no limits on how God might graciously use it to his glory. As God 'has put eternity into man's heart' (Ecclesiastes 3:11), I pray that those who may deny or doubt the very existence of God as they begin to read it will by the time they put it down have been drawn to put their trust in the one who is 'Lord of heaven and earth' (Matthew 11:25).

Some years ago I was in Jerusalem and needed to find a post office. Deep in the confusing little streets and alleyways of the oldest part of the city late one afternoon, I had no idea where to find one. When I asked a shopkeeper for help, he began to give me directions; but when my eyes glazed over he looked at his watch, shrugged his shoulders, locked up his shop and said, 'Come with me, I am the way.' Hundreds of people were swirling all around us, but I clung to him like a limpet until he had taken me safely to where I wanted to go. The dictionary definition of 'hitch-hike' is 'travel by getting free lifts in passing vehicles',[7] and to all intents and purposes I was a hitch-hiker—relying on him to take me to my destination.

When Jesus was speaking to his disciples about heaven he told them, 'I am the way' (John 14:6). Later in the New Testament we find Christians described as 'belonging to the Way' (Acts 9:2), a term that is used five more times in the early history of the church (see Acts 19:9, 23; 22:4; 24:14, 22) and Luke calls the Christian faith 'the way of the Lord' (Acts 18:25) and 'the way of God' (Acts 18:26). The church's persecutors called the Way 'a sect', but Paul made it crystal clear that it was not a heretical innovation but that its followers worshipped 'the God of our fathers' and believed 'everything laid down by the Law and written in the Prophets' (Acts 24:14). These references became more grist to my title's mill!

My original intention was to write a small booklet reminding readers of the twin certainties of death and the afterlife, showing them the eternal realities of heaven and hell, and then pointing to the only way to get right with God. However, I soon discovered that I wanted to say much more about heaven, so I decided on two publications instead of one. The first, a forty-four page evangelistic booklet entitled *Anyone for Heaven?*[8] was published in 2012. You are holding the second one in your hands.

As it goes into circulation I want to express my thanks to Alistair Begg for kindly writing a Foreword, and to Owen Bourgaize, Brian Edwards, Paul Hill, Graham Hind, Betty Thomas and Curtis Thomas, who read the manuscript one chapter at a time and made many valuable suggestions. I am also grateful to Andrew Shrimpton for being such a superb editor. My special thanks to Marlene Williams who meticulously read every word (several times!) and without whose outstanding help this book would not be as it is.

The subject matter of the book guarantees that readers will easily think of areas not covered and of others that are not handled as they would have wished. For all its weaknesses I take full responsibility, but as God once used 'the jawbone of a donkey'[9] to help in accomplishing his purposes I am daring to pray that he will make this book a means of blessing to those who read it.

John Blanchard

Banstead

Surrey

September 2013

Introduction

To celebrate the arrival of the third millennium nearly one million people in Sydney, Australia lined the city's harbour to enjoy one of the greatest firework displays ever seen, a spectacle shared by countless millions on television all around the world.

Sydney has a well-deserved reputation for New Year's Eve fireworks, but this extravaganza beat anything that had gone before, with illuminated barges, laser beams bouncing off the magnificent Sydney Opera House, and rockets that exploded up to a height of a thousand metres. To get a close-up view, spectators crowded on to six thousand boats that jammed Sydney harbour. The dazzling, computer-generated show that saw pyrotechnics fired from the city's iconic harbour bridge, the Opera House, six city buildings and four barges and cost $3.5 million to produce lasted for twenty-four minutes and ended in an unforgettable way when the centre of the massive bridge was lit with one word in copperplate script: 'Eternity'. A remarkable story lies behind the organizers' choice of this word and the style in which it was written.

Arthur Stace was born in the Sydney suburb of Balmain on 9 February 1884 and was raised in poverty as his parents were alcoholics. He survived by eating food he had stolen or found in waste bins. He became a ward of state by the time he was twelve and was serving a prison sentence as an alcoholic criminal in his mid-teens. He earned what money he could by working as a 'cockatoo' (a look-out) for gambling dens and brothels. Later, he enlisted in the Australian Army and served in France, but in 1919 he was medically discharged, suffering from bronchitis and pleurisy.

Eleven years later his life was revolutionized when he was converted to Christ after hearing a sermon in St Barnabas Church, Broadway (now popularly known as 'Barneys') in the heart of Sydney and he immediately became gripped by the reality of eternity. Two years later he heard a well-known Australian evangelist, John Ridley, preach a sermon called 'The echoes of eternity', based on Isaiah 57:15. In the course of the sermon Ridley cried, 'Eternity, eternity! I wish that I could sound or shout that word to everyone in the streets of Sydney. You've got to meet it; where will you spend eternity?' This affected Arthur Stace so deeply that he sensed God calling him to write down the word 'Eternity'. Although he was hardly able to write his own name the word 'Eternity' came out in beautiful copperplate script, leading him years later to confess, 'I couldn't understand it, and I still can't.'

From then on he felt his mission was to share this word with the entire city. He would often leave his home at 5 a.m. to chalk the word 'Eternity' on footpaths and buildings and in countless other places. The city council had rules about defacing pavements, but somehow Stace kept up his 'mission'. It has been estimated that in the course of the following thirty-five years he wrote the word some 500,000 times, always in immaculate copperplate. One of his signs, chalked on a piece of cardboard, is now in Canberra's National Museum of Australia, while a wrought aluminium replica of 'Eternity' in his copperplate writing is embedded in a footpath in Sydney's Town Hall Square as a permanent memorial to a man who became known as 'Mr Eternity' and was a legend in his own lifetime.

Arthur Stace died of a stroke on 30 July 1967 at the age of 83 after bequeathing his body to the University of Sydney for medical science, but he bequeathed much more. Thirty-two years later, at midnight on 31 December 1999, millions of people all over the world had their attention taken away from thoughts about millennia, centuries, decades, years, months, weeks, days, hours, minutes and seconds, and suddenly focused on the single word 'Eternity' emblazoned in copperplate lettering on Sydney Harbour Bridge—a one-word summary of something towards which every living person is moving.

The American theologian Albert Barnes (1798–1870) once wrote, 'Life, if properly viewed in any aspect, is great, but mainly great when viewed in its relation to the world to come.'[10] Germany's Count Bismarck once said, 'Without the hope of eternal life, this life is not worth the effort of getting up in the morning.'[11] For Christians, the word 'eternity' should have a significance that is literally impossible to grasp in all its fullness, as for them it is virtually a synonym for heaven, when in a way that far surpasses anything they ever experience in this life, 'God ... will dwell with them, and they will be his people, and God himself will be with them as their God' (Revelation 21:3). Yet as an anonymous member of a religious community has said, 'For most Christians, life in heaven is no more than a supplement— of which they have but a very hazy notion—to life on earth. Life in heaven is seen somewhat as a postscript, an appendix, to a book whose text is formed by earthly life. But it is the opposite which is true. Our earthly life is but the preface to the book. Life in heaven will be its main text, and this text is endless. To make use of another image, our earthly life is but a tunnel, narrow, dark—and very short—which opens onto a magnificent, sunlit landscape. We think too much of what our life now is. We do not think enough of what it will be.'[12]

The prospect of life in heaven should constantly be filling our hearts with wonder, love and praise, but many Christians can spend a lot of time shuffling around in the 'preface' without ever moving on to explore the 'text'. Others may never have studied in any depth what the Bible teaches about heaven or never read a book on the subject, with the result that their ideas are sketchy at best, and may not go far beyond the words of a few hymns on the subject.

Cinderella?

The original story of Cinderella may go back to classical antiquity, but it is still popular today and the word 'Cinderella' has come to mean 'a person or thing that is undeservedly neglected or ignored'.[13] Apart from its first two chapters there is a sense in which the entire Bible is about man's eternal destiny, and in particular the destiny of God's people; yet it would hardly be an exaggeration to call heaven a Cinderella of Christian doctrine.

To begin with, the subject is given very little space in some of Christianity's major creedal statements. *The Apostles' Creed* (which reflects what Jesus' original apostles taught, but was not put together by them) limits what it says on the subject to the two words 'life everlasting'. The *Athanasian Creed* (which may or may not have been written in the fourth century by Athanasius, the twentieth Bishop of Alexandria) merely states, 'They that have done good shall go into life everlasting.' *The Nicene Creed*, which was adopted by the Christian Church at the first Council of Nicaea in AD 325, settles for a phrase referring to 'the life of the world to come'. The *Westminster Confession of Faith*, drawn up in 1646 by 'learned, godly and judicious Divines' on the directions of the English Parliament, refers to the subject on only one or two pages, stating that 'the righteous' will 'go into everlasting life'. The 1689 *Baptist Confession of Faith*, leaning heavily on the Westminster Confession, simply uses the same words.

Perhaps these examples are not too surprising, as the creeds and confessions concerned are meant to be bite-size condensations of major doctrinal truths, not detailed theological statements. What *is* surprising is the small amount of space given to the subject of heaven in some of the best-known volumes of systematic theology. The French Reformer John Calvin (1509–1564) wrote his monumental *Institutes of the Christian Religion*, the original Latin version of which first appeared in 1536 and was later revised and expanded to nearly 1,300 pages in some editions, but it has fewer than two pages directly related to heaven. The British Puritan preacher John Owen (1616–1683) has been called 'the greatest theologian in English history' and his sixteen volumes of concentrated theological exposition take up over nine thousand pages, but I found fewer than twenty pages directly relating to heaven. The American theologian Robert Lewis Dabney (1820–1898), called by his contemporary theologian A. A. Hodge (1823–1886) 'the best teacher of theology in the United States, if not in the world', published the gist of lectures he gave at Union Theological Seminary, Virginia under the shortened title of *Systematic*

Theology. The book runs to just over nine hundred pages, but only two of these are devoted to what he calls 'the nature of eternal life'.[14] The American theologian William Shedd (1820–1894) wrote a three-volume *Dogmatic Theology*, with only two pages on heaven. Another American theologian, Augustus H. Strong (1836–1921) produced a three-volume *Systematic Theology* totalling 1,116 pages, only four pages of which deal with the final state of God's people. The Scottish theologian Stewart Salmond (1838–1905) wrote *The Christian Doctrine of Immortality*, yet with eight hundred subjects listed in its index there is no mention of heaven. The Dutch theologian Louis Berkhof (1873–1957) has a *Systematic Theology* with nearly eight hundred pages, yet gives less than a single page to what he calls 'the eternal abode of the righteous'.[15] The British preacher D. Martyn Lloyd-Jones (1899–1981) based his three-volume *Great Doctrines of the Bible* on lectures he gave at Westminster Chapel, London, yet fewer than two pages deal with believers' eternal state. The contemporary American theologian Robert L. Reymond's *A New Systematic Theology of the Christian Faith* has 1,210 pages, and although the chapter on Biblical Eschatology runs to eighty-five pages, less than a single page describes the final state of believers and the word 'Heaven' is not listed as a subject in the index.

Composers of Christian hymns and songs have also seemed reluctant to concentrate on the subject. A British hymnbook,[16] first published in 1977, has 901 compositions, but only fifteen in the section headed 'Death and Glory'; and of these only two were written later than the nineteenth century. Another hymnbook,[17] first published in 2000 and widely used in evangelical circles, has 976 compositions, but only twelve in the section headed 'Heaven and Glory', and of these only three were written in the twentieth century or later.

Nothing in these paragraphs implies any criticism of those who compiled the words concerned, yet the details seem to sit strangely with the fact that throughout both the Old and New Testaments one writer after another refers to heaven in prophecy and poetry, exhortations and principles, promises and precepts, sometimes briefly and cryptically, but sometimes in extensive passages. Take away all the references, stated or implied, to the eternal destiny of God's people and the Bible would be not merely a mystery but a mockery. The American preacher A. N. Martin is not wide of the mark when he claims, 'If I took a pair of scissors and clipped out every explicit and implicit reference to heaven from Genesis to Revelation I would be left with a very thin Bible.'

Windows on the word

Words like 'heaven' or 'heavenly' are often used to describe something exceptionally enjoyable, such as a deliciously satisfying meal, arriving safely after a long or difficult journey, returning home after a stay in hospital, complete relief from chronic pain, lying on a sunlit beach while on holiday, slumping into a favourite armchair after a hard day's work, or finally collapsing into bed at the end of an exhausting day. Using the words in circumstances like these has no direct bearing on the Bible's teaching about heaven, but the *Oxford Dictionary of English* definition of 'heaven' as 'A place, state, or experience of supreme bliss'[18] helps to confirm that the concept of heaven is embedded into many people's minds. The Bible is an infinitely higher authority and tells us much more.

In the Old Testament, the Hebrew word most often used for 'heaven' is the plural *samayim*, which means 'the heights' or 'upper regions'. In the New Testament, the Greek word most often used for 'heaven' is *ouranos*, which comes from a root meaning 'to lift up' or 'to elevate' and occurs nearly three hundred times, ninety-four times in the plural. The general sense of all the Bible words for heaven is 'that which is above';[19] but in both the Old and New Testaments the words concerned are versatile and their exact meaning becomes clear only when they are read in their immediate context and in the light of what we are told elsewhere in the Bible. A few examples will help to make this clear. The opening verse in the Old Testament tells us, 'In the beginning, God created the heavens [*samayim*] and the earth' (Genesis 1:1). The Hebrews had no word for 'universe' and 'the heavens and the earth' is a way of saying that God created all reality outside of himself; in other words, he created everything that is not God. On the other hand, when God commanded, 'Let birds fly above the earth across the expanse of the heavens [*samayim*]' (Genesis 1:20), the word means only the envelope of air immediately surrounding our planet.

In the New Testament, there are times when 'heaven' simply means the sky, or the earth's immediate atmosphere. For example, Jesus once told his disciples that sometimes 'the sky [*ouranos*] is red' (Matthew 16:3) and on another occasion he spoke of 'birds of the air [*ouranos*]' (Matthew 8:20). In other places it refers to galactic space, such as when the writer of Hebrews reminds his readers that the Old Testament patriarch Abraham's descendants were, as promised by God, 'as many as the stars of heaven [*ouranos*]' (Hebrews 11:12).

It is also used as a metonym, a figure of speech in which a word is used to describe a thing or person associated with it. In the United Kingdom we are sometimes told, 'The Crown says ...' about a statement from the Queen, in the same way that 'Downing Street announces ...' introduces a statement from the

Prime Minister or the Government. When the Old Testament tells us that people in serious trouble 'cried to heaven [*samayim*]' (2 Chronicles 32:20), they were not merely throwing words into space, they were calling upon God. When the prodigal son in Jesus' famous parable comes to his senses and cries, 'I have sinned against heaven [*ouranos*]' (Luke 15:18), he means that he has sinned against God. In the same way, the phrase 'the kingdom of heaven [*ouranos*]', which occurs many times in the New Testament, means the kingdom of God. This comes across very clearly when Jesus uses both phrases to emphasize one particular truth (see Matthew 19:23–24). Used in this way, 'heaven' is a synonym for God, who tells us that he is everywhere: 'Do I not fill heaven and earth?' (Jeremiah 23:24). Theologians call this God's omnipresence, meaning that he is present in every part of the universe at one and the same time. As Louis Berkhof puts it, 'God fills every part of it with his whole Being', yet he 'transcends all space and is not subject to its limitations'.[20] This is what Paul has in mind when he tells community leaders in Athens that God is 'not far from each one of us' and then quotes an ancient Greek poet Epimenides by adding, 'In him we live and move and have our being' (Acts 17:27–28).

While this is true, both the Old and New Testaments specifically speak of heaven as God's dwelling place. One of the Old Testament Psalmists tells us, 'The LORD looks down from heaven; he sees all the children of man' (Psalm 33:13). The prophet Isaiah prays, 'Look down from heaven and see, from your holy and beautiful habitation' (Isaiah 63:15), while a little later God confirms to the prophet, 'Heaven is my throne, and the earth is my footstool' (Isaiah 66:1). In the New Testament, Jesus teaches his followers to pray, 'Our Father in heaven'

(Matthew 6:9), and John refers to God as 'the God of heaven' (Revelation 11:13).

Most importantly, the Bible shows us the unique relationship between Jesus and heaven. He calls himself the one 'who comes down from heaven' (John 6:33) and has no hesitation in saying to his contemporaries, 'You are from below; I am from above. You are of this world; I am not of this world' (John 8:23), making a clear distinction between himself and them. In the course of what has become known as his high priestly prayer he says 'And now, Father, glorify me in your own presence with the glory that I had with you before the world existed' (John 17:5). Shortly afterwards he straightforwardly claims, 'I came from God' (John 8:42). No other human being in all of history could credibly make statements like these. Towards the end of his earthly life he tells his followers, 'I came from the Father and have come into the world, and now I am leaving the world and going to the Father' (John 16:28). Forty days after his resurrection from the dead he had a final meeting with his disciples and was then 'carried up into heaven' (Luke 24:51).

Paul confirms that after his earthly life, Jesus was 'taken up in glory' (1 Timothy 3:16) and is now 'in the heavenly places, far above all rule and authority and power and dominion, and above every name that is named, not only in this age but also in the one to come' (Ephesians 1:20–21). Elsewhere, we are told that Jesus is 'seated at the right hand of the throne of God' (Hebrews 12:2). This tells us that he is in a position of active pre-eminence in heaven. He is not resting, but reigning. He is what we might call the executive director of all the benefits he accomplished for believers through his incarnation, life, death, resurrection and ascension. As John Calvin puts it, Jesus is 'invested with lordship over heaven and earth'.[21]

Nor is this the end of the story. When his disciples were depressed at the thought of him being put to death, Jesus assures them that he is going to 'my Father's house' (John 14:2) to prepare a place for them, then promises, 'I will come again and will take you to myself, that where I am you may be also' (John 14:3). At Jesus' ascension into heaven an angel tells his disciples, 'This Jesus, who was taken up from you into heaven, will come in the same way as you saw him go into heaven' (Acts 1:11). Finally, in a revelation of eternity, the apostle John 'heard every creature in heaven and on earth and under the earth and in the sea, and all that is in them, saying, "To him who sits on the throne and to the Lamb be blessing and honour and glory and might for ever and ever!"' (Revelation 5:13).

It is impossible to miss the implication of the unique links established in these last two paragraphs. Jesus came from heaven; while on earth he was in constant communion with his Father in heaven; at his ascension he returned to heaven; he rules the universe from heaven; he will return from heaven to earth to usher in the end of the present age; he will gather all true believers to be with him in heaven and he will reign triumphantly in heaven for ever. This makes it clear that if we tried to use a compass to find heaven's location the needle would always point to Jesus. Put another way, if we were to take a sheet of paper and make a list of all that defines heaven, the first word to be written would have to be 'Jesus'. Simply put, the presence of Jesus is what makes heaven to be heaven.

A hefty theological tome about heaven may not immediately attract most Christians—and I am not qualified to write it. However, I have for some time sensed the need for a much smaller book setting out basic biblical teaching on the subject arranged in such an accessible way that it will stimulate those whose 'citizenship is in heaven' (Philippians 3:20) to look forward with growing enthusiasm to going home. Such a book should also encourage them to live in a way that reflects their destination and encourages others to join them. The pages that follow are my attempt to meet that need.

I

Heaven now—
and then

Speaking at a meeting of 'Feed the Minds' in Leicester, Donald Coggan, Archbishop of Canterbury from 1974 to 1980, said, 'I do not think I shall ever land on the moon, but I hope to pass it one day on my way higher.' Many people would think this a cute way of describing what they hope will happen to them when they die, but is this true?—and if so, how much higher do they have in mind? On 21 October 2012 William Walker, one of the last surviving Battle of Britain pilots, died in an English hospital, seventy-two years after he narrowly escaped death when his Spitfire was shot down over the English Channel. In paying tribute to him, an RAF spokesman said, 'He has taken to the skies for the last time.'[22] The spokesman clearly had heaven in mind—but where did he think it was? For all their sincerity, the spokesman's words were as ambiguous as those in a hymn by the American songwriter Jessie Pounds that pictures heaven as being

'Land of the true, where we live anew; beautiful isle of somewhere.' We are not to think in these romantic terms, nor in the crassly literal terms used by the sixth-century religious leader who is said to have visited God in heaven and reported back that there was a distance of three days' journey between God's eyebrows.

As I write these words, NASA's Mars rover *Curiosity*, having taken eight months to get there, is wandering around the red planet gathering data and feeding it back to earth. It has been calculated that if we could travel at the speed of light (186,000 miles per second) we would reach the planet Venus in two minutes and eighteen seconds, Mercury in four minutes and thirty seconds and Jupiter in thirty-five minutes. Travelling at the same unimaginable speed it would take us over five hours to reach Pluto—and we would still not have left our solar system. Is heaven somewhere between here and Pluto? Astronomers tell us that what they call the universe extends for more than ten billion light years around us and contains billions of galaxies (some with billions of stars), billions of planets and perhaps billions of biospheres. Is heaven somewhere out there?

No space craft has ever reported seeing heaven, but does this mean that we will have to send one much farther into space if we want to find it? Is it possible that if we were to travel far enough we would eventually get there—and that when we did, we could hope to be welcomed by those living there? Stretching our imagination even further, could we even arrange trips back to earth to visit friends, family members or descendants?

One would hardly expect Christians to toy with these ideas, yet many make the fundamental mistake of thinking that heaven is a place or state somewhere 'up there', missing the vital point that there is no biblical basis for believing that heaven is a remote place beyond the outer limits of what we call 'deep space'. When the Bible uses the words 'up' and 'above' in relation to heaven, direction and distance are not the issues. Our planet is rotating on its axis at over a thousand miles an hour and moving around the sun at about 67,000 miles an hour, which means that (to give just one example) at any given moment what is 'up' in the United Kingdom is 'down' in Australia. Heaven both permeates and transcends space and in biblical terms there is no place on earth (or in space) which is nearer to heaven than any other.

Countless Christians also think that heaven will remain exactly as it is now. When they say of fellow Christians who have died, 'They are now in heaven,' they imagine their situation remaining unchanged for ever, regardless of what may happen to the cosmos. But in saying this they are missing the point that (strange as it may seem to some) the key to understanding the Bible's bottom line about heaven is to grasp what it reveals about the future state of the earth. When we begin to explore this, we find that the Bible paints a very different picture from what is popularly thought. It tells us about *heaven as it is at present* and *heaven as it will be in the future*.

Paradise

As Jesus was being crucified, one of the criminals being executed alongside him cried out, 'Jesus, remember me when you come into your kingdom' (Luke 23:42). This man had already confessed his own sin—he told his fellow criminal, 'We are receiving the due reward of our deeds'—and acknowledged that Jesus had 'done nothing wrong' (Luke 23:41). We can only guess at how much he had heard about him, but from what follows he seems to have sensed that Jesus was to reign as a king.

In a reply that was a wonderful example of God being able to do 'far more abundantly than all that we ask or think' (Ephesians 3:20) Jesus told him, 'Truly, I say to you, today you will be with me in Paradise' (Luke 23:43). Yet at the end of that day Jesus' body was lying in a tomb, where it remained until his resurrection three days later, while the criminal's body had been disposed of in some way. What Jesus promised him was that before the end of that day their *spirits* would be together in Paradise.

As it was Jesus who made this promise, we can be sure that it was fulfilled—and there is another possibility that would add a spine-tingling dimension to what happened. In those days the Valley of Ben Hinnom, outside the eastern wall of Jerusalem, was a public rubbish dump in which the city's garbage and filth was poured, and where the corpses of criminals were often flung and left to rot, be scavenged by wild animals or consumed by the fire that was always burning there. The shortened form of the original name for the Valley of Ben Hinnom was *Ge-hinnom*, of which the Greek translation became *Gehenna*, the very word that Jesus used eleven times when referring to hell. If the criminal's body was flung into the Valley of Ben Hinnom, the end of the first Good Friday saw his spirit with Jesus in Paradise (heaven as it is now), while his body lay in the very place Jesus used to illustrate some of the horrors of hell! Be that as it may, the spirits of Jesus and the criminal were no longer united to their bodies but separated from them and in what Jesus called Paradise.

Our English word 'paradise' translates the original word *paradeisos*, which the Greeks borrowed from the Persians, among whom it meant a beautiful garden or park, the kind of thing often belonging to a king. In the Septuagint (the first

Greek translation of the Old Testament) the word is used of the
setting in which man was first placed at his creation, while later
in the Old Testament a place of great blessing in God's presence
is called 'Eden, the garden of God' (Ezekiel 28:13). Other than in
the Good Friday incident, the word 'paradise' occurs in only two
other places in the New Testament. The first is when the apostle
Paul tells of having been 'caught up into paradise' (2 Corinthians
12:3) and calls it 'the third heaven' (2 Corinthians 12:2). As we saw
in the Introduction, the Bible uses the word 'heaven' in three
different ways (referring to the sky immediately above the earth,
galactic space and God's dwelling place). We can be certain that
it is the third definition that Paul means here and that he was
caught up into heaven *as it is now*. The other use of the word
'paradise' comes in another revelation, this time to the apostle
John. In this, God promises to the church in Ephesus, 'To the
one who conquers I will grant to eat of the tree of life, which is
in the paradise of God' (Revelation 2:7). At creation, man was put
into 'a garden in Eden' (Genesis 2:8) in which God had placed
'the tree of life' (Genesis 2:9). We are not told what this tree was,
but God said that if man ate its fruit he would 'live for ever'
(Genesis 3:22). It was therefore a symbol of the Lord Jesus Christ,
who told his disciples, 'Whoever feeds on my flesh and drinks
my blood has eternal life' (John 6:54). The promise to the
Ephesians was that when by the grace of God they had been
enabled to remain faithful, they would be received into Paradise
to delight in all the blessings that Jesus obtained for them in his
birth, life, death, resurrection and ascension.

Replaced or replenished?

A hugely important passage pointing to the difference between
heaven as it now is and as it will be in the future comes in

Romans 8. Paul begins by pointing out that creation suffers from having been 'subjected to futility' (Romans 8:20). As a result of man's sin, it has been brought down to a condition in which it is no longer fulfilling its intended purpose and no longer a perfect reflection of its Creator's glory. Instead, it is trapped in the vicious spiral of deterioration that science calls the Second Law of Thermodynamics. Ever since its dislocation by sin 'the whole creation has been groaning together in the pains of childbirth' (Romans 8:22). This graphic phrase personalizes nature and pictures it writhing in agony. Earlier in the chapter the same form of language is used; Paul says that at the end of the present age there will be a final, radical division between those who are God's children and those who are not, and that 'creation waits with eager longing for the revealing of the sons of God' (Romans 8:19). In his paraphrase *Letters to Young Churches*, the British minister and author J. B. Phillips (1906–1982) sees creation 'on tiptoe',[23] as if craning its neck to see exactly who will finally be declared to be the true children of God, destined to spend eternity in his eternal kingdom. Creation is doing this because that will be the moment when it will be 'set free from its bondage to corruption' (Romans 8:21). The destinies of creation and man, God's highest creature, are inextricably linked. When man sinned the whole of creation was wrecked, but God plans to banish sin and all its consequences. The present heaven (Paradise) and the present cosmos will not be wiped out, but in a way beyond our understanding will be reconstructed and restored to their pristine perfection, fulfilling God's intention to unite for ever 'things in heaven and things on earth' (Ephesians 1:10). As the American scholar Philip Ryken explains, 'This is the goal for which God has been working since eternity past. Not only are all things *from* God, but they are also *for* God—for his glory in Christ. This goal was frustrated by the fall, but God has not stopped working toward it, and he will reach it in the end. God is no more satisfied with this fallen world than we are, but unlike us he is able to do something about it, and he will.'[24]

When one of his disciples asked Jesus what would eventually become of them in the life to come, as they had left everything to follow him, Jesus said that they could look forward to 'the renewal of all things' (Matthew 19:28, NIV). The phrase he used translates the single Greek word *paliggenesia*, a combination of two words meaning 'again' and 'genesis'. In the only other place in the New Testament in which the identical word occurs Paul uses it to refer to the new birth as 'the washing of *regeneration*' (Titus 3:5, emphasis added). This helps to confirm the Bible's teaching about the new creation. When a person is born again they remain the same person, but one who has undergone a revolutionary change—and the same will be true of the heavens and the earth. They will not be replaced, but will be renewed and redeemed from all the effects of sin. At the beginning of the Bible we find God making the universe; at the end of the Bible we find him remaking it. In his acclaimed *New Testament Commentary* the Netherlands-born Bible commentator William Hendriksen (1900–1982) gets it right when he translates the phrase 'the renewal of all things' as 'the restored universe'.[25] God's ultimate goal is the redemption of the entire cosmos. As Philip Ryken notes, 'Redemption is not separate from creation. It is the very world that God once made—now lost and fallen in sin—that God has a purpose to redeem.'[26]

None of this suggests that creation will be wiped out and replaced; there is a vast difference between being liberated and being liquidated. Commenting on creation's destiny the British author Stuart Olyott writes, 'It will shine out in its proper splendour, telling out the glory of God in a way which far surpasses that of the present creation.'[27] The Second Law of Thermodynamics, dragging everything into entropy and disorder, will no longer exist. There will no shifting of tectonic plates, no tsunamis, no earthquakes, no floods, no hurricanes or other natural disasters. Nor will there be any environmental problems; earth's ecological perfection will exceed the wildest dreams of Greenpeace!

The apostle Peter describes what will take place before this happens:

> 'But the day of the Lord will come like a thief, and then the heavens will *pass away* with a roar, and the heavenly bodies will be burned up and *dissolved*, and the earth and the works that are done on it will be *exposed*. Since all these things are thus to be *dissolved*, what sort of people ought you to be in lives of holiness and godliness, waiting for and hastening the coming of the day of God, because of which the heavens will be set on fire and *dissolved*, and the heavenly bodies will melt as they burn!' (2 Peter 3:10–12, emphasis added).

The key words here are those I have emphasized: 'pass away', 'dissolved' and 'exposed'. At first glance these all seem to point to the present cosmos being wiped out, but closer study shows that this is not so. The words 'pass away' are based on the Greek *parerchomai*, which is used nearly thirty times in the New Testament, without ever meaning that something was annihilated or ceased to exist. The word 'dissolved', used three times in this passage, points in the same direction. It is based on the Greek verb *appolumi*, and although related words appear over forty times in the New Testament it never once means annihilation or non-existence. Examples are numerous and obvious. It is used in three well-known parables Jesus told in Luke 15, in which a sheep, a coin and a son were all said to have been 'lost'—but they were not annihilated, they were found. In another parable, Jesus reminded people what would happen if new wine was put into old wineskins; the wineskins would be 'destroyed' (Mark 2:22). They would not disappear, but they would no longer be able to fulfil the purpose for which they were made. To give another illustration of the meaning of 'destroy', we are told that Jesus came to earth to die, so that 'through death he might destroy the one who has the power of death, that is, the devil' (Hebrews 2:14)—and we all know to our cost and shame that the devil has not been annihilated.

The distinguished American geologist Edward Hitchcock (1793–1864) made some very helpful comments on the subject of the cosmos being burned up. After accepting that God certainly has the power 'partially or wholly to annihilate the material universe' he pointed out that 'heat, however intense, has no tendency to do this; it only gives matter a new form'. He then went on, 'In short, we have no evidence, either from science or revelation, that the minutest atom of matter has ever been destroyed since the original creation; nor have we any evidence that any of it will ever be reduced to the nothingness from which it sprang. We may, therefore, conclude that the Bible does plainly and distinctly teach us that this earth will hereafter be burned up; in other words, that all upon or within it, capable of combustion, will be consumed, and the entire mass, the elements, *without the loss of one particle of the matter now existing*, will be melted; and then, that the world, thus purified from the contamination of sin, and surrounded by a new atmosphere, or heavens, and adapted in all respects to the nature and wants of spiritual and sinless beings, *will become the residence of the righteous*' (emphasis added).[28]

Immediately before the passage we have looked at in these last three paragraphs Peter had reminded his readers of the cataclysm that took place in Noah's day. In rebuking those who imagined that nothing would ever happen to interrupt the world's unending progress he wrote, 'They deliberately overlook this fact, that the heavens existed long ago, and the earth was formed out of water and through water by the word of God, and that by means of these the world that then existed was deluged with water and *perished*' (2 Peter 3:5-6, emphasis added). The word 'perished' has an identical root to the word 'dissolved' discussed above, and Peter emphasizes the point he is making: 'But by the same word the heavens and earth that now exist are stored up for fire, being kept until the day of judgement and destruction of the ungodly' (2 Peter 3:7). The world of Noah's day was not annihilated by the flood; nor will the present world be annihilated when the fire of God's final judgement falls upon it.

The meaning of the verbs being used is underlined in yet another way when Peter adds that the coming cataclysm will usher in 'the day of judgement and *destruction* of the ungodly' (2 Peter 3:7, emphasis added). Again, the word 'destruction' has the same root as the verbs we are studying—but nowhere does the Bible teach annihilationism and say that at the final day of judgement the ungodly will be wiped out of existence. Pulling all of this together, we can be sure that there will be no such thing as the end of the world, but only *the end of the world in its present ruined form*. It is destined for destruction, but also for restoration. We were born on the earth, we live on the earth and we cling to what we have on the earth as long as we can—yet as Christians our final dwelling place will not be on the earth as it now is, but on a renewed earth and under new heavens. We are not only made *from* the earth, but *for* the earth.

The destiny of God's people is inextricably linked in the Bible with the destiny of the entire cosmos. To limit redemption to one section of humanity is to ignore the New Testament's clear testimony, which says, 'The creation itself will be set free from its bondage to corruption and obtain the freedom of the glory of the children of God' (Romans 8:21). The British scholar F. F. Bruce writes, 'If words mean anything, these words of Paul denote not the annihilation of the present material universe and its replacement by a universe completely new, but the transformation of the present universe so that it will fulfil the purpose for which God created it.'[29] Christians have a vested interest in the new earth!

Early indications

Then what is to happen? The first hint comes near the very beginning of the Bible. In the so-called *protoevangelion*, God warns Satan (represented in the form of a serpent), 'I will put enmity between you and the woman, and between your offspring and her offspring; he shall bruise your head, and you shall bruise his heel' (Genesis 3:15). This is 'the first glimmer of the gospel'.[30] The woman's offspring was to be Jesus, and the bruising of his heel foresaw the suffering he was to endure in order to redeem God's people. The bruising of the serpent's head predicted the fact that although he had ruined God's perfect creation Satan would eventually be utterly defeated. This is the first indication of God's promise that the curse placed on earth would one day be removed and that all of creation, including our planet, on which the catastrophe occurred, would be restored to its former glory.

Later, in his covenant of salvation with Abraham, God promises him and his descendants 'all the land of Canaan, for an everlasting possession' (Genesis 17:8), yet the only part of Canaan that Abraham ever owned was a burial cave he bought from the Hittites (see Genesis 50:12–13). Nevertheless, this covenant was not broken. We are told 'By faith [Abraham] went to live in the land of promise, as in a foreign land, living in tents with Isaac and Jacob, heirs with him of the same promise. For he was looking forward to the city that has foundations, whose designer and builder is God' (Hebrews 11:9–10). Abraham, Isaac and Jacob clearly looked forward to more than a sliver of land on the south-east coast of the Mediterranean Sea as their promised inheritance. The writer of Hebrews makes that clear: 'These all died in faith, not having received the things promised, but having seen them and greeted them from afar, and having acknowledged that they were strangers and exiles on the earth. For people who speak thus make it clear that they are seeking a homeland. If they had been thinking of that land from which they had gone out, they would have had opportunity to return. But as it is, they desire a better country, *that is, a heavenly one.* Therefore God is not ashamed to be called their God, for he has prepared for them a city' (Hebrews 11:13–16, emphasis added).

It is clear from the New Testament that in the covenant with Abraham the 'inheritance' was not limited to ethnic Israelites but applied to 'the Israel of God' (Galatians 6:16), believers of every land and age in history, and it is equally clear that 'the land of promise' was not restricted to Canaan, but included the whole earth. This is the broader picture that Paul has in mind when he assures Galatian believers, 'If you are Christ's, then you are Abraham's offspring, heirs according to promise' (Galatians 3:29). When we grasp this we can begin to make sense of magnificent

Old Testament promises like these: 'It shall come to pass in the latter days that the mountain of the house of the LORD shall be established as the highest of the mountains, and shall be lifted up above the hills; and all the nations shall flow to it' (Isaiah 2:2); 'For the earth shall be full of the knowledge of the LORD as the waters cover the sea' (Isaiah 11:9); and 'Be glad and rejoice for ever in that which I create; for behold, I create Jerusalem to be a joy, and her people to be a gladness' (Isaiah 65:18).

All things new

Towards the end of his prophecy Isaiah paints these promises on a broader canvas, as God tells him, 'For behold, I create new heavens and a new earth' (Isaiah 65:17); and in the New Testament the apostle Peter repeats it: 'But according to his promise we are waiting for new heavens and a new earth in which righteousness dwells' (2 Peter 3:13). Then, in a God-given vision of the future, John sees 'a new heaven and a new earth, for the first heaven and the first earth had passed away' (Revelation 21:1) and hears God say, 'Behold, I am making all things new' (Revelation 21:5). The key to understanding whether these are promises that the earth will be replaced or that it will be restored obviously turns on the meaning of the word 'new'. There are three Greek words with the general meaning of 'new' in English translations of the New Testament—*prosphatos, neos,* and *kainos.* The first two are used to speak of something new in relation to time, or replacing something that no longer exists, as we can see by looking at some examples of their use.

- The writer of Hebrews reminds his readers about the Old Testament religious system with its endless round of 'sacrifices and offerings and burnt offerings' (Hebrews 10:8), then goes on to tell them that in his death on their behalf

Jesus had 'offered for all time a single sacrifice for sins' (Hebrews 10:12). They can therefore have 'confidence to enter the holy places by the blood of Jesus, by the *new* and living way that he opened for us' (Hebrews 10:19–20, emphasis added). The word 'new' is *prosphatos*, which literally means 'newly-killed', and the writer is using exactly the right word to highlight the fact that the death of Jesus was totally different from the old sacrifices. It did not merely improve or modernize them, it replaced them. As the British author Edgar Andrews comments, people coming to the Old Testament sacrifices 'were *reminded* of their sin, not *relieved* of it'.[31] In total contrast, those who now trust in the shed blood of Christ can come to God 'with a true heart in full assurance of faith' (Hebrews 10:22).

• The second Greek word—*neos*—is the basis of a number of different words in our English Bibles, but as with *prosphatos* we can use the teaching of Hebrews to illustrate its basic meaning. The writer says that Christians are those who have put their trust in 'Jesus, the mediator of a new (*neos*) covenant' (Hebrews 12:24). This new covenant is not a revamped version of the old one; it completely replaced the one which was done away with. Edgar Andrews puts it well: 'The contrasts between the two covenants could not be greater. The first marks and condemns transgression; the second redeems the transgressor. Those bound under the old covenant could look forward only to death, for it was "the ministry of condemnation" (2 Corinthians 3:9). But under the new covenant it is Christ who dies, atoning for our sin. *The first covenant held promise only of an earthly homeland; but the new promises and guarantees an eternal inheritance*' (emphasis added).[32]

Soon after the nineteenth-century American missionary Adoniram Judson began his ministry in Burma (now Myanmar), he was captured by natives and flung into a filthy prison, where he was strung up by his thumbs. When they mocked him by asking, 'And now what are your plans to win the heathen to Christ?' Judson calmly relied, 'My future is as bright as the promises of God.' Every Christian can say the same, and one of the promises is, 'Blessed are the meek, for they shall inherit the earth' (Matthew 5:5).

- When Peter and John speak of new heavens and a new earth, they are using the third Greek word—*kainos*—which in the New Testament is used of 'something new as opposed to old or former and hence also implying better because different'.[33] For example, when we read of Jesus telling his disciples, 'A new commandment I give to you, that you love one another' (John 13:34), the word 'new' translates *kainos*. We might be tempted to wonder what is new about it, as many centuries before God's clear commands to his people included, 'You shall love your neighbour as yourself' (Leviticus 19:18). What is more, Jesus' summary of the Ten Commandments distilled the last six into exactly the same single sentence (see Mark 12:31). However, his meaning becomes clear when we read of him adding, 'Just as I have loved you, you also are to love one another' (John 13:34). The command to love one another was not a replacement of the previous commandment to do the same thing—but 'new' in that it gave it a much greater motive, one based on the greatest possible example.

This helps us to understand the true meaning of new heavens and a new earth. The picture is not of something brand new, but of a reconstruction of something that previously existed. In the original creation the entire universe was in perfect harmony until sin ruined it. But God will reverse the curse, and in the consummation of the kingdom of God the whole of creation will be purged and perfected. The new, remodelled universe will be free from sin and its harmony will be restored, fulfilling God's original purpose. It will not be a creation *ex nihilo* (out of nothing) but the renewal of a creation that already exists. The result will be what the American preacher John MacArthur calls 'a magnificent kingdom where both heaven and earth unite in a glory that surpasses the limits of human imagination and the boundaries of earthly dimensions.'[34] As someone has neatly put it, 'In the beginning was the end'; if we want to know what the new creation will be like in the end, when sin has been banished for ever, we must try to imagine what it must have been like in the beginning, before sin existed.

There is also a powerful theological reason for believing that creation is to be renewed and not destroyed. Were God to annihilate the present cosmos and create another one, it would mean that Satan had wrecked it beyond remedy, forcing God to abandon Plan A and go to Plan B. But God has no Plan B, and his restoration of creation will show his complete dominion by renewing what Satan has ruined. To defeat Satan finally and completely God must restore everything to its original condition, and as he has all the materials of the original creation to hand there is no reason to suppose that he will make the creation out of nothing. We need to pursue this much further, and will do so as we look at the Bible's most vivid and dramatic definitions of heaven. It should come as no surprise to find that these are in the last of the Bible's sixty-six books. Although the books are not placed in their exact chronological order in the Bible, there is strong evidence to suggest that the closing book, Revelation, was the final one to be written (between AD 90 and

95). This would make it God's last written word on heaven or on any other subject—an added reason for us to give it our close attention.

Because of the form of language in which it is written, Revelation is one of the most difficult books in the Bible to understand, and it will therefore be useful for us to step aside and get an overview of it before we go any further. When we do, we should find ourselves agreeing with J. B. Phillips, who found the task of translating it 'in the true sense of that threadbare word, thrilling. For in this book the translator is carried into another dimension—he has but the slightest foothold in the Time-and-space world with which he is familiar. He is carried, not into some never-never land of fancy, but into the Ever-ever land of God's eternal Values and Judgements.'[35] It is time for us to see what Phillips means—and then to discover what Revelation tells us about the new heavens and the new earth.

2

Unwrapping Revelation

When a fairly recent poll asked Christians on which book of the Bible they would most like to hear a series of sermons preached, Revelation came top of the poll. Another poll asking preachers on which book of the Bible they would least like to develop a series of sermons produced the same result! These findings are hardly surprising, as the book is full of exotic symbolism, sometimes featuring curious beasts with unusual numbers of heads and horns, while other phenomena include hail and fire mixed with blood, blood flowing from a wine press, the greatest earthquake in the world's history and a horse being ridden by someone with a sword coming out of his mouth. Then there is the unusual use of certain numbers. Why does the number seven appear fifty-five times, referring to things such as spirits, lampstands, stars, angels, trumpets, bowls, plagues and beasts' heads and horns? Why does the number four appear

eighteen times, and the number twelve nine times? What are we
to make of the two numbers that usually attract most attention,
the mysterious 666 and the enigmatic 144,000? (This second
number has been wrongly commandeered by the Watchtower
Bible and Tract Society, which heads up the non-Christian cult
Jehovah's Witnesses). In 1880 the British preacher C. H.
Spurgeon (1834–1892) told his London congregation,

> There are some things in the Word of God which are
> undoubtedly true which must be swallowed at once by an effort of
> faith, and must not be chewed by perpetual questioning. You will
> soon have I know not what of doubt and difficulty and bitterness
> upon your soul if you must needs know the unknowable, and have
> reasons and explanations for the sublime and the mysterious. Let
> the difficult doctrines go down whole into your very soul, by a
> grand exercise of confidence in God. I thank God for a thousand
> things I cannot understand. When I cannot get to know the reason
> why, I say to myself, "Why should I know the reason why?"[36]

Theologians have treated Revelation in interesting ways. The
German Reformer Martin Luther (1483–1546) once thought it
'unedifying for the ordinary believer' and in 1522 wrote that he
considered it 'neither apostolic nor prophetic' and could 'in no
way detect that the Holy Spirit produced it',[37] though later in life
he changed his mind. Although John Calvin believed Revelation
to be canonical (that is, part of the Word of God), it was the only
New Testament book on which he never wrote a commentary.
Yet Revelation appears to say more about heaven than any other
book in the Bible, and heaven is the subject we are researching
here. When the American theologian R. C. Sproul was in
seminary he button-holed the distinguished professor John

Gerstner and asked him, 'What's heaven like?', hoping for a reply teeming with deep spiritual insight. Instead, Sproul writes that Gerstner 'gave me a strange look, as if to say, "How am I supposed to know? I haven't been there."'[38]

Gerstner's glance said a great deal.

Countless books have been written by people who claim to have been to heaven in the course of a so-called 'near-death experience' (NDE). A Gallup poll reported that in the United States alone nearly eight million people claim to have had one. These claims are usually made by people who have been pronounced clinically dead—which makes a '*near*-death experience' a strange term to use! Whatever we make of such testimonies, the fact is that nobody living here on earth can give us an authoritative, first-hand description of heaven or tell us exactly what happens there. The only reliable information we have is that which God has provided in his Word, and it should come as no surprise to discover that the most detailed passages are in the last book in the Bible.

In the previous chapter we read that at one point the apostle Paul had been 'caught up into paradise' (2 Corinthians 12:3), which he called 'the third heaven' (2 Corinthians 12:2), yet even he did not go on to describe what it was like. Instead, he testified that while he was there he heard 'things that cannot be told, which man may not utter' (2 Corinthians 12:4). Paul was an intellectual giant and a powerfully effective preacher, but when he was in some way given a revelation of heaven as it is now he saw and heard things that God prevented him from putting into words. As the British preacher Philip Arthur comments, 'Glory caressed him, bathed him and left his mind so swamped by sheer splendour that one of the greatest intellects of the first century was dazzled to the point of incoherence.'[39] Simply put, Paul was in some way given a revelation of heaven *as it now is*.

The Bible mentions 'heaven' nearly 250 times, though often only in a few words and giving little or no indication of what it is like. In Revelation we get several longer passages, but before we examine these an overview of the book will enable us to see the Bible's picture of heaven in its proper context as part of God's final written word to man. It will also help us to clear away many myths and misunderstandings about it.

Revelation records a series of visions received by the apostle John on 'the island called Patmos' (1:9), about fifty miles west of Asia Minor (now western Turkey). Today, it is a popular holiday resort, but John was not there as a tourist, or on a religious retreat, but as a high-profile prisoner. In those days Patmos had a penal colony—a kind of first century Alcatraz—designated for people the Roman Empire considered a threat to good public order. The Romans saw the rapidly-growing Christian church as a seedbed of rebellion, which is why John tells the believers to whom he is writing that he is on Patmos as 'your brother and partner in the tribulation' (1:9). This 'tribulation' was the vicious persecution of the early Christian church by the Roman Empire, especially under the Emperors Nero (AD 54–68) and Domitian (AD 81–96). We are not sure which one of these was in power when John was on Patmos (most scholars favour Domitian), but either way John makes it clear that he was in exile 'on account of the word of God and the testimony of Jesus' (1:9). In other words, he was banished to this remote island because of his faithful preaching of the Christian gospel.

Persecution by the Romans was not the only problem for these early churches. They faced the false teaching of 'the Nicolaitans' (2:6, 15), who professed to be Christians, but who sanctioned sexual immorality and the eating of food that had been sacrificed to idols. They were also slandered by 'those who say that they are Jews and are not' and whose evil was such that John describes them as 'a synagogue of Satan' (2:9). Several church members had been killed for their faith (see 2:13; 6:9), and worse was to come (see 2:10; 13:7–10).

The visions John describes in Revelation were given while he was 'in the Spirit on the Lord's Day' (1:10), John's way of claiming that the Holy Spirit was controlling what he saw, thought, felt and wrote. The divine origin of Revelation is confirmed in its opening verse, when John calls it, 'The revelation of Jesus Christ, *which God gave him* ... by sending his angel to his servant John' (1:1, emphasis added) and by an angel twice telling the apostle, 'These words are trustworthy and true' (21:5; 22:6).

At this time, the Roman Empire marked 'Emperor's Day' in honour of the ruling Caesar, who was treated as if he were divine. To celebrate the day on which Jesus rose from the dead, early Christians (most of whom were devout Jews) changed their day of worship from the Sabbath (which had been for centuries the day on which their ancestors had met for worship) to 'the first day of the week' (Acts 20:7), which we now call Sunday. In Revelation, John calls this 'the Lord's Day' (the only place in the Bible in which it is given this name). John addressed the book to 'the seven churches that are in Asia' (1:4), which was then a Roman colony. These churches are identified as being in Ephesus, Smyrna, Pergamum, Thyatira, Sardis, Philadelphia and Laodicea (see 1:11), and separate instructions are given to each of them, geared to their particular situations. However, all of the messages conveyed principles that would have been significant not only to the other churches in Asia Minor at the time but to all contemporary Christian communities, and as part of the 'living and abiding word of God' (1 Peter 1:23) they remain relevant today. This becomes clear when we see that each message to an individual church ends with the phrase, 'He who has an ear, let him hear *what the Spirit says to the churches*' (Revelation 2:7, 11, 17, 29; 3:6, 13, 22, emphasis added).

That is fairly straightforward: now it gets trickier, and the book's very first word in the original Greek in which it was written should prepare us for what follows. The word is *apokalupsis*, which means removing a veil, or exposing to open view something that has been hidden. This means that by definition Revelation is apocalyptic, a distinct kind of writing that is highly symbolic. The British scholar Alister McGrath suggests 'Heaven is perhaps the supreme example of a Christian concept that is mediated directly through images.'[40] Revelation is also 'prophecy' (1:3, 22:7, 10, 18, 19), the only New Testament book defined in this way. As an apocalyptic prophecy it uses symbolic language similar to that found in Old Testament prophetic books such as Ezekiel, Daniel and Zechariah, and includes some of the most arresting and dramatic material in the entire Bible. It tells of creatures with six wings, a pale horse ridden by Death, the sun turning black and the moon turning to blood, a red dragon with seven heads and ten horns, unclean spirits like frogs, stars falling out of the sky, and a plague of hailstones each weighing about 100 pounds. These passages have spawned a bewildering and bizarre variety of interpretations. For example, it has been said that the locusts mentioned in chapter 9 are prophetic images of helicopters! This kind of whimsy gives Revelation a bad name. In the same way, the number 'seven', used over fifty times in Revelation, has been linked to many exotic ideas, avoiding the simple fact that the number 'seven' is almost invariably used in the Bible to speak of completeness or fullness. The Australian biblical scholar Leon Morris (1914–2006) writes about 'the fantastic schemes of prophecy which some exegetes find in it, and whose ingenuity is matched only by their improbability'.[41]

Students of Revelation have approached it in radically different ways, some of which can be noted here.

The first is the *preterist* approach (from the Latin *praetor*, meaning 'past'). This claims that except for the final two chapters Revelation is all about events that were already taking place or would do so very soon. These included the Roman persecution of the Christian church, the sacking of Jerusalem in AD 70 and the destruction of its temple. This would make the book powerfully relevant to John's first readers, but for the most part not having the same immediate significance for later generations, though they could of course draw important lessons from it.

The second is the *futurist* approach, which goes to the other extreme. It claims that except for the first three chapters, the events prophesied in Revelation will all take place in the future, culminating in a relatively short time of great crisis just before the Second Coming of Christ. This view produces the exact opposite result to that of the preterist view. It means that the events it prophesied had no urgent relevance to those who first read them, and that only now (or at some unknown time in the future) will they be significant.

The third is the *historicist* approach. It states that except for eight chapters (the first three and the last five) Revelation gives a chronological outline of the history of the Christian church from its beginnings until the Second Coming of Christ. This approach links certain prophecies to events such as Muslim expansion in Europe, the rise of the papacy, the sixteenth-century Protestant Reformation, the French Revolution, the re-establishment of the state of Israel and a coming military clash in the Middle East. The difficulty with this view is that there have been wagonloads of historicist opinions as to which events Revelation has in mind—and its first readers could never have known which were to be proved valid. This would also seem a complex and confusing way of stating such important truths!

The fourth is the *idealist* approach. This steers away from linking statements in Revelation to specific times, events or people and says that it highlights the opposition that the Christian church will face and the spiritual warfare in which it will be involved until Christ returns, and sets out principles that are true at all times, especially the eventual victory of good over evil.

These four views all have their strengths (or they would not have been adopted) and their weaknesses (or others would not have been preferred). However, there is another approach, one that prepares us in a much more logical way for the great statements about the new heavens and earth. The bulk of Revelation can be divided into seven cycles or visions. This approach (sometimes known as *progressive parallelism*) says that they are not to be read in chronological order, nor to be confined to New Testament times or the end of the world. Instead, it sees them as running parallel to each other, with successive visions restating the essence of earlier ones but adding further detail. For example, this approach points out that each of the seven visions mentions one or more of the events that will take place at the end of the world, all of them coming to a climax in the seventh vision, which depicts the final day of judgement and the ultimate and eternal triumph of God over all his enemies.

It is impossible to produce an accurate analogy of what this means, but let me give an easily understandable illustration. Of all the golf courses I have ever played, the finest may well be Royal Portrush, in Northern Ireland—though it seems to get more difficult every time I play it!—and its scenery is awe-inspiring. Superbly situated on the North Antrim coast, this masterpiece of golf course architecture has been voted one of the top twelve in the world. The most spectacular views of most golf courses are from the air, and Royal Portrush is no exception. Seen from the west, the background is the massive limestone cliffs known as White Rocks and the medieval ruins of Dunluce Castle. From the east, the course is set against the hills of Inishowen. From the south, the backdrop is the Atlantic Ocean, giving glimpses of the Scottish islands of Islay and Jura, while from the north it is the lush landscape of North Antrim. Each viewpoint has a different part of the course in the foreground— but every one forms part of the complete picture. In Revelation, each of the seven cycles or visions provides a different emphasis (or 'view'), but reveals the same overarching picture of God's eternal triumph.

Some interpreters insist that everything in Revelation must be taken literally unless it is clearly symbolic, while others insist that everything must be taken symbolically unless it is clearly literal. Over the centuries there have been countless explanations of certain words and phrases. This led C. H. Spurgeon to say, 'Only fools and madmen are positive in their interpretations of the Apocalypse.'[42] He may have been exaggerating, but dogmatism is not synonymous with truth. There is room for differences of opinion on matters such as the precise end-of-the-world timetable and the sequence of the events that will take place then. But these are of secondary importance, as no-one's eternal destiny rests on their opinion about them. J. C. Ryle (1816–1900), the first Anglican Bishop of Liverpool, struck the right note: 'All portions of Scripture … ought to be approached with deep humility, and earnest prayer for the teaching of the Spirit. On no point have good men so entirely disagreed as on the interpretation of prophecy. On no point have the prejudices of one class, the dogmatism of a second, and the extravagance of a third, done so much to rob the church of truths, which God intended to be a blessing.'[43]

In a radio broadcast on 1 October 1939, Winston Churchill, then First Lord of the Admiralty, famously said, 'I cannot forecast to you the action of Russia. It is a riddle, wrapped in a mystery, inside an enigma.' Many feel the same about Revelation, and as a result have tended to steer clear of it, or to read it without paying close attention to its meaning. At the opposite extreme, many spend extravagant hours trying to squeeze detailed explanations out of every statement, running the risk of being unable to see the wood for the trees. These approaches are dangerously flawed. The all-important thing when reading Revelation is to look for the big picture, which gathers up the entire teaching of the Bible (its twenty-two chapters have some five hundred allusions to the Old Testament alone) and brings it to a triumphant climax. The British preacher Gary Benfold goes so far as to claim, 'I believe that Revelation is by far the easiest book in the New Testament to understand! Easy, that is, if we will content ourselves with getting the general picture... If we forget that Revelation is full of symbolism, or if we become obsessed with the meaning of individual symbols, we will soon find ourselves lost in the by-ways of a thousand fabulous interpretations. More importantly, we will inevitably miss the point of the book.'[44]

The American preacher Kim Riddlebarger underlines this important point about the book's overall context: 'Revelation is not a handy guide to explain the evening news; rather, it is a commentary on the Old Testament in light of the person and work of Jesus Christ.'[45] This brings us to the reason for getting an overview of Revelation. As God's last written word to man it is not given to satisfy our curiosity, but to increase our faith and to change our lives by realigning them to focus on the glorious outcome he has prepared for us.

When I was compiling a compendium of thousands of notable quotations on hundreds of subjects (which eventually became *The Complete Gathered Gold*), a friend in Oklahoma told me that he had come across one I could include. Always keen to add to my hoard, I asked him what it was. His reply has been embedded in my mind ever since: *the main thing is to make sure that the main thing remains the main thing.* This is certainly the best possible advice when reading Revelation. One should begin by accepting that it is a single 'revelation', not a collection of revelations—and then grasp that that revelation points to God as being in sovereign control of the universe, of history, and of human destiny, guiding and protecting the church of his beloved Son the Lord Jesus Christ, in whom he will bring all things to their triumphant consummation.

Revelation should be read as if handling a telescope, not a microscope. To use another analogy: it has been said that to dip into the book, focussing on single statements about things like symbols or numbers and basing one's understanding of the book on these is as dangerous as grasping a razor-sharp knife by the blade instead of the handle. It is not the right way to go about things! As Alister McGrath rightly states, 'The book of Revelation is not a timetable, but a prophetic vision, concerned above all with demonstrating the final and total victory of God, despite all the trials and tribulations of his people at present.'[46] God's promise is that when the curse of sin is finally removed and his original goal for creation is fulfilled, the new heavens and new earth will ring with the cry, 'The kingdom of the world has become the kingdom of the Lord and of his Christ, and he shall reign for ever and ever' (11:15). We can see this at the beginning of Revelation when we notice that each of the letters sent to the seven Asian churches not only deals with a specific local situation but ends with a promise related to a different aspect of heaven. Here are those promises:

- The letter to the church in Ephesus ends, 'To the one who conquers I will grant to eat of the tree of life, which is in the paradise of God' (2:7).
- The letter to the church in Smyrna ends, 'Be faithful unto death, and I will give you the crown of life' (2:10).
- The letter to the church in Pergamum ends, 'To the one who conquers I will give some of the hidden manna, and I will give him a white stone, with a new name written on the stone that no one knows except the one who receives it' (2:17).
- The letter to the church in Thyatira ends, 'The one who conquers and who keeps my works until the end, to him I will give authority over the nations ... and I will give him the morning star' (2:26, 28).
- The letter to the church in Sardis ends, 'The one who conquers will be clothed ... in white garments, and I will never blot his name out of the book of life. I will confess his name before my Father and before his angels' (3:5).
- The letter to the church in Philadelphia ends, 'The one who

conquers, I will make him a pillar in the temple of my God' (3:12).

- The letter to the church in Laodicea ends, 'The one who conquers I will grant to sit with me on my throne, as I also conquered and sat down with my Father on his throne' (3:21).

Each one of these seven promises relates to all true believers, not merely to those in the churches to which John originally wrote, and they set the tone for all that follows in Revelation. The American theologian Martin Franzmann (1907–1976) gives this excellent summary of John's reason for writing as he did: 'He writes in order to strengthen them in their trials, both internal and external, to hold before them the greatness and certitude of their hope in Christ, and to assure them of their victory, in Christ, over all the powers of evil now let loose upon the world and, to all appearances, destined to triumph on earth.'[47] The American preacher Thomas N. Smith elaborates: 'Revelation never ceases to remind us in the most graphic and compelling images in the New Testament that, despite the worst that fallen man and the Devil can do on earth, the true and triune God reigns in heaven and shall reign on the earth. With calculated repetition it tells us that this reign is being conducted because of the triumph of the slaughtered Lamb, and that because of this triumph, the Lamb, and not the Dragon, shall finally prevail. It announces that the world shall not end in either a bang or a whimper, but the shout of the blood-stained but victorious King of Kings and Lord of Lords. It sets before us the eschatological hope that the destroyers of the earth will not succeed, but that *the Creator will recreate the earth he loves as the eternal home place for the people he loves*' (emphasis added).[48]

Perfection restored

The truth of these words can be clearly seen by contrasting statements made in Revelation with those made in Genesis. Here are some of these:

- Genesis records, 'In the beginning, God created the heavens and the earth' (Genesis 1:1). In Revelation, John's vision of heaven was 'a new heaven and a new earth' (Revelation 21:1).
- In Genesis, man was told that if he disobeyed God, 'you shall surely die' (Genesis 2:17). Revelation tells us that in heaven 'death shall be no more' (Revelation 21:4).
- In Genesis, Satan caused man to sin (see Genesis 3:1–7). In Revelation, he is cast out 'for ever and ever' (Revelation 20:10).
- In Genesis, Adam and Eve 'hid themselves from the presence of the LORD God' (Genesis 3:8). In Revelation, God's redeemed people 'will see [God's] face' (Revelation 22:4).
- In Genesis, God 'sent [man] out from the Garden of Eden' (Genesis 3:23). In Revelation, 'the dwelling place of God is with man' (Revelation 21:3).
- In Genesis, God told Adam, 'cursed is the ground because of you' (Genesis 3:17). In Revelation, God promises, 'No longer will there be anything accursed' (Revelation 22:3).
- In Genesis, God barred man's way to 'the tree of life' (Genesis 3:24). In Revelation, God's redeemed people have 'the right to the tree of life' (Revelation 22:14).

Revelation may record visions that were received over an extended period of time. This and its divine origin means that we should hardly expect John to have written a book that would be as clinical, formal and polished as a solicitor's letter. Instead, it employs an astonishing variety of symbols to drive home this message and ends with the most breathtaking passages about the new heaven and the new earth to be found anywhere in the Bible. We can turn to them now and should do so with some of John's opening words ringing in our ears: 'Blessed is the one who reads aloud the words of this prophecy, and blessed are those who hear, and who keep what is written in it' (Revelation 1:3).

3

The bride and
the city

The phrase 'Heaven on Earth' has such an exciting ring to it
that many have latched onto its commercial appeal. A
company called Heaven on Earth claims to be 'the most
prestigious florist in London'. In Lancashire, the Heaven on
Earth hair and beauty salon promises, 'When you walk out of the
door you will truly feel that you have experienced a taste of
heaven without costing you the earth.' In the same county the
Heaven on Earth massage and beauty parlour offers 'holistic,
natural and organic treatments combined with the most
luxurious techniques to completely nourish the body, soul and
spirit'. Finally, when no life-enhancing services are of any further
value to you, the Bristol-based Heaven on Earth funeral
directors claim to offer 'the first green funeral service' and will
dispose of your body in whatever legal way your family wishes.
Yet, as we are about to see, heaven on earth is a thoroughly

biblical truth; not a sales pitch that never matches up to the hype, but a firm promise God makes to his redeemed people. In the previous chapter we saw that by definition Revelation is apocalyptic, a distinct kind of writing that is highly symbolic. It should hardly surprise us that God uses this form of language to tell us about the world to come and about heaven on earth in particular.

In his book *A Biblical Doctrine of Heaven*, the American preacher Wilbur Smith calls certain chapters in Revelation, 'The most extensive revelation of the eternal home to be found anywhere in the Scriptures.'[49] In this chapter we will concentrate on the following two passages, which illustrate what he meant.

> Then I saw a new heaven and a new earth, for the first heaven and the first earth had passed away, and the sea was no more. And I saw the holy city, new Jerusalem, coming down out of heaven from God, prepared as a bride adorned for her husband. And I heard a loud voice from the throne saying, 'Behold, the dwelling place of God is with man. He will dwell with them, and they will be his people, and God himself will be with them as their God. He will wipe away every tear from their eyes, and death shall be no more, neither shall there be mourning nor crying nor pain any more, for the former things have passed away' (Revelation 21:1-4).

> Then came one of the seven angels ... and spoke to me saying, 'Come, I will show you the Bride, the wife of the Lamb.' And he carried me away in the Spirit to a great, high mountain, and showed me the holy city Jerusalem coming down out of heaven from God, having the glory of God, its radiance like a most rare jewel, like a jasper, clear as crystal (Revelation 21:9-11).

Passages like these have been called 'the playground for the wild fantasies of some popular preachers', and we must do all we can to avoid adding to them. Then what do we make of the details we are given about the heavenly city called new Jerusalem? Regarding them as being literally true produces all kinds of problems, but seeing the city as symbolic reflects truth we read elsewhere in the Bible.

The bride

In the first passage, the new Jerusalem is said to be 'prepared as a bride adorned for her husband' (Revelation 21:2), while in the second it is specifically called 'the Bride, the wife of the Lamb' (Revelation 21:9). One of the most beautiful biblical pictures of the relationship between God and his church is to say that they are married to each other, with the church as the bride. This comes across in the instructions, 'Wives, submit to your own husbands, as to the Lord. For the husband is the head of the wife even as Christ is the head of the church' (Ephesians 5:22–23) and 'Husbands, love your wives, as Christ loved the church and gave himself up for her' (Ephesians 5:25). In his heavenly vision John heard a great multitude crying out, 'Hallelujah! For the Lord our God the Almighty reigns. Let us rejoice and exult and give him the glory, for the marriage of the Lamb has come, and his Bride has made herself ready' (Revelation 19:6–7). God's purpose has always been to draw the elect to himself, and the marriage of the Lamb brings wonderful closure to the plan. As Gary Benfold delightfully puts it, 'Now, at last, that purpose is complete and the whole universe is able to sing, "Here comes the bride."'[50]

These pictures echo something we read in the heart of the Old Testament, where God says to his people in Judah, 'Your Maker is your husband, the LORD of hosts is his name' (Isaiah 54:5). One can only imagine that Paul had this truth in mind when he explained to the church in Corinth the ultimate purpose of his ministry: 'I betrothed you to one husband, to present you as a pure virgin to Christ' (2 Corinthians 11:2). The reference to the holy city as a bride is a lovely picture of believers' eternal intimacy with God in heaven, where they will revel in their relationship with him.

When we look more closely at the heavenly city of the new Jerusalem we will be left in no doubt as to believers' eternal security; but before we do this it is worth looking again at the promise made to the church in Philadelphia, in which God uses a remarkable picture to establish this. In full, the promise reads, 'I am coming soon. Hold fast what you have, so that no one may seize your crown. The one who conquers, I will make him a pillar in the temple of my God. Never shall he go out of it, and I will write on him the name of my God, and the name of *the city of my God, the new Jerusalem*, which comes down from my God out of heaven, and my own new name' (Revelation 3:11–12, emphasis added).

The Christians in Philadelphia would have had no difficulty in getting the message, as they would have linked it to Israel's history. Solomon's temple in the capital city of Jerusalem had been the centre of the nation's worship and its main features included elaborately designed pillars (see 1 Kings 7:13–22). But for all its magnificence the temple was destroyed by the Babylonians in 586 BC, whereas God's promise to faithful Christians was that they would become pillars in God's temple, one which could never be destroyed. The Dutch theologian Herman Hoeksema (1886–1965) helps us to get the message: 'If temple is taken literally, pillars must also be taken in the same sense. And it would be a poor consolation indeed for the people of God to learn that they all will be changed into pillars in the future. No, the sense is symbolical. Temple is symbolic of the dwelling of God with man, of *his most intimate communion and union with himself* ... To be made pillars in the temple of God, therefore, is to enter lastingly and abidingly into the eternal covenant communion with God, the God of Jesus Christ our Lord'(emphasis added).[51] This 'most intimate communion and union' with God reflects exactly the picture of believers as 'the Bride, the wife of the Lamb'.

Elsewhere in the New Testament, we are told that 'Christ is the head of the church, his body, and is himself its Saviour' and that 'Christ loved the church and gave himself up for her' (Ephesians 5:23,25). Not all hymnology is good theology and not all hymns about heaven give a true picture of what the Bible teaches on the subject, but the British clergyman Samuel J. Stone (1839–1900) struck all the right notes when he wrote these lines:

> The church's one foundation
> Is Jesus Christ, her Lord;
> She is his new creation
> By water and the word;
> From heaven he came and sought her
> To be his holy bride;
> With his own blood he bought her,
> And for her life he died.

The city

The picture of God's redeemed people as his bride enjoying eternal fellowship with him prepares the way for us to lay hold of something that opens up the meaning of the passages highlighted earlier, and about which Herman Hoeksema suggests that we can only 'stammer out a few words of explanation'.[52] As we read the passages concerned in the context of the rest of Scripture, we can see them underlining the fact that 'the holy city, new Jerusalem' is not a massive celestial metropolis but a biblical definition of God's redeemed people, with God himself in their midst. As Albert Barnes points out, the earthly Jerusalem, the site of the temple in which the worship of God was celebrated, 'came to be synonymous with the church, the dwelling place of God on earth'.[53] Revelation's holy city, the new Jerusalem, symbolizes the church triumphantly redeemed and glorified. Elsewhere in Revelation it is called 'the beloved city' (20:9), and the adjective points to the only reason its members have been redeemed. The picture of God's people as his bride fits perfectly with them being called 'beloved', and the central truth that comes across loud and clear in Revelation is not that they *live* in the new Jerusalem, but that they *are* the new Jerusalem. A local church here on earth is not a building but a gathering of God's people, and the holy city in Revelation is not property but people. It is the entire glorified Christian church; its members are not in the city, *they are the city*!

As we work our way through the city's dimensions and details we should bear in mind this comment by the American pastor John Gilmore: 'It would dishonour the heavenly Architect to contend that its dimensions were meant to be taken literally.'[54] Later he adds, 'The calculations are precise, but only to convey the sense of immensity. They are meant to convey how huge, how grand, how glorious and how lavish life in heaven will be.'[55] This comes across as we examine some of these details.

The dimensions
The city John saw in his vision measured '12,000 stadia' and 'its

length and width and height are equal' (Revelation 21:16). A stadion was almost exactly 607 feet, which means that the city was about 1,380 miles in length, width and height. Taken literally, this produces the staggering picture of a massive cube of real estate with a length and width almost exactly the same as the distance between London and Athens. From my home in Banstead I can see Britain's tallest building, The Shard, in London, which has seventy-two habitable storeys. If the city in Revelation is taken literally (and if we allow a generous fifteen feet for a single storey) it would have 492,000 storeys. Are we to think of it literally sitting on our planet?

However, it is important to notice that the city's measurements meant that it was a perfect cube. At first glance this may not seem particularly significant, but it should get our attention when we realize that the only other perfect cube in Scripture is the Holy of Holies in Solomon's temple, which measured 'twenty cubits long, twenty cubits wide, and twenty cubits high' (1 Kings 6:20) and housed the Ark of the Covenant, which symbolized God's presence with his people.

When God called Israel as a people they formed twelve tribes. Multiply this by 1,000 (which in biblical terms means perfection or completeness) and it seems clear that a heavenly city measuring 12,000 stadia in length, width and height symbolizes the completed number of all God's chosen people, the new, spiritual Israel, in his eternal presence. This fits perfectly with John being told, 'Behold, the dwelling place of God is with man. He will dwell with them, and they will be his people, and God himself will be with them as their God' (Revelation 21:3).

The wall
The city's surrounding wall measured '144 cubits' (Revelation

21:17). A cubit is eighteen inches, which means that the wall measured 230 feet. If this was its height, such a wall around a city that was 1,380 miles high would be what Leon Morris calls 'curiously low'![56] If 230 feet refers to its width, it would hardly sustain a wall 1,380 miles high.

It seems clear that symbolic language is being used here and that the wall symbolizes something other than security, especially as we are specifically told that the city's gates 'will never be shut' (Revelation 21:25). What is more, there will be no enemies outside the new Jerusalem trying to force their way in (nor, for that matter, any inside the city capable of stirring up rebellion or wanting to get out). The eternal security of God's people is guaranteed not by a structure of any kind but by God himself—'The LORD surrounds his people, from this time forth and for evermore' (Psalm 125:2).

In biblical times the number 12 was another expression of perfection or completeness, which would point to the wall's measurement of 144 (12 x 12) underlining the gathering of all of God's elect into their Saviour's secure and eternal presence.

The gates

The walls had 'twelve gates, and at the gates twelve angels, and on the gates the names of the twelve tribes of the sons of Israel were inscribed' (Revelation 21:12). The mention of the twelve tribes of Israel points once again to the complete ingathering of God's people. The fact that there were twelve angels at the gates (obviously one at each gate) torpedoes the popular notion that the apostle Peter is a heavenly gatekeeper with authority to decide who should be allowed in. Stories about Peter standing at the pearly gates acting as a celestial bouncer and deciding people's destiny are all absurd. They have no biblical basis, but rely on a skewed interpretation of an incident in the New Testament.

When Jesus asked the disciples who people thought he was, Peter confessed, 'You are the Christ, the Son of the living God' (Matthew 16:16). In reply, Jesus told him, 'You are Peter, and on this rock I will build my church, and the gates of hell shall not prevail against it' (Matthew 16:18). The original word for Peter is the masculine name *Petros*, but the original word for 'rock' is the feminine *petra*, and refers not to Peter but to the truth of his declaration that Jesus was the Christ, the Son of the living God. Writing to believers at Corinth about the Christian church, Paul said, "No one can lay a foundation other than that which is laid, which is Jesus Christ' (1 Corinthians 3:11). Peter was undoubtedly one of Jesus' original disciples, but he never claimed to be their leader, only a fellow elder. When a Roman centurion 'fell down at his feet and worshipped him', Peter hauled him up and told him, 'Stand up; I too am a man' (Acts 10:25–26). There is no biblical evidence that Peter has any special position in heaven, let alone being a security guard there.

The foundations

The wall of the city had 'twelve foundations, and on them were the twelve names of the twelve apostles of the Lamb' (Revelation 21:14). This ties in perfectly with the fact that Christians are called 'members of the household of God, built on the foundation of the apostles and prophets, Christ Jesus himself being the cornerstone' (Ephesians 2:19–20). This does not mean that the apostles and prophets built the foundations, but confirms that the church is not built on the apostles but on the truth of the God-given message they brought. The British preacher John Stott (1921–2011) explains why this is relevant today: 'In practical terms this means that the church is built on the New Testament Scriptures. They are the church's foundation documents. And just as a foundation cannot be tampered with once it has been laid and the superstructure is being built upon it, so the New Testament foundation of the church is inviolable and cannot be changed by any additions, subtractions or modifications offered by teachers who claim to be apostles or prophets today.'[57]

Other details
The dimensions, wall, gates and foundations give us the general 'shape' of the city. In John's vision we are given several other details.

- Not only was 'the street of the city ... pure gold, transparent as glass' (Revelation 21:21), but the entire city was 'pure gold, clear as glass' (Revelation 21:18). As gold is not transparent, but dense, the references to glass may emphasize the precious metal's perfect purity. As far as we know, the purest gold is 24-carat, but in the new Jerusalem the word 'pure' breaks through chemical analysis and 'combines to convey, as far as it is possible to express, the infinite and inexpressible beauty and perfection of heaven.'[58]

- Two major features of the new Jerusalem refer to water. One of these is to its absence and the other to its presence, but an understanding of what they symbolize removes any confusion. In the first, John saw that 'the sea was no more' (Revelation 21:1). One might wonder why the first statement about the city refers to something that is not there, but there is a straightforward explanation. Time and again in Scripture the sea is symbolic of powerful enemies, massive problems and times of great danger and destruction. One psalmist links a time of trouble with a raging sea whose waters 'roar and foam' (Psalm 46:3). Facing a dire situation, another cries out, 'The floods have lifted up, O LORD, the floods have lifted up their voice; the floods lift up their roaring' (Psalm 93:3). The prophet Isaiah says, 'The wicked are like the tossing sea; for it cannot be quiet, and its water toss up mire and dirt' (Isaiah 57:20). In a picture of an outbreak of evil at the end of the present age John sees 'a beast rising out of the sea' (Revelation 13:1). John's vision of a setting where 'the sea was no more' did not mean the absence of a vast amount of water, but the complete and permanent absence of evil of any kind, as by then the devil had been cast into the lake of fire. In the new creation God's people will face no enemies, no problems, no dangers and no spiritual battles. C. H. Spurgeon claimed that the word 'difficulty' did not appear in heaven's dictionary.

• In the second reference to water, John sees 'the river of the water of life, bright as crystal, flowing from the throne of God and of the Lamb' (Revelation 22:1). There is one other biblical reference to a river in the city of God, and reading it in context helps to understand the meaning of this one. Psalm 46 was obviously written at a time when Israel was facing an overwhelming crisis. The writer pictures things getting so bad that it would be as if 'the earth gives way,' mountains would be 'moved into the heart of the sea', its waters would 'roar and foam' and the mountains 'tremble at its swelling' (Psalm 46:2-3). Yet he follows up these powerful pictures with another: 'There is a river whose streams make glad the city of God, the holy habitation of the Most High. God is in the midst of her; she shall not be moved' (Psalm 46:4-5). The city mentioned here was Jerusalem, which had some tiny streams but no river. This tells us that the Psalmist is using symbolic language to assure his fellow believers that whatever crises they faced they would not be overwhelmed and could enjoy a continual flow of God's blessing because of his living presence with them. The absence of the sea but the presence of the river combine to tell us that in the new Jerusalem all danger is over and nothing but blessing remains. Believers will rejoice in the never-ending outpouring of the river of the water of life flowing from God's throne. As the British preacher and commentator Matthew Henry (1662–1714) wrote, 'The church shall survive the world, and be in bliss when that is in ruins.'[59]

• On either side of new Jerusalem's river John sees 'the tree of life with its twelve kinds of fruit, yielding its fruit each month' and records that 'the leaves of the tree were for the healing of the nations' (Revelation 22:2). The Bible tells us that at creation 'The tree of life was in the midst of the garden' (Genesis 2:9). God has not told us what this tree was, but it was a symbol of God's intention that man should always know his Maker's blessing. Yet when Adam rebelled, 'the LORD God sent him out from the garden of Eden' so that he could not 'take ... of the tree of life and eat, and live for ever' (Genesis 3:22–23). God then took steps to 'guard the way to the tree of life' (Genesis 3:24) to show that there was no way in which man could re-enter the garden and have access to the tree of life by his own efforts. He stood condemned and powerless, shut out from God's presence because of his own sin.

Later on in the Old Testament, God took other steps to press home this fundamental truth. For example, he directed that throughout the forty years of wandering in the desert a curtain should surround the holiest place in the tabernacle.

This was God's special dwelling place with his people, and the curtain was a visual aid, reminding them that their sin separated them from the holiness of God, who is 'of purer eyes than to see evil' (Habakkuk 1:13). When the Israelites had settled in the Promised Land, God directed that for the same reason curtains should separate the Most Holy Place from the rest of the sanctuary in the Jerusalem temple. But at the very moment Jesus died, making atonement for the sins of all those in whose place he was put to death, God provided a stunning visual aid to show what the death of Jesus accomplished: 'the curtain of the temple was torn in two, from top to bottom' (Matthew 27:51). From that moment on, those who put their trust in him 'have confidence to enter the holy places by the blood of Jesus, by the new and living way that he opened for us through the curtain, that is, through his flesh' (Hebrews 10:19–20).

A revised version of a hymn by the British minister and prodigious hymn writer Charles Wesley (1707–1788)—who is said to have written 8,989 hymns!—has a phrase about this. In a verse bursting at the seams with glorious truth that includes several other wonderful benefits accomplished by the death of Christ, it declares:

The temple curtain is torn down,
The living way to heaven is seen;
Through Christ, the middle wall has gone
And all who will may enter in.
The ancient shadows are fulfilled,
The law's harsh sentence is applied,
The sinless Lamb of God is killed,
The covenant is ratified.[60]

- These marvellous truths are all confirmed by the fact that the new Jerusalem's life-giving river flows from 'the throne of God *and of the Lamb*' (Revelation 22:1), an unmistakable reminder that the death of Jesus, 'the Lamb of God' (John 1:29), is the source of the believer's life. Those still living on earth have a 'sure and steadfast anchor of the soul, a hope that enters into the inner place behind the curtain, where Jesus has gone as a forerunner' (Hebrews 6:19–20). In the new Jerusalem that glorious hope is fulfilled!

- As the new Jerusalem has 'no need of sun or moon' (Revelation 21:23) and therefore no calendar months, the trees John saw along the banks of the river yielding fruit 'each month' (Revelation 22:2) point to God's abundant and unending provision of all his people's needs. The leaves of the trees are said to be 'for the healing of the nations' (Revelation 22:2), but in the new Jerusalem there is no sickness or sin from which healing is needed. Instead, the leaves of the trees can be seen as symbolizing the perfect spiritual wholeness enjoyed by God's redeemed elect drawn from 'every tribe and language and people and nation' (Revelation 5:9).

The transition

As well as giving us all these details of the holy city, John also tells us of a breathtaking transition that is to take place; he sees 'the holy city, new Jerusalem, coming down out of heaven from God' (Revelation 21:2). As we saw earlier, the angel's promise to the church in Philadelphia uses a similar phrase and tells believers about 'the new Jerusalem, which comes down from my God out of heaven' (Revelation 3:12). In his vision John sees the eventual fulfilment of that promise.

An Old Testament narrative illustrates the delay between a divine promise and its fulfilment. The prophet Jeremiah served God for more than twenty years while Judah was being threatened by Assyria and Egypt, and for even more years after Judah had been overcome by Babylon. In the course of three invasions the cream of its population was deported, but false prophets told the captives that they would be delivered very quickly. God told Jeremiah to warn the exiles that these prophets were lying. The exiles were then reminded that they had been deported because of their sin and that they should accept their punishment, settle down in Babylon, and even pray for the welfare of their pagan overlords. Yet Jeremiah also brought this wonderful promise from God: 'For I know the plans I have for you, declares the LORD, plans for welfare and not for evil, to give you a future and a hope' (Jeremiah 29:11).

Christians in crisis sometimes 'claim' this promise as a word from God that he is on the brink of intervening to solve their personal problems, whether they are financial, physical, relational, vocational, social or of any other kind. God may indeed be about to bless them in some significant way and use this word to focus their attention on his grace and goodness, but the more important thing is to grasp the principles that lie behind it. Firstly, the promise was not to an individual but to 'all the people' (Jeremiah 29:1), that is, to God's exiled people as a whole. Secondly, it was not to be fulfilled until 'seventy years are completed for Babylon' (Jeremiah 29:10). Many who received the message would no longer be alive then; nor would Jeremiah, who had been taken to Egypt, where tradition says he was martyred. The promise was made to several generations. Thirdly, the way in which the promise was to be fulfilled was clear: 'I will bring you back to the place from which I sent you into exile' (Jeremiah 29:14).

This clearly links to man's fall into sin, God driving him into 'exile' from the garden of Eden, the life-long struggle against sin that he has brought upon himself and the gospel promise to all of God's redeemed people that in his good time they will be brought safely home to the new heaven and the new earth. This scenario perfectly reflects the truth behind the word given through Jeremiah, and includes the promise we are now considering.

In the midst of all the exotic language about this transition, only two adjectives describe God's people—they are 'the *holy* city, *new* Jerusalem'. It is not difficult to explain the use of 'holy'. Of all the Bible's words used to speak of God's attributes, 'holy' occurs more than any other; and in two places in the Bible the word is repeated twice. In Isaiah's vision of heaven he saw God 'sitting upon a throne, high and lifted up', surrounded by angels crying, 'Holy, holy, holy is the LORD of hosts; the whole earth is full of his glory' (Isaiah 6:1, 3); and in John's vision he saw celestial beings surrounding God's throne and crying out, 'Holy, holy, holy is the Lord God Almighty; who was and is and is to come' (Revelation 4:8).

Its relevance in the passage we are studying is well put by the American preacher John Piper: 'The holiness of God is the absolutely unique, infinite value of his majestic glory. To say that our God is holy means that he is beautiful beyond degree in the magnificence of his glory, and that his value is infinitely greater than the sum of the value of all created things.'[61] Then why does John use the same word about God's redeemed people during the transition we are reading about? The British preacher Richard Brooks puts it beautifully: 'The glory of God is at last imparted to the glorified church and thoroughly reflected in her. All God's infinite perfections and virtues, all his knowledge and grace and righteousness and love and holiness and wisdom and goodness are reflected in the church. The church is adorned with the glory of God, radiated with it, filled with it—aglow with it!'[62] If that does not get your pulse racing, I am not sure what will!

The second word is 'new'. In the first chapter we looked closely at the Bible's use of this word. Here it translates the Greek word *kainos*, which as we saw means not something brand new but something better because different; it means new in kind, not new in time. What a perfect word to describe God's people in heaven! They have been transformed by God's power and grace and in wonderful fulfilment of Paul's promise to the church at Corinth, they 'bear the image of the man of heaven' (1 Corinthians 15:49).

During his vision John hears 'a loud voice from the throne' (Revelation 21:3) with a message that lies at the very heart of all the Bible's teaching about the life of the believer in heaven: 'Behold, the dwelling place of God is with man. He will dwell with them, and they will be his people, and God himself will be with them as their God' (Revelation 21:3). It is impossible to miss the way in which God emphasizes the fundamental feature of heaven—*his intimate presence with his people.*

Before the fall, God's relationship with our first parents was up close and personal. After the fall, God dwelt among his chosen people, though throughout Old Testament times their relationship was mediated through a God-given nexus of rituals and ceremonies, the focal point of his presence being the Ark of the Covenant in the tabernacle and later the Holy of Holies in the temple. When Jesus came, 'the Word became flesh and dwelt among us' (John 1:14). The word 'dwelt' has precisely the same root as the heavenly promise that in heaven God will 'dwell' with his people—and Jesus fulfilled to perfection Isaiah's prophecy that Messiah would be '"Immanuel" (which means, God with us)' (Mathew 1:23). When Jesus returned to heaven, he sent the Holy Spirit to indwell and empower believers, so that Paul was able to tell those in Rome, 'The Spirit of him who raised Jesus from the dead dwells in you' (Romans 8:11).

In a passage about church discipline (with the aim of bringing an offender to repentance), Jesus outlines a situation in which the cause for concern was eventually brought before the local church. He assures the disciples that in such a situation they could look to him for wisdom and guidance, 'For where two or three of you are gathered in my name, there am I among them' (Matthew 18:20). Most Christians are not aware of the context, but they can nevertheless extend its truth beyond the matter of church discipline and look for an assurance of his spiritual presence when believers meet for worship. At his ascension, Jesus widens this pledge and tells them, 'Behold, I am with you always, to the end of the age' (Matthew 28:20). The time-span covered by this pledge shows that it was not restricted to the first disciples but extends to every Christian between then and the moment when the present age ends and the new age is inaugurated by the glorious return of Jesus to the earth.

This means that as Christians living today we can be sure that God's relationship with us is real, but as we know only too well our fellowship with him is flawed because even at our best we 'fall short of the glory of God' (Romans 3:23). As we shall see in detail in the coming chapters, there are no such flaws in the new Jerusalem as it blends into the new heavens and earth and God fulfils his promise to make all things new (Revelation 21:5).

Matthew Henry comments, 'He that in the beginning finished the heavens and the earth, and all the hosts of both, will finish all the blessings of both to his people. God does nothing by halves. He will give them to see the expectation, that end which they desire. He will give them not the expectations of their fears, nor the expectations of their fancies, but the expectations of their faith.'[63]

God's promise to his people about their destiny is not that they will spend eternity in some vague spatial environment, but that they will 'inherit the earth' (Matthew 5:5), 'in which righteousness dwells' (2 Peter 3:13) and which will be 'full of the knowledge of the glory of the LORD' (Isaiah 11:9). What a staggering contrast to today's world! As I write, nearly three billion people in up to ten thousand people groups have never had the gospel preached to them even once in any form and have no obvious access to the gospel. Of some 6,500 different languages, four thousand have no portion of God's Word, while 250 ethnic groups with populations of more than ten thousand people have no Christian worker planned for them.

Yet the Bible's emphasis is not on describing the renewed heaven and earth in terms of a place, state or condition, but on *the presence of God with his people*, and this is what the Bible means when it promises, 'He will dwell with them, and they will be his people, and God himself will be with them as their God' (Revelation 21:3).

There is a precise parallel between the language the Bible uses about the new earth and the new Jerusalem. In speaking of the resurrection of God's people, the Bible does not paint a picture of disembodied spirits floating around for ever somewhere in outer space. Martyn Lloyd-Jones writes of 'a wonderful renovation that is to take place even in the creation', when 'you and I who are children of God are destined to dwell in that kind of world, under those new heavens and on this new earth.'[64] Later in the same chapter, he is even more specific: 'We shall live in the body on this renewed, renovated, regenerated earth.'[65] The American scholar Paul Marshall has co-authored a book provocatively entitled *Heaven is not my Home* and on one of the first pages he explains what he means: 'Our destiny is an earthly one: a new earth, an earth redeemed and transfigured. An earth reunited with heaven, but an earth, nevertheless.'[66]

Famous last words

The prophetic book of Ezekiel is closely related to Revelation, which takes up many of its themes and includes forty-eight direct or indirect quotations from that particular Old Testament book. One scholar has even traced over eighty points of contact between the two. Like Jeremiah, Ezekiel pronounces God's judgement on his disobedient people, but also promises their restoration under a new covenant. By means of visions, parables, prophecies, allegories, signs and symbols an angel gives Ezekiel a guided tour of the restored city of Jerusalem, and with almost ninety references to his book in the gospels the Messianic dimension is clear. This makes it all the more significant that at the very end of his forty-eight chapters Ezekiel sums up his vision of the eternal state of God's redeemed people in just four words: 'The LORD Is There' (Ezekiel 48:35). As we shall see later in these pages, this is the ultimate truth about the new heavens and the new earth—and the ultimate answer to the default prayer of countless millions of believers for the last two thousand years: 'Your kingdom come, your will be done, on earth as it is in heaven' (Matthew 6:10).

It has always been God's intention that as part of a cosmos of utter perfection our planet should be governed for ever by human beings who reflect his glory in everything they are and in everything they do. At first glance his plans might seem to have been derailed, this is not the case. They are eternally secure and will be worked out in his perfect timing. Christians hoping to spend eternity somewhere on the other side of the Andromeda Galaxy should revise (but not lower!) their expectations. The city and the bride are symbols of God's redeemed people who will make that final transition to the new heavens and the new earth, the reconstructed and perfected cosmos where they will live and reign with God for ever.

4

Getting there

As I returned home from an engagement in Albania, my flight was within a few miles of its scheduled arrival at London's Gatwick Airport when the pilot announced that because of snow on the runway we had been diverted to Bournemouth, eighty miles to the west. Plans for me to be met at Gatwick were wrecked, yet another travel glitch to add to the many I have experienced in over fifty years in an itinerant ministry. Those who invite me to speaking engagements obviously need to know my estimated time of arrival, either at an airport, a railway station or an address to which I am driving; yet sometimes factors beyond my control upset the best-laid plans. Anybody reading this book will be able to add their own examples of disrupted travel plans, even when travelling a relatively short distance.

Then when (and how) can a believer expect to arrive in

heaven? In a delightful *Peanuts* cartoon Lucy asks, 'When you die and go to heaven, do they take you there in a school bus?' Linus replies, 'No, they pick you up in a golden chariot ... silver if you come second.' This may be harmless enough in a cartoon, and in context is more acceptable than the claims made by the American television evangelist Jessie Duplantis, who claims that he went to heaven in 'something like a cable car' in 1988.[67] He also claims that when there he put out his hand to comfort Jesus, who seemed to be hurting, only for Jesus to tell him, 'I need you Jesse'.[68] We can safely ignore such blasphemous nonsense, but it is important to know the answers to our double-barrelled question, which are not straightforward, as a human being is a unity of 'soul and body' (Matthew 10:28) and death separates one from the other.

When do the souls (or spirits) of believers reach heaven? The apostle Paul refers to Christians who have died as 'those who are asleep' (1 Thessalonians 4:13), while we are told that as Stephen, the first Christian martyr, was being stoned to death he prayed that God would forgive his murderers, then 'fell asleep' (Acts 7:60). Statements like these have led Jehovah's Witnesses, Mormons and others to teach that after death there is such a thing as 'soul sleep', but this is not the case. When somebody dies, the person concerned has no further earthly experiences or sensations, and there are times when at first glance he or she gives every appearance of being asleep. When nurses came into a hospital ward where my stepmother, a devout Christian, was critically ill, they had begun to adjust her position in the bed to make her more comfortable before they realized that she was no longer asleep, but dead. However, her soul was still very much alive, and immediately in heaven.

To say that the soul of a believer who dies is asleep raises some very awkward questions. How can people in heaven 'serve [God] day and night in his temple' (Revelation 7:15) if they are asleep? How can they sing, 'Worthy is the Lamb who was slain, to receive power and wealth and wisdom and might and honour and glory and blessing' (Revelation 5:12) if they are unconscious? There is no biblical evidence to support any kind of post-mortem hibernation. When believers die they are (literally) 'dead to the world', but their souls cannot die and are instantly in God's glorious presence. Death for believers is a cloud with the most wonderful silver lining.

The moment a believer dies his or her body begins to degrade, yet nowhere are we told that the dead person's soul is affected. We have a clear pointer in the Old Testament, where we read that at death, 'the dust [that is, the body] returns to the earth as it was, and the spirit returns to God who gave it' (Ecclesiastes 12:7). The difference is obvious and dramatic. The moment the believer's soul leaves the body it joins those of all believing predecessors in the presence of God. The American preacher Paul Wolfe paints this delightful picture of the Christian's journey to heaven: 'When a man first comes to Christ he has one foot in heaven, one foot left on earth. But then, for the rest of his life, he slowly shifts his spiritual weight. With the passing of time he grows in love for God, even as he grows nearer to the day when he will enter the presence of God. Finally, in death, he lifts his back foot from earth entirely and steps fully into the world above. At last he is both *of* heaven ... and *in* it too.'[69] Although (as we have already seen in earlier chapters) this is not the full and final picture of believers' heavenly existence, they will immediately begin to enjoy an infinitely deeper relationship with God than they could possibly know in this present life.

This is confirmed by Paul's testimony to the Christians in

Philippi. He tells them that he is torn between wanting to go on living, so that he can have further 'fruitful labour', and longing 'to depart and be with Christ, for that is far better' (Philippians 1:22–23). The precise language he uses shows that he sees no gap between departing (dying) and being 'with Christ' (in heaven). The two are so closely linked that they have been called 'two sides of the same coin'.[70] Elsewhere, Paul expresses this by telling Christians at Corinth, 'While we are at home in the body [that is, still living on earth] we are away from the Lord', so that for the time being 'we walk by faith, not by sight'; but he then adds, 'we would rather be away from the body and at home with the Lord' (2 Corinthians 5:6–8). When this transition takes place believers will no longer walk by faith, as they will be in their Saviour's immediate presence.

Writing about this, R. C. Sproul lets his imagination off the leash and says, 'It certainly doesn't violate any principle of Scripture to say that at the moment we die we meet an escort, and that the escort or escorts are the angels.'[71] Referring to the presence of angels at Jesus' ascension into heaven (see Acts 1:9–11), he adds, 'I like to think that this is normative ... and that we, as his people, can look forward to an escort service that transcends any liveried limousine we ever might enjoy in this world.'[72] This would be exciting, though we need to bear in mind that although people often refer to 'going to heaven' as if on a journey, the Bible never uses this kind of language. Nothing we read there suggests that when a believer's soul leaves the body it zooms through trackless space until it reaches heaven.

There is, however, an even more exciting possibility than that of an angelic escort, one which the British preacher Charles Price put to me like this when he was reading an early manuscript of this book: 'I think we can go one better than

[Sproul's suggestion] with John 14:3, where Jesus says, "And if I go and prepare a place for you, I will come again and take you to myself, that where I am you may be also." Most commentators see here a reference to the Second Coming of Christ, but it may be a reference to death, and Jesus himself receiving us to himself. I think there is a valid reason to believe that this is its meaning. After all, to be "away from the body" is to be "at home with the Lord", so why may it not be the Lord himself who comes back to take us? Stephen's dying words, "Lord Jesus, receive my spirit" (Acts7:59), may confirm this too. It's a thought that I have shared with people at death, or with close relatives after death, and it has always been very meaningful.'

Whether or not we envisage 'escorts', and whether we think of them as being angels of the Lord or the Lord of the angels, we can be certain of one thing: the moment believers die, their souls are 'away from the body' and instantaneously in God's immediate presence. As John MacArthur says, 'It is a graceful, peaceful, painless, instantaneous transition.'[73]

As we saw in chapter 1, the incident between Jesus and the criminal being put to death alongside him is a brilliant illustration of this. When the criminal cried, 'Jesus, remember me when you come into your kingdom' (Luke 23:42), Jesus promised, '*Today* you will be with me in Paradise' (Luke 23:43, emphasis added). As we also saw in that chapter, 'Paradise' is one of the Bible's words for heaven as it is at present, and the dying criminal was promised that his soul would be there the moment he died.

Whatever causes the deaths of believers, their bodies remain here on earth but their souls are immediately in their Saviour's presence, an experience often called 'the intermediate state'. The Bible does not have a detailed description of what this will mean. The only thing we are told is about the condition of believers' souls after death, and that is that they will be 'with Christ' (Philippians 1:23). This led the Dutch theologian G. C. Berkouwer (1903–1996) to write that the most information we have about the intermediate state is 'the clear whispering of the New Testament'.[74] Yet even this is enough to tell us that the souls of those who die in Christ instantly begin an indescribably glorious experience in the company of 'the spirits of the righteous made perfect' (Hebrews 12:23). The word 'perfect' is based on a verb which means 'to complete, make perfect by reaching the intended goal'.[75] As the Scottish theologian John Murray (1898–1975) wrote, they enjoy 'the highest bliss conceivable or possible for disembodied souls who are waiting for the liberty of the glory of the children of God to be dispensed at the resurrection'.[76]

Redemption
The next question to ask is *when do the bodies of believers who have died reach heaven?* The Greek philosopher Plato, who lived about four hundred years before Jesus was born, made a famous statement, '*Soma, sema*' ('a body, a tomb'), his way of saying that the human spirit reached its ultimate destiny when it broke free from the body at death. In the same way, Greek and Roman ideas in New Testament times held out no hope for dead bodies. It seems that this kind of thinking had made inroads into the church, leaving some Christians with serious concern about the future state of the bodies of believers. Paul is glad to reassure them: 'But we do not want you to be uninformed, brothers, about those who are asleep [that is, dead], so that you may not grieve as others do who have no hope. For since we believe that Jesus died and rose again, even so, through Jesus, God will bring

with him those who have fallen asleep' (1 Thessalonians 4:13–14). While 'others' (unbelievers) have 'no hope' as far as dead loved ones are concerned, Christians should be filled with hope and should not 'grieve as others do'. It is natural for us to grieve over the loss of loved believers, but we know that our separation from them is only temporary—and that their souls are already in Paradise.

Nor is our hope for their bodies wishful thinking; it is based on what Jesus did for them. Jesus not only died on behalf of those who trust in him, he also rose physically from the dead on their behalf, guaranteeing that they would also rise from the dead. Paul assures his readers that as their fellow believers had died trusting in Christ their whole persons, body and soul, would eventually share in his glory. *His* resurrection secured *theirs*. They will be part of the holy city, the new Jerusalem, and when Jesus returns to the earth *they* will come with *him*. Centuries before, the prophet Zechariah was given a vision of the day when, 'The LORD my God will come, and all the holy ones with him' (Zechariah 14:5). Paul assures the Thessalonians that their believing dead will be among them.

The Bible's specific answer to the question about the bodies of believers who have died is linked to the moment when Jesus will return physically and visibly to the earth. Usually called the Second Coming of Christ, it is mentioned over three hundred times in the New Testament (equivalent to once in every thirteen verses) and always as something sure to take place. Forty days after his resurrection from the dead, Jesus gave his disciples some final instructions and then 'he was lifted up, and a cloud took him out of their sight' (Acts 1:9). As the disciples stood gazing upwards, two angels stood by them and said, 'Men of Galilee, why do you stand looking into heaven? This Jesus, who was taken up from you into heaven, will come in the same way as you saw him go into heaven' (Acts 1:11). As we shall see later in this chapter, there has been endless speculation as to when this will be, and countless volumes have been written by those claiming to have worked out a timetable; but Jesus warns that 'concerning that day and hour no one knows, not even the angels in heaven' (Matthew 24:36). All we do know is that he *will* come: 'The Lord himself will descend from heaven with a cry of command, with the voice of an archangel, and with the sound of the trumpet of God' (1 Thessalonians 4:16).

At that unimaginable moment, 'All who are in the tombs will hear his voice and come out', either 'to the resurrection of life' or 'to the resurrection of judgement' (John 5:28–29). The word 'life' is the 'eternal life' (John 5:24) to which Jesus had referred earlier, and clearly means life in heaven. As far as the bodies of believers are concerned, whether they have been buried or cremated, lost at sea, pulverized in an explosion, swept away by avalanches, tornadoes or tsunamis, or disappeared without trace, they will be resurrected and united to their souls, so that they will spend eternity in God's presence as complete persons. When Christians were martyred in Lyons, France from AD 175–177, their pagan persecutors, knowing their victims' beliefs about the resurrection of the body, burned their bodies and then threw the ashes into the River Rhône, believing this would make doubly sure that there were no bodies to be raised. Little did they realize that whenever this kind of thing is done, 'He who sits in the heavens laughs; the Lord holds them in derision' (Psalm 2:4).

Almost unbelievably, *TIME* reported in 1997 that of Americans who said they believed in the resurrection of the dead two thirds said that their bodies would not be involved.[77] It would be difficult to think of a more outrageous oxymoron because, as the American author Randy Alcorn puts it, 'A non-physical resurrection is like a sunless sunrise.'[78] If only the body has been laid in the grave, what else but the body can be raised from it? In a commentary on the 1649 Westminster Confession of Faith, A. A. Hodge sets out what will happen: 'There are many changes in the material elements and form of the human body between birth and death, and yet no one can for a moment doubt that the body remains one and the same through it all. There is no difficulty in believing, upon the authority of God's Word, that in spite of the lapse of time and of all the changes, whether of matter or of form, it undergoes, the body of the resurrection will be in the same sense and to the same degree one with the body of death as the body of death is one with the body of birth.'[79] Cutting to the chase—not always the practice of the Puritans!— the British preacher Thomas Watson (1620–1686) writes, 'We are not so sure to rise out of our beds as we are to rise out of our graves.'[80]

The personal identities of those raised from the dead will be preserved, but their bodies will be dramatically changed to fit their new, eternal environment. It is impossible to imagine this, let alone understand it, but as God created the universe out of nothing—he simply 'spoke, and it came to be' (Psalm 33:9)—it will be a simple matter for him to bring back to life dead bodies that have degraded, disintegrated or disappeared. He can do this more easily that we can wake up a person who is asleep. As John Calvin writes, 'Since God has all the elements ready at his bidding, no difficulty will hinder his commanding earth, waters, and fire to restore what they seem to have consumed.'[81]

Anticipating this, Paul declares that at that moment these believers—who received 'the firstfruits of the Spirit' the moment they trusted Jesus as their Saviour—will then receive their 'adoption as sons, *the redemption of our bodies*' (Romans 8:23, emphasis added). The Greek word translated 'adoption' is *huiothesia*, which literally means 'the placing of a son'. Believers' adoption by God means that they are then given what we could call legal status within God's family, enabling them to enjoy all the rights and privileges involved. However, the full enjoyment of this status will not be theirs until the redemption of their bodies. In biblical terms, redemption means release from captivity through the payment of a ransom. The moment they trust Jesus as their Saviour, believers receive eternal life as 'the free gift of God' (Romans 6:23) and are delivered from the penalty of sin, but they are not yet released from its effects and their bodies remain subject to deterioration, decay, disease and death. Yet at the Second Coming the bodies of believers who have died will be redeemed and so set free from all the effects of sin. Paul assures the believers at Ephesus that the moment they trusted Christ they were 'sealed for the day of redemption' (Ephesians 4:30). This is the only time the phrase is used in the Bible and it assures believers that nothing can interfere with God's purpose and plan that their bodies will share in the glories of heaven.

In making his point, Paul adds 'For in this hope we were saved' (Romans 8:24); but as John Stott dares to say, we were only 'half saved, in hope of a full salvation in the end (to include our bodies)'.[82] Even if we begin counting from when Paul wrote Romans, the souls of millions of believers have already gone to heaven, *but only to heaven as it now is*—that is, to Paradise—as in one form or another their bodies remain on earth. Only when their bodies are fully and finally delivered from mortality and corruption will their salvation be complete. Their souls are in Paradise until then, but not yet in heaven as it will eventually be.

Even the unimaginable glory believers now enjoy in the immediate presence of their God and Saviour is only an intermediate experience. As A. A. Hodge explains 'There is something incomparably higher and more complete to look forward to—when all the redeemed will pass for ever from under the power of death, and each entire person, instinct with life and glorified, shall be completely conformed to the likeness of his Lord and adjusted to his environment in the new heavens and the new earth.'[83]

As with the new creation, the Bible shows us that the redemption of believers' bodies is not replacement but renewal. In a major passage on the subject of resurrection, Paul writes, 'What is sown [that is, the body that has been buried] is perishable; what is raised is imperishable. It is sown in dishonour; it is raised in glory. It is sown in weakness; it is raised in power. It is sown a natural body; it is raised a spiritual body' (1 Corinthians 15:42–44). This is the fullest treatment in Scripture of the subject, and describes a number of clear contrasts between our present bodies and our resurrection bodies. Our present bodies are 'perishable', subject to decay and disease and eventually to death; our resurrection bodies will be beyond all of these. Our present bodies are 'sown in dishonour', as there is something ignominious about lowering a human body into a grave; as an unvarnished comment by the British preacher John Flavel (1628–1691) puts it: 'That body, which was fed so assiduously, cared for so anxiously, loved so passionately, is now tumbled into a pit, and left to the mercy of crawling worms.'[84] In complete contrast, our resurrection bodies will be glorious, as far surpassing the body that was buried as a beautiful flower surpasses the seed from which it emerged. Our present bodies are characterized by 'weakness', often becoming tired, constantly running down and eventually lifeless and helpless; our resurrection bodies will never deteriorate. Our present bodies are 'natural', suited only for the present life and guided by our earthly impulses; our resurrection bodies will be totally in tune with the new, spiritual reality. Philip Arthur says, 'Every time I preach it is as though I looked out upon a congregation of caterpillars, each one guaranteed to turn into a butterfly.'[85]

Yet the bodies raised to glory will be those that were laid in the grave. They will be the same bodies of the people who lived, worked, played, sinned, deteriorated and died here on the earth. There is no suggestion in the Bible that the buried bodies will be annihilated and new ones created to replace them. As Paul makes clear later in the same chapter, 'For *this perishable body* must put on the imperishable, and *this mortal body*, must put on immortality' (1 Corinthians 15:53, emphasis added). John Murray linked this with the resurrection of Jesus and he put it so well that I can do no better than to quote him in full:

> The body that was raised from the tomb on the third day was the same body as was laid in the tomb. But it was endowed with new qualities. So it is with the resurrection of believers. There is unity and continuity. The usage of Scripture with respect to both Christ and believers is noteworthy in this respect. It was not a body that was laid in the tomb of Jesus: it was *he* as respects his body. *He* was buried, *he* lay in the tomb, and *he* rose from the dead. So it is with believers. *They* die and *they* are laid in their graves. At the resurrection day *they* will be raised up; *they* will hear Jesus' voice and will come forth. This identification of their persons with what was laid in the grave underlines the continuity. *The person buried is the person raised*' (emphasis added).[86]

On a lovely May day in 1972 the American preacher Vance Havner (1901–1986) took a photograph of his wife Sara. By the time he had finished the film, some eighteen months later, Sara had died. Four months after her death he took the film to be developed (those were pre-digital days), fearing that it might have deteriorated. To his great delight the photograph turned out beautifully, showing Sara with the kind of smile that had gladdened his heart for thirty-three years. Telling the story, he said that the camera was rather like Sara's grave; one day God will open it and from the negative produce a glorious positive, a new body transformed by God's resurrection power. Paul makes it clear that the resurrection of the body is not a 'maybe' but a 'must'—'This perishable body *must* put on the imperishable, and this mortal body *must* put on immortality.' At their conversion, Christians are 'sealed with the promised Holy Spirit, who is the guarantee of our inheritance until we acquire possession of it, to the praise of [God's] glory' (Ephesians 1:13–14). Human guarantees are sometimes loosely given and can prove worthless; but this guarantee is made by God, and the Holy Spirit dwells in the believer, not merely as a pledge of what is to follow, but as a first instalment.

Known unknowns

At a press briefing on 12 February 2002, in reply to a question about weapons of mass destruction in Iraq, United States Secretary of Defence Donald Rumsfeld told reporters, 'There are known knowns; there are things we know we know. We also know there are known unknowns; that is to say we know there are some things we do not know. But there are also unknown unknowns—there are things we do not know we don't know.' Journalists and others had a field day at his expense, and he was ridiculed by some for abusing the English language; but the distinguished linguist Geoffrey Pullum said that Rumsfeld's words were 'completely straightforward' and 'impeccable'. Be that as it may, we can make use of one particular 'Rumsfeldism' when reflecting on the eternal destiny of believers.

Although their destiny is secure, there are two obvious 'known unknowns' that are certain to take place before believers' eternal salvation will be fully and finally experienced, but about which we are presently in the dark. The first is an individual's date of death (something equally true of both believers and unbelievers). This is so obvious that we can deal with it in a few paragraphs. Writing to people used to making detailed business plans, a New Testament writer warns them not to take the future for granted because 'you do not know what tomorrow will bring', before adding, 'What is your life? For you are a mist that appears for a little time and then vanishes' (James 4:14). This is true at every stage of life and ultimately of death, regardless of a person's age. As the French abbot Bernard of Clairvaux (1090–1153) wrote, 'Death is oftentimes as near to the young man's back as it is to the old man's face.'

Jesus illustrates this in a parable about a wealthy farmer As his barns could no longer hold his crops, he decided to tear them down, build much bigger ones, store all his grain and goods, and then sit back and relax 'for many years', taking as his motto, 'relax, eat, drink, be merry' (Luke 12:19). But God intervened and told him that he had only hours to live—'This night your soul is required of you' (Luke 12:20). History has many examples of the same kind of thing. Early in the eighteenth century, Britain's Queen Anne had Blenheim Palace built near Oxford as the nation's gift to John Churchill, 1st Duke of Marlborough, following a famous military victory over the French in 1704 (though this was actually at Blindheim, not Blenheim). With three hundred rooms spread over seven acres, and set in 22,000 acres of prime land, it outshone any of Britain's royal palaces. The American author Bill Bryson describes it as a 'colossal explosion of magnificence' and as 'the greatest monument to vanity that Britain had ever seen'.[87] In 1719 the Duke and Duchess were able to move into the east wing of the unfinished palace, and may have anticipated many years of living in its vast splendour—but within three years the Duke was dead, long before the building was even finished.

An Old Testament writer warns us, 'No man has power to retain the spirit, or power over the day of death' (Ecclesiastes 8:8). For all his own authority and power Israel's King David acknowledges to God, 'My times are in your hand' (Psalm 31:15). Just as God determined the moment of our birth, so he knows exactly when we will die; he has no 'known unknowns'.

The second 'known unknown' is the timing of the Second Coming of Christ. As this determines when the bodies of believers who have died will go to heaven, the obvious question is, 'When will this take place?' As we saw earlier, not even Jesus (within the self-imposed limitations he accepted when he added humanity to his deity and came to live on our planet) knew the time of his return, yet many people have confidently claimed to know more than he did.

In 1533 Michael Stifel, an associate of Martin Luther, persuaded some of his followers to sell their property immediately as the world would end very soon. Followers of the American preacher William Miller endured what became known as The Great Disappointment when his prediction that the world would end on 22 October 1844 proved false. Leaders of the religious organization Jehovah's Witnesses declared that it would happen in 1874, then opted for 1914 and have since added 1915 and 1975 to their playlist. The American evangelist and author Hal Lindsey wrote a best-seller entitled *The Late Great Planet Earth*, which claimed that the world would end within one generation of the present State of Israel being established in 1948. In 1988, ex-NASA engineer Edgar Whisenant published a book listing eighty-eight reasons why the world would end in 1988 and claimed, 'Only if the Bible is in error am I wrong.' Human gullibility meant that the book quickly sold 4.5 million copies, but 1988 came and went. Later Whisenant publications, revising the date to 1989, then 1993, then 1994, all failed to make the best-seller lists. Many cults forecast that the end of the world would coincide with what was commonly celebrated as the turn of the millennium on 31 December 1999. More recently, the American radio broadcaster Harold Camping, who had previously predicted that the world would end in 1994, confidently went on air to predict that this would happen on 11 May 2011, his radio station spending $100 million to advertise the forecast. He said that he would not do any media interviews should it not happen (and of course would not have been available to do any if it had!). On 12 May 2011 he said that he was 'flabbergasted' that he was still alive on the earth and later revised his prediction to 21 October in the same year. One assumes that on 22 October he was even more flabbergasted.

The simple truth is that nobody on earth is qualified to give us details of the world's terminal timetable, and all claims to do so can be safely ignored. William Hendriksen put it well when he said, 'Curiosity is wonderful. For nosiness, intrusiveness, impertinence there is no excuse.'[88] We can be absolutely certain that God knows the precise moment when Jesus will return to the earth—and we can be equally certain that nobody on earth knows.

What we *do* know is that in fulfilment of God's promise the final 'day of the Lord' *will* come, bringing unspeakable horror to those who reject him and unimaginable joy to those who trust him. As we shall see in the final chapters, the certainty of Christ's Second Coming and all that will follow should profoundly affect God's people. The British preacher John Trapp (1601–1669) went so far as to say, 'This is pinned as a badge to the sleeve of every true believer—that he looks and longs for Christ's coming to judgement.'[89] Near the end of his life, the seventh Earl of Shaftesbury (1801–1885), a prominent social reformer, added this personal testimony: 'I do not think that in the last forty years I have lived one conscious hour that was not influenced by the thought of our Lord's return.'[90] Instead of pointless speculation about the event, Christians should be committed to passionate preparation for it, so that they will not 'shrink from him in shame at his coming' (1 John 2:28). As the British author C. S. Lewis (1898–1963) puts it, 'Precisely because we cannot predict the moment, we must be ready at all moments.'[91]

The survivors

We should now be clear on how and when the souls and bodies of believers who have died before Jesus returns reach heaven, but that leaves another question: *what of the millions who will be living on earth when he returns?* This question is so important that we need to get a clear grasp of what the Bible teaches on the subject. Paul gives us the answer in his first letter to the Thessalonians:

For this we declare to you by a word from the Lord, that we who are alive, who are left until the coming of the Lord, will not precede those who have fallen asleep. For the Lord himself will descend from heaven with a cry of command, with the voice of an archangel, and with the sound of the trumpet of God. And the dead in Christ will rise first. *Then we who are alive, who are left, will be caught up together with them in the clouds to meet the Lord in the air, and so we will always be with the Lord* (1 Thessalonians 4:15–17, emphasis added).

We are so locked into putting related events into strict chronological order that when we try to get a clear grasp of the Bible's teaching about issues as important as this we are in danger of paralysis by analysis. When Peter is writing about the Second Coming and rebuking sceptics who doubted whether it would ever happen, he reminds his readers that 'with the Lord one day is as a thousand years, and a thousand years as one day' (2 Peter 3:8). As God created time he is not controlled by it, cramped in it or confined to it. We need to bear this in mind as we read what Paul is saying about Christians who are alive when Jesus returns. We should throw away our calendars, clocks and stopwatches and focus on the facts, which are these:

- Paul is writing 'a word from the Lord' (as if to emphasize that he is not merely giving his own opinion) and says that when Jesus returns believers still alive at the time 'will not precede those who have fallen asleep'. Some of his readers seem to have thought that if they were alive when Jesus returned they would have some kind of advantage over believers who had died; Paul tells them that this will not be the case.
- Jesus will 'descend from heaven with a cry of command, with

the voice of an archangel, and with the sound of the trumpet of God'. The cry of command ties in exactly with what Jesus tells his disciples about his return: 'An hour is coming when all who are in the tombs will hear his voice and come out' (John 5:28-29). We are not told which archangel is involved—Jesus speaks of the Son of Man coming in glory 'and all the angels with him' (Matthew 25:31). Earlier he said that at his coming he would 'send out his angels with a loud trumpet call, and they will gather his elect from the four winds, from one end of heaven to the other' (Matthew 24:31). Nor are we told what words the archangel speaks or what 'the trumpet of God' means, but William Hendriksen is right to say that the Second Coming will be 'not only visible but also audible'.[92] He dismisses those who say that these events have no meaning, then comments that they must at least mean 'that in addition to the shouted command of our Lord ... a reverberating sound will actually pervade the universe', although 'what forces of nature will be employed to produce this sound has not been revealed'.[93]

- Paul then says that 'the dead in Christ will rise'. Jesus' command will be as clear and effective as the one he gave at his friend's tomb in Bethany when he cried, 'Lazarus, come out' (John 11:43). Just as surely, the bodies of the billions of believers who have died will miraculously obey the Lord's command.

- We are next told that the dead in Christ will rise 'first'. This is where thinking crippled by chronology can get us into trouble. How long will it take God to raise dead bodies? Will it take longer to raise someone who died in Old Testament times than to raise someone who died a few days (or a few minutes) before Jesus returns? The questions are irrelevant, but the basic truth is clear.

- Paul now adds, 'Then we who are alive, who are left, will be caught up together with them'. This raises more chronology issues! What does 'then' mean? Is there a time-lag between the last of the dead being raised (or the moment when they are all raised simultaneously) and living Christians being caught up with them? How long will it take for believers living when Jesus returns to be 'caught up' with those who have died earlier? At what moment does everyone receive a resurrection body? The Bible's answer to the questions asked in these two paragraphs is given in six words in a statement Paul makes to Christians at Corinth: 'We shall not all sleep, but we shall all be changed in a moment, *in the twinkling of an eye*, at the last trumpet. For the trumpet will sound, and the dead will be raised imperishable, and we shall be changed' (1 Corinthians 15:51–52, emphasis added).

As we saw earlier, Jesus supplies further details: his return will be 'with power and great glory' and that 'he will send out his angels with a loud trumpet call, and they will gather his elect from the four winds, from one end of heaven to the other' (Matthew 24:30–31). This emphasizes that regardless of when Jesus returns, no Christian will be overlooked. Those living at that moment will be 'caught up' with the reintegrated believers who have died so that together they will form the completed holy city, the new Jerusalem. Nor will this be a long drawn-out process—can we time a twinkle?

In a follow-up letter to the Thessalonians, the apostle writes of that glorious day when Jesus returns and all of his people will be 'gathered together to him' (2 Thessalonians 2:1). For believers who are living when Jesus returns there will be no intermediate state (with their bodies remaining on earth while their souls are in heaven). Instead, when the bodies of believers who have died have been raised and reintegrated with their souls (which have been in Paradise waiting for that moment), those still alive will also receive new bodies as they are 'caught up together with them in the clouds to meet the Lord in the air'. From that moment on every believer throughout history will 'always be with the Lord', living in his glorious presence as the new Jerusalem takes its place in the new heavens and the new earth. The American theologian Wayne Grudem writes, 'Christians often talk about living with God "in heaven" for ever. But in fact the biblical teaching is richer than that: it tells us that there will be new heavens and a new earth—an entirely renewed creation—and we will live with God there' and adds that there will be 'a new kind of unification of heaven and earth ... a joining of heaven and earth in this new creation, and there we will live in the presence of God.'[94] His is a much clearer understanding of the Bible's teaching than the one we find in gospel songs with lines such as, 'Away far beyond Jordan we'll meet in that beautiful land' and 'When the roll is called up yonder I'll be there'. The melody for the song 'This world is not my home, I'm just a passing through. My treasures are laid up, somewhere beyond the blue' is available as a mobile phone ringtone; thoughtful Christians should be glad that the words are not included!

After so clearly assuring the Thessalonian Christians that the deaths of their fellow believers mean only an interruption of the intimately personal relationships they had with them here, and that these would be renewed at even greater depth and in an indescribably superior environment, Paul adds, 'Therefore encourage one another with these words' (1 Thessalonians 4:18).

I hope that readers coming to the end of the present chapter will be stimulated to do exactly that. The Dutch theologian Anthony Hoekema (1913–1988) reflects what I have tried to say:

> The Bible assures us that God will create a new earth on which we shall live to God's praise in glorified, resurrected bodies. On the new earth, therefore, we hope to spend eternity, enjoying its beauties, exploring its resources, and using its treasures to the glory of God. Since God will make the new earth his dwelling place, and since where God dwells there heaven is, we shall then continue in heaven while we are on the new earth. For heaven and earth will no longer be separated as they are now, but will be one. But to leave the new earth out of consideration when we think of the final state of believers is greatly to impoverish biblical teaching about the life to come.[95]

The full meaning of the Old Testament promise, 'The meek shall inherit the land' (Psalm 37:11) is unwrapped by Jesus in the Sermon on the Mount: 'Blessed are the meek, for they shall inherit the earth' (Matthew 5:5). R. C. Sproul makes the point precisely: 'The expectation of the New Testament, ultimately, is that heaven will be here after the earth has been transformed.'[96] History is not meaningless, nor is it going round and round in circles. God is utterly in control and 'works all things according to the counsel of his will' (Ephesians 1:11). However dark the picture may be in the world at large or in our own lives, we can be absolutely certain that God is orchestrating every event and moment and that the time is coming when, as we saw in an earlier chapter, 'the earth will be filled with the knowledge of the glory of the LORD as the waters cover the sea' (Habakkuk 2.14).

5

Can we be sure?

The American author Samuel Clemens (1835-1910)—better known by his pen name Mark Twain—is sometimes quoted as having said, 'Nothing in the world causes so much misery as uncertainty.' Whether or not he coined the phrase—Martin Luther is another candidate—there is a certain amount of truth in the statement. Waiting for the result of an important examination, an interview for a job, an application for a mortgage, or to hear a jury's verdict or a consultant's diagnosis are some of many situations that can cause anxiety.

Although Christians are not exempt from these things, they should be able to handle them better than those with no understanding of God's sovereignty, wisdom and grace, who are without any credible testimony to his involvement in their lives. Yet many believers are plagued at times with the greatest uncertainty: in spite of all they believe and how they try to live, can they be confident of going to heaven when they die? Their doubt may be fuelled by remembering a particularly sinful episode in the past, or by repeated failure to overcome what some Puritans called a 'darling sin', or by finding at times that their love for Christ is so feeble and their commitment to him so weak that it causes them to wonder whether they have strayed beyond the boundaries of his promises.

The unbreakable chain

Some Christians have been influenced by teaching on the issue that allows for the possibility of a fatal fall from grace. While on a preaching tour in the United States I came across an example of this very thing. A pastor asked me whether I would meet with a church member who, in spite of his profession of faith in Christ, had chronic doubts as to whether he would go to heaven when he died. He was a brilliant medical practitioner, at the top of his profession and honoured nation-wide. As I was later to discover, the walls of his surgery (Americans would call it his office) were lined with citations reflecting his brilliance and the high esteem in which he was held. An appointment was arranged and a few days later I was able to spend an hour or so with him.

To his great credit, he was completely honest and open with me. He was sure that he was trusting Christ for his salvation, but was not certain that after death he would spend eternity in his presence. As soon as he had finished explaining his situation I asked him to turn with me to what many Christians would call their favourite sentence in the Bible: 'And we know that for those who love God all things work together for good, for those who are called according to his purpose' (Romans 8:28). I then asked him if he knew why the apostle Paul could be so sure about this, especially when he had just said that all of creation was 'in bondage to corruption (Romans 8:21) and that Christians had to endure 'the sufferings of this present time' (Romans 8:18). When he admitted that he had no idea, I turned with him to the next words in Paul's letter: 'For those whom he foreknew he also predestined to be conformed to the image of his Son, in order that he might be the firstborn among many brothers. And those whom he predestined he also called, and those whom he called he also justified, and those whom he justified he also glorified' (Romans 8:29–30).

As he took out a notebook and pen I pointed out that the first word—'For'—means 'Because' and that what followed was therefore an explanation of exactly *why* Paul was so certain that God was utterly in control and would ensure that whatever their circumstances or feelings, everything would work out for the eternal good of those who loved him. I could already sense that this was an eye-opener to him; it was time to work our way through Paul's explanation phrase by phrase. The gist of what I told him is included in the following paragraphs.

'For those whom [God] foreknew ...' Some Christians limit the meaning of this to saying that God knows ahead of time what people will do in response to the gospel; but while this is true— God is 'perfect in knowledge' (Job 37:16) and 'knows everything' (1 John 3:20)—the meaning of 'foreknew' goes far beyond that. As C. H. Spurgeon told his Metropolitan Tabernacle congregation, 'a reader must wear very powerful magnifying spectacles before he will be able to discover that sense in the text.'[97] There is never a time when anything past, present, or future is not fully known to God, including all the events in a person's life. David cries out, 'Your eyes saw my unformed

substance; in your book were written, every one of them, the days that were formed for me, when as yet there was none of them' (Psalm 139:16).

This points us towards a crucially important truth. Paul does not say that God merely foreknew what certain individuals would do (specifically, that they would become Christians). His foreknowledge in the verse we are studying is of *people*, not of things that happen in their lives. To say that God foreknew people is to say that he set his heart upon them before history ever began to unfold. The parallel word in the Old Testament is sometimes translated 'chosen' or 'known' and there is a perfect example of its use when God tells the people of Israel, 'You only have I *known* of all the families of the earth' (Amos 3:2, emphasis added). This obviously does not mean that God was not aware of any other families (that is, nations) in the world. Instead, it means that he had marked Israel out from all the rest of the human race and set his love upon her as his chosen nation. He knew *about* all other people, but had not chosen to do so in a loving, intimate way. The Dutch theologian Herman Bavinck (1854–1921) called it God's 'active delight'.[98] Including himself with the Christians in Ephesus, Paul places God's choosing of his people beyond the parameters of time, declaring that God 'chose us in him[the Lord Jesus Christ] *before the foundation of the world*' (Ephesians 1:4, emphasis added).

Some Christians think of their conversion in terms of having 'made a decision' for Christ, but they would never have done so had God not first made a decision about them! In believers' salvation, God is pro-active. Before time began God set his love upon them (a love that was unaffected by anything that would happen to them during their earthly lives). Paul tells the Christians of his day that God chose them 'not because of our works but because of his own purpose and grace, which he gave us in Christ Jesus before the ages began' (2 Timothy 1:9), another indication that their salvation was eternally secure. Those foreknown by God were sovereignly and lovingly chosen before the creation of the cosmos and he will not disown even one of them when the present cosmos is replaced by new heavens and new earth. Rather than question or resist this Christians should rejoice in it. Why God should do this is utterly baffling. C. H. Spurgeon's response to the mystery was not to question it, but to confess,

> I believe the doctrine of election, because I am quite certain that, if God had not chosen me, I should never have chosen him; and I am sure he chose me before I was born, or else he never would have chosen me afterwards; and he must have elected me for reasons unknown to me, for I never could find any reason in myself why he should have looked upon me with special love.[99]

The British theologian J. I. Packer adds, 'If you, a Christian, should ask, why did God choose me? ... the Bible answer is, because in his mercy he was pleased to—and that is the end of the matter.'[100]

'he also predestined to be conformed to the image of his Son'. This tells us the purpose for which God called his people. Some Christians have a blind spot about the biblical doctrine of predestination and feel uncomfortable about even trying to grasp what it means, but it is difficult to understand why this is so. Martin Luther wrote that 'all objections to predestination proceed from the wisdom of the flesh'.[101] Be that as it may, it is strange that Christians should not rejoice in their

predestination, as they have no problem in rejoicing in the 'end product'. The apostle John makes the amazing statement that when believers die and go to heaven they will not only be with Jesus but will be 'like him' (1 John 3:2). This statement is so staggering that we shall drill down into it in a later chapter. Yet in the verse we are studying, Paul says that God's purpose in predestining Christians is precisely that: 'to be conformed to the image of his Son'. Predestination ensures that all whom God foreknew will eventually be conformed to the likeness of Christ and believers should gratefully grasp that in love God 'predestined us for adoption as sons through Jesus Christ, according to the purpose of his will, to the praise of his glorious grace' (Ephesians 1:5–6).

When Gentiles in Antioch heard Paul and Barnabas preaching, 'they began rejoicing and glorifying the word of the Lord, *and as many as were appointed to eternal life believed*' (Acts 13:48, emphasis added). Writing about God's choice of Jacob and not Esau, Paul anchors it not in anything either of them did but in God's own eternal purposes and says that he did so 'though they were not yet born and had done nothing either good or bad—in order that God's purpose of election might continue, not because of works but because of him who calls' (Romans 9:11).

'*And those whom he predestined he also called*'. God's foreknowledge and predestination predate time; Paul now moves to two lifetime events. The first is that believers are 'called'. The Bible speaks of two ways in which God calls people. One is an *outward* call, given to everyone who hears or reads the gospel, and the other is an *inward* call, given to those whom God moves to respond to the gospel by turning to him and putting their trust in Christ. Theologians speak of this as 'the effectual call'. Imagine two unconverted friends hearing an evangelistic sermon, with two very different results. Both are called outwardly, but only the one who is called inwardly comes to faith. For him the difference is utterly life-changing and determines his new destiny.

I spend countless hours in airports all around the world and constantly hear (and ignore) public address announcements that are mostly irrelevant to me; but whenever I hear one that begins, 'Will Dr John Blanchard, a passenger on ...' I am all ears and nothing prevents me responding to it. At the same time hundreds of other people hear the same message but understandably ignore it. This gives a faint picture of the difference between an outward gospel call and an inward one. Yet response to an inward call is not self-generated; it is 'the gift of God ... so that no one may boast' (Ephesians 2:8–9). The inward, effectual call is a clear indication that the person concerned has been foreknown and predestined to be conformed to the likeness of Christ. This is exactly what happened to Lydia, a businesswoman in Thyatira who was one of those who heard Paul preaching in Philippi; 'The Lord opened her heart to pay attention to what was said by Paul' (Acts 16:14). His preaching reached not only her ears (the outward call) but also her heart (the inward call), and that is why she responded and was later baptized as a follower of Jesus Christ.

'and those whom he called he also justified'. The second lifetime event for the believer is that he is justified. To be justified by God is to be declared righteous in his sight on the basis of what Christ has done. The death of Christ in his place paid the penalty God rightly demands for the sinner's disobedience, and

the perfect life of Christ is credited to the sinner as if it were his own. The guilt and penalty of his sin is removed from him and the righteousness of Christ is bestowed upon him. This is why Paul is able to say elsewhere that 'there is therefore now no condemnation for those who are in Christ Jesus' (Romans 8:1). The justified sinner is not merely declared 'Not Guilty', but is brought into God's favour and family and received as though he had met all the demands of God's holy law. To be justified means not only to be made right with God immediately, but to remain so for all eternity. Paul Wolfe is not exaggerating when he writes, 'To be justified is to possess the same right to heaven that belongs to those who are already there.'[102]

In 1941 Bruce Hunt, an American missionary, was working among Koreans in Manchuria when the country was overrun by invading Japanese forces. On 21 October of that year he was arrested and after some time in solitary confinement put on trial on a series of obscure charges in relation to the Law for the Control of Religions. After hours of interrogation, the judge's verdict, which was translated by a Korean interpreter, left Hunt puzzled. 'What is it?', he asked the interpreter, 'I don't quite understand it.' The interpreter replied, 'You are without crime.' Hunt could hardly believe his ears, as other missionaries facing similar charges had been found guilty. 'Is this a suspended sentence?', he asked. 'No,' his interpreter replied, 'it is not a suspended sentence. It is a two-year suspended judgement. It means that they have not found you guilty. And if for two years you don't get into trouble, everything will be all right. They have not found you guilty. You are without crime.' 'Then why the two-year suspended judgement?' Hunt asked. The interpreter explained, 'That means that while they have not found you guilty, neither do they declare you not guilty. The judgement one way or another has been left hanging. If nothing comes up within the next two years the case is dropped. And now you can go home to your family.'[103] When God justifies a believer, nothing is 'left hanging', nor are we put on probation. God's declaration is clear, unqualified and final.

'and those whom he justified he also glorified'. Paul now moves beyond time. Simply put, those who are made right with God are eventually received into heaven, where they will not only be with Christ but will, as Paul puts it earlier in the chapter, be 'glorified with him' (Romans 8:17). Elsewhere, Paul calls this 'an eternal weight of glory beyond all comparison' (2 Corinthians 4:17). It is impossible to capture the full sense of the original Greek phrase used here in the same number of words, but The Amplified Bible points us towards its meaning: 'an everlasting weight of glory—beyond all measure, excessively surpassing all comparisons and all calculations, a vast and transcendent glory and blessedness never to cease!'

After I had explained these statements to my friend I asked him to tell me in what tenses they were written. I went through them one by one and he correctly told me that 'foreknew', 'predestined', 'called' and 'justified' were obviously all in the past tense. He wrote this down and then stopped. When I asked him to carry on and tell me the tense in which 'glorified' was written he replied, 'Well, of course, that must be in the future tense, as the people to whom Paul was writing were still living on earth— and so are we as we read these words.' I waited for a moment, then said, 'Look again at the wording—"those whom he justified he also glorified". Although Paul's readers were obviously not yet in heaven, Paul was so certain they would eventually be there that he wrote as if they were already there. The word *"glorified" is in the past tense!'*

I will never forget what happened next. As tears gathered in his eyes he put down his pen, looked me straight in the eye and said, 'Thirty years of doubt have just rolled away!' It was a precious moment for me and even more precious for him. Correspondence in the months that followed confirmed that God had graciously removed the doubt that for many years had clouded his vision and weakened his testimony.

The truths I shared with him that day have been called 'the golden chain of salvation' that binds every Christian to God. Unbelievers often reject it because it strikes a fatal blow to human pride and makes it clear that salvation is *only* by the sovereign grace of God. Because they are sometimes misunderstood by Christians, it is important for us to be clear on what the statements are saying and about how they hang together. To say that the people of whom Paul wrote were foreknown means that before the creation of the universe God marked them out and set his love upon them in a way that applied to no other people. With that as a given, there is a case for saying that the key word in the entire passage is 'whom', as it links together what John Stott calls five 'undeniable affirmations'.[104] Everyone foreknown is predestined; everyone predestined is called; everyone called is justified; and everyone justified is so certain to be glorified in God's presence in heaven that Paul uses a past tense (in this case a so-called 'prophetic past tense') to drive the truth home. He uses exceptional grammar to highlight extravagant grace. As Herman Bavinck puts it, 'Because Christ is a perfect Saviour, who brings not only the possibility but also the actuality of salvation, he cannot and may not and will not rest before those who are his own have been bought by his blood, been renewed by his Spirit, and brought where he is, there to be the spectators and sharers of his glory.'[105]

This unbreakable chain was forged by God before the sun, moon and stars were hung in space. Jesus underlines this when declaring that on the day of final judgement he will say to all who have put their trust in him, 'Come, you who are blessed by my Father, inherit the kingdom prepared for you *from the foundation of the world*' (Matthew 25:34, emphasis added). No Christian ever has grounds for doubting this staggering truth. As the Welsh preacher Geoff Thomas writes, 'The golden chain is God's. He designed it and made each link. He didn't make the links and then depend on man's ability to connect them up into a chain, but forges the chain together himself through his own power, purpose and love.'[106] The chains of condemnation have been broken and replaced by golden chains drawing God's people to heaven.

God graciously used the passage in Romans to rescue my new-found friend from decades of doubt, but there are other places in the Bible that are full of the same liberating truth. Here is just one:

> Blessed be the God and Father of our Lord Jesus Christ! According to his great mercy, he has caused us to be born again to a living hope through the resurrection of Jesus Christ from the dead, to an inheritance that is imperishable, undefiled, and unfading, kept in heaven for you, who by God's power are being guarded through faith for a salvation ready to be revealed in the last time (1 Peter 1:3–5).

People who trust Jesus as their Saviour yet sometimes have

doubts as to whether they will 'stay the course' and eventually go to heaven need to read the last paragraph again—*slowly!* Notice what it is saying:

- It is God who in his great mercy causes a person to be 'born again'. They could no more have brought about their spiritual birth than they could their physical birth. God worked a miracle in their life, opening deaf ears to hear the truth of the gospel, opening blind eyes to see its meaning and softening a hardened heart to yield to it. Paul reminds his Christian readers that they were 'dead in the trespasses and sins in which you once walked' but that now, by God's sovereign grace, they had been 'made alive' (Ephesians 2:1-2,5).

- This means that Christians have 'a living hope'. In common use, the word 'hope' always has an element of doubt attached to it, and sometimes is not much more than wishful thinking; but whenever the Bible uses the word 'hope' in speaking about salvation it means absolute certainty. Paul speaks of the 'hope of eternal life, which God, who never lies, promised before the ages began' (Titus 1:2) and elsewhere tells believers that their hope is 'laid up for you in heaven' (Colossians 1:5). This hope (absolute certainty) of eternal life is not dependent on emotions or mood swings, but is grounded in God's promise to all who trust in Christ.

- The believer's hope of eternal life rests on 'the resurrection of Jesus Christ from the dead'. He not only came, lived and died on behalf of all who were to put their trust in him, *he also rose from the dead on their behalf*. All these were what theologians call 'federal' acts, things done on behalf of others. Adam's fall into sin was a federal act, as a result of which God pronounced the curse of death upon the entire human race. The death of the sinless Jesus was also federal; in dying he bore that curse on behalf of all those whose place he took. As a result, 'God raised him up, loosing the pangs of death, because *it was not possible for him to be held by it*' (Acts 2:24, emphasis added). This comes across with great power when Paul writes, 'Jesus our Lord ... was delivered up *for* our trespasses and raised *for* our justification' (Romans 4:24–25, emphasis added). In both cases, the word 'for' means 'on account of' or 'because of'. It was because of people's sins that Jesus was delivered up to death, and in his death sin's penalty was paid in full, so that those in whose place he died are made right with God; as Paul later confirms, they are 'justified by his blood' (Romans 5:9). This is why he can say that Jesus 'was raised *for* (because of) our justification'. His resurrection is a stupendous visual aid, proving that because he was raised all who trust in him and are right with God will also be raised at the last day. Believers are called Christians just three times in the New Testament, but they are said to be 'in Christ' nearly 200 times, and their union with him in his death and resurrection guarantees their resurrection to the fullness of eternal life.

• The believer has an inheritance that is 'imperishable, undefiled, and unfading'. The Bible teaches that God has not only 'raised us up with [Christ]' but has 'seated us with him in the heavenly places in Christ Jesus' (Ephesians 2:6). Christians are united with Christ not only in his resurrection but also in his ascension into heaven (another federal act), and so are spiritually present with him already. Jesus makes this crystal clear: 'Truly, truly, I say to you, whoever hears my word and believes him who sent me *has* eternal life. He does not come into judgement, but *has passed* from death to life'

(John 5:24, emphasis added). Headstones on graves sometimes have the words 'Entered into eternal life' after the person's date of death, but even if that person were a Christian this is misleading. Believers enter into eternal life the moment they put their trust in Jesus Christ as their personal Saviour, not when they die. This glorious inheritance is guaranteed never to suffer from inflation, recession or anything else that ravages earthly inheritances. It is not only secure but can never be devalued in any way.

When my friend and fellow preacher Derick Bingham was diagnosed with acute myeloid leukaemia early in 2009, he was told he had only two days to live. He survived for another year, and at one point wrote, 'As a Christian I have an incorruptible inheritance as the world economy collapses, as millions lose employment, as wealth flies away like an eagle in a storm, none of this can touch my inheritance in Christ. Even as death stalked me in my first chemotherapy course, it was touch and go, but I made it. I am told that I have a 5–10% chance of living, but through it all my inheritance remains reserved for me and it is untouchable by anything.' Every Christian can have the same assurance!

• This spiritual inheritance is being 'kept in heaven for you'. The word 'kept' has the sense of being reserved. It is the word used in the story of the wedding at Cana when Jesus turns water into wine and the unsuspecting host tells the bridegroom that he has 'kept the good wine until now' (John 2:10). The Christian's inheritance in heaven is not merely promised, it is reserved! Writing to Christians at Colosse, Paul calls them 'the saints and faithful brothers *in* Christ *at* Colossae' (Colossians 1:2, emphasis added). It is as if he sees them having two addresses that overlap. While they are living physically here on earth they are already living spiritually with Christ in heaven, in that they share in his resurrection life and look forward to the time when they will be there in a fuller and final sense. The writer of Hebrews tells his readers to be 'grateful for receiving a kingdom that cannot be shaken' (Hebrews 12:28). Membership in the kingdom of God is not something that believers receive and enjoy only when or after they die, but something they have while they are still living on earth. Believers become members of the kingdom of God the moment they trust in Christ.

His ascension is their ascension. Their unity with him is organic in the sense that they can never be separated from him. It is also dynamic, because in spite of their failures, they have 'tasted the goodness of the word of God and the powers of the age to come' (Hebrews 6:5), and every experience they have of his presence, love and power increases their assurance of eternal salvation. The British preacher Thomas Brooks (1608–1680) writes, 'To have grace, and to be sure that we have grace, is glory upon the throne, it is heaven on this side of heaven.'[107] As the American hymn writer Fanny Crosby (1820–1915) puts it, it is 'a foretaste of glory divine'![108] If heaven is seen as a feast (and the Bible does speak of 'the marriage supper of the Lamb', Revelation 19:9), Christians still living on earth are already tasting the *hors d'oeuvre!*

• By God's power believers are being 'guarded through faith'. The word 'guarded' is a military term, one that was used of the vigilant defence of a fortress in order to safeguard those who occupied it. God is committed to preventing Satan, the enemy of their souls, from ever prising believers out of his grip; yet they are responsible for exercising faith in his power to do so. They are called to 'take up the shield of faith', so as to 'extinguish all the flaming darts of the evil one' (Ephesians 6:16), whose evil work will continue until they are finally with God in heaven.

- Believers have a 'salvation' that is 'ready to be revealed in the last time'. In this context salvation means complete, full and final deliverance from the penalty, power and presence of sin when Christ's eternal triumph is declared. The day will come when the glorious inheritance demonstrating this will be revealed to the entire universe. As the American scholar Simon Kistemaker says, 'Everyone will see the inheritance, but only the believers shall possess it.'[109]

I have just seen a full-page advertisement placed by a High Street bank in one of our national newspapers. The headline reads, 'After your personal best comes your personal best ever' and the entire advertisement is splashed over the picture of a tennis player sinking to his knees—obviously after achieving his greatest-ever victory. The text goes on to speak of the bank's extensive experience of working with clients 'who set the bar high, and having reached it, set it even higher'. It then speaks of expanding one's horizons, assuring the readers that it has the resources to help them reach new goals. However, after all that enticement, the advertisement does have a significant bottom line which warns that, because of market fluctuations, 'You may get back less than you invest.' In complete contrast, Christians 'investing' their lives in Christ by trusting everything to him can be said to get back infinitely more than they 'invest', including the fulfilment of this unbreakable promise: 'I give them eternal life, and they will never perish, and no one will snatch them out of my hand' (John 10:28).

The Burial Service in the 1662 Book of Common Prayer has the minister saying these words: 'Forasmuch as it has pleased Almighty God of his great mercy to take unto himself the soul of our dear brother/sister here departed, we therefore commit his/her body to the ground; earth to earth, ashes to ashes, dust to dust; in sure and certain hope of the Resurrection to eternal life, through our Lord Jesus Christ; who shall change our vile body, that it may be like unto his glorious body, according to the mighty working, whereby he is able to subdue all things to himself.' When these words are said of people who had put their trust in Christ, the 'sure and certain hope' will one day be fulfilled. The English hymn writer Augustus Montague Toplady (1740–1778) puts it perfectly:

My name from the palms of his hands
Eternity will not erase;
Impressed on his heart it remains
In marks of indelible grace;
Yes, I to the end shall endure,
As sure as the earnest is given;
More happy, but not more secure,
The glorified spirits in heaven.[110]

Everlasting rest!

The delightful story is told of a woman in the United States who was diagnosed with terminal cancer and told that she had three months to live. She called her pastor and asked him to visit her, as she wanted to put certain things in order before she died. They talked for some time, planning the funeral and tidying up all kinds of loose ends. As the pastor was about to leave, she called him back and said she had forgotten two important things. The first was that she wanted to be buried with her Bible inside the coffin. When he assured her that this would be done, she added, 'Secondly, I want to be buried with a fork in my right hand.' As the pastor struggled to know how to respond, the woman explained her request. 'I have gone to so many church suppers, and when the main course was over and someone came to clear the table they would always say, "Keep your fork." That was my favourite part of the meal, because I knew there was something better coming. It might be a chocolate cake or a deep-dish apple pie, but I knew it would be wonderful and substantial.' She then went on, 'I want to be laid out at the viewing with a fork in my right hand, so that people will leave wondering, "Why does she have a fork?" Then at the funeral service you can tell the congregation, "Keep your fork; the best is yet to come!"' The story may be apocryphal, but the sentiment is superbly scriptural!

Part of the 'best' the believer is certain to know in heaven is an experience of rest that eludes everyone in this life, yet of which at one point Jesus gave his followers a foretaste. Few of the promises he made to the Jewish people of his day would have had a more immediate impact than 'Come to me, all who labour and are heavy laden, and I will give you rest,' especially as he added the assurance that if they did so 'you will find rest for your souls' (Matthew 11:28–29). They were crushed by the massive accumulation of rules and regulations concocted by the scribes and Pharisees, who insisted that only when these were obeyed could anyone get right with God. Later on, Jesus referred to this in saying, 'They tie up heavy burdens, hard to bear, and lay them on people's shoulders' (Matthew 23:4). He then swept all these man-made restrictions aside and instead of a rulebook offered them a relationship. He promised that if they would put their trust in him, the burden of trying to get right with God by their own efforts would be lifted and they would find that love for their Saviour made them glad to live in a way that was pleasing to God. The British scholar R. V. G. Tasker (1895–1976) explains the impact of Jesus' words: 'Certainly Jesus does not promise his disciples a life of inactivity or repose, nor freedom from sorrow and struggle, but he does assure them that, if they keep close to him, they will find relief from such crushing burdens as crippling anxiety, the sense of frustration and futility, and the misery of a sin-laden conscience.'[III]

Jesus' words have meaning far beyond the particular circumstances of the people to whom he was speaking at the time, and they are as relevant now as they were then. People of different faiths, or without faith in a god of any kind, share a common longing to have peace of heart and mind and face many obstacles to enjoying it. Busy lifestyles, crowded schedules, financial pressures, physical concerns, moral conflicts, fractured relationships, a guilty conscience and a sense of personal failure in some areas of life are among the many things that can rob people of inner peace—and so can nagging thoughts about death and uncertainty about what may happen to them after that.

R.I.P?

The human longing for rest runs so deeply that headstones on millions of graves in countless cemeteries all over the world have the letters 'R.I.P.' engraved on them. These three initials represent the Latin words *Requiescat in Pace* (Rest in Peace). This headstone inscription—often repeated on wreaths, memorials, and condolence cards—expresses either the hope that the deceased has found rest from the pains and pressures of life on earth or the prayer that they will do so. It represents the heart-felt cry of those left to grieve and a longing for the deceased person to enjoy everlasting peace far beyond anything they knew while they were living. No doubt the words are sincerely meant, but it is vitally important that we ask a fundamental and inescapable question: *do they achieve anything?* As God is the only one who can grant the request, we need to turn to Scripture, not sentiment, to find the answer. There are four different cases in which the words are used.

- When the deceased and the mourners are unbelievers. This is the saddest case of all—for two reasons. Firstly, the Bible teaches, 'There is one God, and there is one mediator between God and men, the man Christ Jesus' (1 Timothy 2:5), which means that only by trusting in him can people bring their needs to God. (That said, we can be thankful that there have been countless times when God has graciously used the death of a loved one to bring otherwise careless people to think seriously, not only about their loss but about their own spiritual condition, and has drawn them to faith in Christ.) Secondly, although their concern for the deceased is perfectly understandable, that person's eternal status was sealed by God the moment they died, and no amount of longing or pleading by those left behind, however earnest and heartfelt, can change this. In a striking metaphor, the Bible likens death to a tree uprooted by a storm and says, 'In the place where the tree falls, there it will lie' (Ecclesiastes 11:3). Death never changes character; it simply seals it for ever.

- When the deceased and the mourners are believers. This is an unlikely case, as the mourners should rejoice in the assurance that their loved one's eternal status is already so glorious that they lack nothing. There is no need to pray for a deceased believer to rest in peace, or to hope that they will, because they already do. As the American theologian Loraine Boettner (1901–1990) writes, 'To petition God to change the status or condition of his loved ones in glory, or to suggest that he is not doing enough for them, is, to say the least, highly presumptuous, even though it may be well intended' (emphasis added).[112] Death is the last and greatest earth blessing God grants to believers, because it ushers them into the immediate presence of their Saviour.

- When the deceased is an unbeliever and the mourners are believers. There is no point in believers hoping or praying that the deceased unbeliever may rest in peace because, as we have already seen, the deceased's eternal (and dreadful) status has already been sealed and settled by God and can never be changed. When an athlete has crossed the finishing line, there is nothing he can do to improve his position in the field. Those who have not found peace with God in this life can never find it in the next, however passionately loved ones here on earth may long for them to do so.

- When the deceased is a believer and the mourners are unbelievers. We have already seen that it is pointless for unbelievers to pray in this way, as only those who are trusting in Christ can 'with confidence draw near to the throne of grace' (Hebrews 4:16). Any such prayer is also unnecessary as the deceased believer already has perfect, unchangeable and eternal peace in the presence of his God and Saviour. Nor is this something they received after they died. From the moment they come to faith they have 'peace with God through our Lord Jesus Christ' (Romans 5:1). This peace goes far beyond what is commonly called 'peace of mind'. Instead, it means a right relationship with God, not as a reward for moral or spiritual achievement of any kind, but because the righteous punishment their sin deserved has been paid for in the death of Jesus on their behalf. The souls of believers who have died are therefore in heaven because they have peace with God, and to pray that they might receive it is both pointless and foolish. As the Irish scholar Alec Motyer puts it, praying for the believing dead means 'denying the reality and efficacy of Christ's saving work; we are acting as though Calvary is insufficient'.[113]

Mourning the loss of a loved one is totally understandable but, as we saw in chapter 4, Christians grieving the loss of a fellow believer should also be filled with hope, as they can be assured that their separation is temporary. 'R.I.P' as a prayer for God to grant peace after death to someone who did not know 'peace with God through our Lord Jesus Christ' (Romans 5:1) during their lifetime is well-meaning but futile.

Rest on earth?

At the beginning of his famous *Confessions*, the North African philosopher and theologian Augustine of Hippo (354–430) addresses God with the words, 'Thou hast formed us for Thyself, and our hearts are restless till they find rest in Thee.'[114] They may be the most famous words he ever wrote and they reflect a basic biblical truth. The Bible frequently speaks of human longing for such rest and elsewhere David provides a dramatic example of this. At one point he is facing such powerful enemies and intolerable pressure that he cries, 'The terrors of death have fallen upon me ... horror overwhelms me' (Psalm 55:4–5). Even though he is a spiritual giant—God was to call him 'a man after my heart' (Acts 13:22)—he feels that he can stand the pressure no longer, and longs to get away from it all: 'Oh that I had wings like a dove! I would fly away and be at rest ... I would hurry to find a shelter from the raging wind and tempest' (Psalm 55:6, 8).

New Testament teaching underlines this constant longing for rest—and our frequent failure to find it. The book of Hebrews was originally written to Jews who had professed faith in Christ. Concerned that they should stand firm, the writer urges them to 'pay much closer attention to what we have heard, lest we drift away from it' (Hebrews 2:1). At one point he does this by quoting from Psalm 95, in which God reminds the writer of his people's repeated unbelief and rebellion during their forty years of wandering in the desert (Numbers 14:22 tells us that they treated God with contempt and dared to put him to the test ten times). They taxed God's patience to the point at which he determined, 'They shall not enter my rest' (Psalm 95:11). By this he meant the promised land of Canaan, which God called 'the rest ... the inheritance that the LORD your God is giving you' (Deuteronomy 12:9). God's promises and warnings were all proved genuine. Those living at the end of the forty desert years and who remained faithful to God entered the Promised Land, their painful years of wandering finally behind them. All the others died in the desert, disinherited by their disobedience.

Yet even those who made it to the Promised Land never had complete rest. They were promised, 'Ask for the ancient paths, where the good way is; and walk in it, and find rest for your souls' (Jeremiah 6:16); but they often turned a deaf ear to the God of their fathers. As a result, they wavered between success and failure, war and peace, prosperity and poverty. Plagued by their own inconsistency and betrayed by compromising or corrupt leaders, they found that God's promise turned into a threat, and as a result they never found complete rest.

The Bible emphasizes this by saying that the measure of rest God's people did manage to enjoy in Canaan is not the whole story: 'If Joshua [who led them into Canaan] had given them rest, God would not have spoken of another day later on' (Hebrews 4:8). 'Another day later on' refers to what is said in Psalm 95, which was written by David many years after Joshua. The writer of Hebrews is so passionately concerned that his readers learn the lesson that he quotes Psalm 95 three times

(Hebrews 3:11; 4:3, 5). These verses tell us that the 'rest' God has planned and promised for his people goes far beyond what was enjoyed by even the most faithful believer in Canaan all those centuries ago. He puts God's warnings and promises in a higher, spiritual context and encourages his readers by saying, 'We who have believed have entered that rest' (Hebrews 4:3). Those trusting Christ to save them have rest on earth *from trying to get right with God by their own moral, spiritual or religious efforts.* They are secure in the knowledge that they can join all other Christians in saying, 'Since we have been justified by faith, we have peace with God through our Lord Jesus Christ' (Romans 5:1).

However, although their salvation is secure, Christians never find complete rest on earth from everything that could disturb them, and they sometimes find themselves in situations that can threaten to overwhelm them. They all know of times when they would love to get away from everything they feel the world is throwing at them and find a place where they could be perfectly at rest. They have an unbreakable relationship with Christ, but not always unbroken fellowship with him, though this should always be their aim. The writer of Hebrews urges his readers, 'Let us therefore strive to enter that rest, so that no one may fall by the same sort of disobedience' (Hebrews 4:11). The apostle Peter strikes the same note when he exhorts his fellow Christians, 'Be all the more diligent to make your calling and election sure' (2 Peter 1:10). Whatever progress we have made, we must never slacken our determination to 'press on towards the goal for the prize of the upward call of God in Christ Jesus' (Philippians 3:14).

Rest in heaven

Nobody enjoys perfect, uninterrupted rest in this life—and for unbelievers there is even worse to come, as in the next life they will have 'no rest day or night' (Revelation 14:11). This is one of the defining differences between them and God's redeemed people, who in heaven will 'rest from their labours' (Revelation 14:13). Heaven as a place of rest is such a fundamental biblical truth that the more one thinks about it the more captivating it becomes. The English preacher Richard Baxter (1615–1691) was possibly the most prolific English theologian of all time. In his early thirties, and not expecting to reach his next birthday, he wrote that he was 'sentenced to death by the physicians'. He therefore began to think more intensely than ever before about his eternal future. As a result, he started to spend thirty minutes a day meditating on the subject of heaven, a practice that he continued until he died in 1691, soon after his seventy-sixth birthday. He had hoped that his early notes on the subject might help to produce 'a sermon or two', but they eventually formed the basis of a best-selling book, *The Saints' Everlasting Rest*, which was first published in 1650 and ran to nearly 700 pages.

In its original Greek form, the word 'labour' John uses in Revelation often meant the kind of activities that bring pressure, weariness or pain. As only God's people will be in heaven, we can be sure that their 'rest' means they will no longer face the unique demands of being a Christian living in the present world. There will be work to do, but none of it will involve fighting against opposing forces. Their 'rest' will cover many things, of which the following are some.

- They will have complete and everlasting rest from the devil's attention and attacks. The greatest pressures and pains Christians experience here on earth stem from the fact that they are constantly exposed to 'the schemes of the devil' (Ephesians 6:11). The Bible warns, 'Be sober-minded; be watchful. Your adversary the devil prowls around like a roaring lion, seeking someone to devour' (1 Peter 5:8). Elsewhere, the danger they face is spelled out in more detail: 'For we do not wrestle against flesh and blood, but against the rulers, against the authorities, against the cosmic powers over this present darkness, against the spiritual forces of evil in the heavenly places' (Ephesians 6: 12). There is no room in this book to unwrap the detailed meaning of these words— Martyn Lloyd-Jones confessed that 'they almost baffle description'[115]—but even listing them should be enough to convince us that the Christian life is not a playground but a battleground, with deadly enemies viciously bent on dragging believers down, mocking their faith, weakening their testimony and dimming their hope of heaven. No Christian is totally untouched by these attacks, but in heaven they will be over for ever and believers will have complete rest from needing to defend themselves from 'the flaming darts of the evil one' (Ephesians 6:16) and the relentless attacks of his agents.

• They will have complete and everlasting rest from the opposition which comes from living in an alien culture. Jesus tells his followers, 'If you were of the world, the world would love you as its own; but because you are not of the world, but I chose you out of the world, therefore the world hates you' (John 15:19). Later, he warns them, 'In the world you will have tribulation' (John 16:33). Paul drives the same message home when he tells Timothy, 'All who desire to live a godly life in Christ Jesus will be persecuted' (2 Timothy 3:12). The word 'persecuted' implies 'repeated acts of enmity'[116] and no

Christian is totally exempt from these. For nearly two thousand years the most severe persecution has resulted in millions being martyred for their faith (more in the twentieth century than in the previous nineteen put together); but opposition to Christians has also taken countless other forms, including torture, imprisonment and exile. Lower levels of persecution (though still painful) have included being refused employment or being passed over for promotion, and being fired for verbally expressing one's Christian faith or for wearing a Christian symbol. Many Christians suffer ridicule within their own family circle; Jesus specifically warned that there would be times when a believer's enemies would be 'those of his own household' (Matthew 10:36). Others are cold-shouldered by neighbours or belittled in social settings. In heaven, there will be no persecution, ostracism, pressure or abuse from enemies of the gospel, as everyone there will be of the same God-honouring mind and spirit. As Richard Baxter says, 'This is the time for crowning with thorns; that, for crowning with glory.'[117]

They will have complete and everlasting rest from battling against the relentless undertow of their sinful natures. At the peak of his ministry Paul confesses, 'I do not do the good I want, but the evil I do not want is what I keep on doing' (Romans 7:19). He is not suggesting that he never did what was right and always did what was wrong, but that there were times when he found himself doing sinful things which he hated because he knew they were contrary to the law of God, which was 'holy and righteous and good' (Romans 7:12). He then gives us the explanation for this: 'I know that nothing good lives in me, that is, in my sinful nature'

(Romans 7:18, NIV). Elsewhere, he explains what happens as a result: 'For the sinful nature desires what is contrary to the Spirit, and the Spirit what is contrary to the sinful nature. They are in conflict with each other, so that you do not do what you want' (Galatians 5:17, NIV). Unbelievers also face moral issues, but for Christians there is never-ending warfare between the indwelling Holy Spirit and their sinful nature, which remains adamantly opposed to God. Not only is this battle fierce and unrelenting, but the closer Christians seek to walk with God the more aware they become of their inbuilt sinfulness and of their longing to have done with sin of every kind. In heaven, the deepest desires of their hearts will be granted, as their nature will be utterly transformed. Sin will no longer live in them, and they will have nothing to fear from the coldness, indifference and treachery of divided hearts that sometimes plague them here.

• They will have complete and everlasting rest from constantly fighting temptation of any kind. The temptation to sin is something we must never excite but always expect, as we never reach such a stage of spiritual maturity that we may be tempted less, or not tempted at all. Commenting on this constant warfare, the British preacher William Gurnall (1617–1679) confessed, 'I expect to lay down my sword and my life together.' Death puts Christians out of Satan's reach for ever. In heaven they will have complete and everlasting rest from the constant need to be watchful, disciplined and ready to defend themselves against temptation, whether subtle or blatant. Life on earth is a constant battle against the world, the flesh and the devil, but in heaven the fight will be over and life there will be very different. In a jointly-authored book, the American theologian K. Scott Oliphint joins the Scottish theologian Sinclair Ferguson in saying, 'In a body that is adapted completely to a life of holiness and fellowship with God through the Spirit, obedience will be natural. Indeed, it will be easy!'[118]

• They will have complete and everlasting rest from the sorrow, heartache and pain of seeing the evidence and effects of sin. Peter tells us that centuries earlier Abraham's grandson Lot (hardly a paragon of virtue) was nevertheless 'greatly distressed by the sensual conduct of the wicked' (2 Peter 2:7). One of the Psalmists cries out to God, 'My eyes shed streams of tears, because people do not keep your law' (Psalm 119:136). Realizing where Jerusalem's sin was leading, Jesus 'wept over it' (Luke 19:41). When visiting Athens, Paul's spirit was 'provoked within him as he saw that the city was full of idols' (Acts 17:16). No Christians should be unaffected by blatant sin in the society in which they live. Wars, other armed conflict, massacres, murder, corruption in the corridors of power, rampant greed, blatant injustice, serial dishonesty and the epidemic spread of adultery, drug and alcohol abuse, reckless sexual behaviour, child abuse and pornography are constantly hitting the headlines, while millions openly reject the very existence of God. These things all grieve godly believers, but as heaven will be a society without sin, there will be total rest from such pain.

Sadly, there are often causes for concern within the Christian church, and as no church is perfect this has always been the case. Grieved about some of the things going on in the church at Corinth, Paul writes to the Christians there with 'much affliction and anguish of heart and with many tears' (2 Corinthians 2:4). So today (though without being destructively judgemental), Christians should feel pain when they see blemishes in the church, the body of Christ.

To take this one step further, a sure mark of growing godliness in Christians is the way in which they mourn when they themselves fail to live in a way 'worthy of the gospel of Christ' (Philippians 1:27). David cries out, 'I confess my iniquity; I am sorry for my sin' (Psalm 38:18). Although Job is described as someone who 'feared God and turned away from evil' (Job 1:1), there is a point at which he finds himself driven to his knees and crying out, 'I despise myself, and repent in dust and ashes' (Job 42:6). It is totally out of character for true Christians to treat sin lightly, commit sin deliberately or remember sin cheerfully. As my late friend Mary Wood, wife of Frederick P. Wood, founder of the National Young Life Campaign, used to say, 'For Christians, sin is not the done thing!' Sadly, 'not the done thing' is done too often and there are times when Christians find themselves echoing Paul's heartfelt testimony, 'Wretched man that I am!' (Romans 7:24). In heaven there will be no need for such a confession.

- They will have complete and everlasting rest from the doubts, fears, anxieties, uncertainties and conflicts of conscience that often plague their lives here on earth. No honest Christian can claim that he has never experienced any of these. The American preacher William S. Plumer (1802–1880) used to say, 'Satan loves to fish in muddy water'; and there are many times when he finds murky puddles or even depths in the lives of Christians struggling against confusing or challenging circumstances. In heaven such things do not exist.

- They will have complete and everlasting rest from the

pressure of unsatisfied desires. Even enjoying the good things people long for in life here on earth is never completely satisfying. Christians also have spiritual highs and lows. There are blissful times which they wish would never end, and other times when they feel 'down', out of sorts, unfulfilled or dissatisfied. In heaven there will be no such ebbing and flowing emotions.

- They will have complete and everlasting rest from the disciplines God requires from his people while they are living on earth. Paul instructs Timothy, 'Train yourself for godliness' (1 Timothy 4:7), and urges Christians, 'Keep alert with all perseverance' (Ephesians 6:18); 'Put to death what is earthly in you' (Colossians 3:5); and 'Walk in wisdom towards outsiders' (Colossians 4:5). Elsewhere, believers are told, 'Leave the elementary doctrine of Christ and go on to maturity' (Hebrews 6:1). These and other disciplines call for never-ending determination on a Christian's part; in heaven there will be no further need for them, as believers' hearts will be completely and constantly in tune with God's.

- They will have complete and everlasting rest from life-long efforts to extend the kingdom of God. There will be no services, rallies, missions or other evangelistic events, and no Sunday Schools, Bible classes, youth camps, young people's fellowships, children's clubs or other church-based auxiliaries. There will be no need to prepare sermons, talks or lessons, and no need to respond to letters or emails enquiring about how to get right with God. Nor will there be any need to write books explaining the Bible's teaching, either to believers or unbelievers (I say this with some feeling!). There will be no missionaries and no need to raise funds to sponsor them, to sustain the local church or to support Christian work of any kind. There will be no church business meetings to discuss practical or spiritual problems (a 'rest' that will bring heart-felt bliss to many!) Every one of God's redeemed people will be in heaven and the day of grace will be over.

- They will have complete and everlasting rest from the demands of pastoral care. Believers in pastoral office will be relieved of all the burdens they bear in caring for members of the church or fellowship in which they serve. Lay leaders in churches—elders, deacons and others—will have none of the responsibilities they now have. There will be no call for them or for other Christians to spend time, effort and resources in counselling or in seeking to meet the needs of the sick, the dying, the bereaved, the poor, the homeless, the unemployed, the neglected, the disadvantaged or the victims of crime, as there will be no such problems in heaven.

- They will have complete and everlasting rest from seeking and exercising the means of grace. This is a very different kind of rest, but nevertheless a real and significant one. There will be no church services, conventions, conferences, seminars or Bible study groups to attend. In the words of the Scottish clergyman Thomas Boston (1676–1732), these will be 'honourably laid aside'.[119] Nor will there be any need to seek God's face in prayer, to confess sin, to fast, or to strive after holiness. There will be no sin to confess and nothing lacking for which to pray, no need for self-denial, no need to seek for guidance and no need to plead with God for 'grace to help in time of need' (Hebrews 4:16). All of these will be replaced by direct, perfect and uninterrupted communion with God.

In the closing sentences of his classic book *The City of God*, Augustine strikes exactly the right note: 'There we shall rest and we shall see. We shall see and we shall love. We shall love and we shall praise. Behold what shall be in the end and shall not end. For what other thing is our end, but to come to that kingdom of which there is no end.'[120]

Questions

Yet the picture of a life of complete and everlasting rest in heaven triggers at least four questions.

The first relates to the intermediate heaven: '*Will Christians not be saddened because of the spiritual state of the world?*' Randy Alcorn suggests, 'It's also possible that even though joy would predominate in the present heaven there could be periodic sadness because there's still so much pain and evil on earth.'[121] Is this really the case? This begs the question as to whether Christians presently in heaven can see and reflect on what is happening in the world. If they can, they see one that is saturated in pain and evil 24/7; there is never a second when the most appalling evil is not happening and when terrible pain is not being suffered. 'Periodic sadness' in heaven would seem a strange response to this. Christians might wonder how perfect rest in heaven can co-exist with sin and its consequences on the earth, but they are not at liberty to edit what God reveals in his Word when he assures them that in heaven 'God will wipe away every tear from their eyes' (Revelation 7:17).

The second question, also relating to the intermediate heaven, is more specific. Will Christians not be saddened as they see churches and individual believers on earth being persecuted or going through difficult times? Isobel Kuhn (1901–1957), a Canadian missionary to China who worked among the Lisu people on the China-Burma (now Myanmar) border, once quipped, 'When I get to heaven they aren't going to see much of me but my heels, for I'll be hanging over the golden wall keeping an eye on the Lisu church!'[122] Nobody who reads her story can question her passionate concern for the church in which she invested her missionary life, but (bypassing the presumption that the intermediate heaven has walls!) her amusing comment raises the serious question as to whether Christians already there feel sadness as churches and individual believers here on earth suffer while the ungodly flourish.

The apostle John reveals that in his vision of heaven, 'I saw under the altar the souls of those who had been slain for the word of God and for the witness they had borne. They cried out with a loud voice, "O Sovereign Lord, holy and true, how long before you will judge and avenge our blood on those who dwell on the earth?"' (Revelation 6:9–10). This is sometimes taken to mean that Christians in heaven agonize over difficulties faced by fellow believers still on the earth and caused by enemies of the gospel, but a closer look shows that this is not true. Firstly, we can be sure that John's vision is about the intermediate heaven, as in the future heaven these martyrs will themselves dwell on the renewed earth, 'in which righteousness dwells' (2 Peter 3:13)—and God will by then have taken righteous vengeance on all who have persecuted the church throughout history and not repented, condemning them to 'the eternal fire reserved for the devil and his angels' (Matthew 25:41). Secondly, their cry is to the 'Sovereign Lord', the only time this title is used in Revelation. This points to God as being the supreme judge of all mankind, the one who determines every person's destiny, who is 'righteous in all his ways' (Psalm 145:17) and who will 'judge the world in righteousness' (Acts 17:31). These martyrs were not crying out for bloodthirsty revenge. They would have prayed for their persecutors while on earth—as Stephen, the first New

Testament martyr did as he was being stoned to death (see Acts 7:60). If this was the spirit in which they lived and died, they would hardly have become spitefully vengeful in heaven.

They were not even asking for the consummation of God's eternal purposes, when his perfect justice will be worked out, as they were sure this would happen; their cry was not, 'Will it?', but, 'How long ...?' Nor were they losing patience with God or questioning his timing. Instead, as Richard Brooks puts it, their cry expressed 'a deep, passionate and agonizing longing for the day when the church of God will be delivered and triumphant in the face of its enemies, the day when the people of God (and not least the martyrs and their testimony) will be vindicated, and the day, most of all, when God (the "Sovereign Lord, holy and true") will be glorified, his kingdom established, his name adored, and his will and law no longer flouted'.[123] There is no hint of sadness in this.

The third question relates both to the intermediate and future heaven and asks, '*Will Christians not be saddened when they remember all the sins they committed while they lived on earth?*' Remembering past sins is a miserable business, and there are times when even for mature Christians dark stains that may date back many years seep into the memory with depressing effect. Some wonder whether the same will be true in heaven and whether memories of past sins might sometimes come flooding back with miserable consequences.

Like the others, the answer to this question must be governed by what God has told us in Scripture and not by our own speculation. In a double-barrelled Old Testament prophecy (one true in both an immediate and ultimate sense), God says of his people, 'They shall all know me, from the least of them to the greatest ... For I will forgive their iniquity, and I will remember their sin no more' (Jeremiah 31:34). It is significant that the writer of Hebrews quotes this when reminding his readers that in making atonement for their sins Christ 'perfected for all time those who are being sanctified' (see Hebrews 10:12–17). God's word to Jeremiah does not mean that God will suspend his omniscience, but that he will purposefully choose not to remember his people's sins. God, whose memory is infallible, will infallibly forget. If we can dare to say so, he will have a self-imposed mental block as far as his people's sins are concerned.

In a brilliant anticipation of this David is led to write, 'As far as the east is from the west, so far does [God] remove our transgressions from us' (Psalm 103:12). God underlines this promise with the promise, 'For behold, I create new heavens and a new earth, and the former things shall not be remembered or come into mind' (Isaiah 65:17). Alec Motyer takes this one step further and writes, 'Not only its sorrows but everything about the old order will be gone in this total renewal ... Divine forgetfulness ... *will be matched by general amnesia* (emphasis added).'[124] The *Oxford Dictionary of English* describes regret as 'A feeling of sadness, repentance or disappointment over an occurrence or something that one has done or failed to do.'[125] The Bible gives no basis for believing that heaven will include regret of any kind. If everything God's people do there will be part of their unceasing praise, what room is left for trawling through the years when they lived as 'sons of disobedience' and 'children of wrath' (Ephesians 2:2,3) and for dredging up the sins they committed then? We can rest assured that in heaven believers will know all that they need to know, and their reaction to what they know will be perfectly in tune with their heavenly Father's will.

Nowhere do we read that in heaven God's people have bouts of depression as they mull over their past sins. Instead, we read of them singing praise to their Saviour because he has 'ransomed people for God from every tribe and language and people and nation' (Revelation 5:9). Their focus is entirely on Christ; even the worst aspects of their previous life on earth are wiped out by the wonder of their redeemed life on the new earth.

The fourth question relates in particular to the future heaven and asks, *'Will Christians not be saddened by knowing that there are family members, friends or loved ones who are not in heaven and are therefore in hell?'* This is the most sensitive question of all, and the knee-jerk reaction is to say, 'Yes, they will!'; but this is because we address the question on the basis of what the human mind thinks is logical or reasonable, rather than what the Bible teaches. Theologians have wrestled with this question for centuries—and sometimes tied themselves in emotional knots in the process—so we need to look carefully at the issue. A passage in Revelation points towards the right answer:

In his vision of heaven John hears 'what seemed to be the voice of a great multitude, like the roar of many waters and like the sound of mighty peals of thunder, crying out, "Hallelujah! For the Lord our God the Almighty reigns"' (Revelation 19:6). In the same passage John hears 'what seemed to be the loud voice of a great multitude in heaven, crying out, "Hallelujah! Salvation and glory and power belong to our God, for his judgments are true and just"' (Revelation 19:1–2).

It is sometimes said that at the first performance of Handel's *Messiah* in London on 23 March 1743 King George II stood to his feet during the singing of the 'Hallelujah' chorus, and that as he did so the entire audience followed royal protocol and also stood—though it has also been suggested that he may have done this to relieve his gout! In fact, there is no convincing evidence that he was even present at the time. Yet for over 250 years audiences have traditionally stood for the 'Hallelujah' chorus, and I recently joined with five thousand others in doing so in London's Royal Albert Hall when a massed choir of five hundred voices joined the Royal Philharmonic Orchestra in a performance of *Messiah*. The chorus includes the words, 'For the Lord God omnipotent reigneth', which are taken straight from Revelation 19, where 'Hallelujah' occurs four times.

The word literally means 'Praise ye Ya' (Ya being the shortened form of Yahweh, that is, Jehovah, or God). It occurs twenty times in the Psalms, where it is translated 'Praise the LORD', and one reference is particularly relevant. One of the Psalmists cries out to God, 'Let sinners be consumed from the earth, and let the wicked be no more! Bless the LORD, O my soul! *Praise the LORD!*' (Psalm 104:35, emphasis added). He is longing for the time when creation will no longer be ruined by sin, *or by the presence of sinners*, so that God can once again declare it to be 'very good' (Genesis 1:31), as he did before sin entered the world. In John's vision the Psalmist's longing is realized. By then God's judgement has fallen, creation is cleansed and God's name is glorified in the outworking of his perfect justice, including the damnation of the lost—and as a result God's redeemed people all join in crying, 'Praise the Lord!'

This is the context in which Christians should face this question. Nobody can think seriously about hell and remain emotionally and psychologically unaffected, and to think of family members, loved ones or friends exposed to God's relentless anger for ever is unbearable—but it will be a different matter in heaven, when all thoughts and emotions will be completely conformed to God's, so that everything is seen from his perspective. Christians will then see that God is as greatly glorified in the eternal punishment of the wicked as in the salvation of the righteous. After Egypt's pursuing hordes were drowned in the Red Sea, enabling God's people to escape and eventually make their way to the Promised Land, Moses and the people of Israel sang, 'I will sing to the LORD, for he has triumphed gloriously; the horse and his rider he has thrown into the sea. The LORD is my strength and my song, and he has become my salvation; this is my God, and I will praise him, my father's God, and I will exalt him ... Your right hand, O LORD, glorious in power, your right hand, O LORD, shatters the enemy' (Exodus 15:1–2,6). If Christians find it right (as they do) to praise God when they see him defeating his enemies here on earth, sometimes in answer to specific prayer, and feel that they honour him in doing so, how much more will they honour him in heaven when they share in his final triumph over all his enemies!

What is more, doing so will add to their rejoicing at the wonder of his saving grace. The believer's place in heaven is not secured by the quality of his life but by the perfect life and substitutionary death of his Saviour. It is a gift from God, the ultimate fulfilment of his promise to grant a 'Sabbath rest for the people of God' (Hebrews 4:9), and he will not allow even the catastrophic fate of others to dim the glory of heaven for those on whom he sets his saving love. The British preacher Edward Donnelly says that the answer to the question about believers in heaven sorrowing for loved ones in hell is 'clear, but inexpressibly solemn ... They will not be our loved ones any more. Our friendship with them will have ended and we will neither miss them nor sorrow over them. The saints in heaven praise God for the display of his justice in punishing sin.'[126]

The answer to these four massive questions has ultimately to be seen through the prism of the truth that when God's people reach heaven, 'He will wipe away every tear from their eyes' (Revelation 21:4). The presence of God will guarantee the absence of grief. There is (literally) no earthly way in which we can know how this will be the case, but C. H. Spurgeon had the right approach: 'I don't know what handkerchief the Lord will use—it's none of my business to guess'!

7

Conquests
and crowns

In previous chapters we have seen that there is an important distinction between heaven as it now is and as it will eventually be. We know that those who are trusting Jesus Christ as their Saviour can be sure of going to heaven when they die, not as a reward for their own moral or spiritual efforts, but by God's amazing grace. In Edward Donnelly's words, 'Sooner could a worm aspire to be a brain surgeon than a sinner expect to work his own passage to glory.'[127] As the Bible makes clear, it was God alone 'who saved us ... not because of our works but because of his own purpose and grace, which he gave us in Christ Jesus before the ages began' (2 Timothy 1:9). Yet it is difficult to imagine that there are any Christians who have never wondered what heaven is like and what it will be like to be there.

The American theologian Reinhold Niebuhr (1892–1971) wrote, 'It is unwise for Christians to claim any knowledge of ... the furniture of heaven.'[128] If that is so, we can do no more than flounder around in a fog when trying to get a grasp of what God's people will experience there, but as Neibuhr did not even believe in the resurrection of the body he hardly qualifies as a reliable guide. In particular, he totally misses the point that the Bible *does* tell us something about heaven; not in great detail, but sufficient to strengthen our faith and bring a glow to our expectations. We can respond to this by first noticing what will *not* be in heaven, and in John's vision one short sentence covers a great deal: 'Death shall be no more, neither shall there be mourning nor crying, nor pain any more, for the former things have passed away' (Revelation 21:4).

These four 'absentees' plague all of humanity, and a world in which none of them exists would be bliss. Yet the statement is not reflecting wish-fulfilment on the apostle's part, but comes to him in 'a loud voice from the throne' (Revelation 21:3). John does not identify the voice, but it clearly comes from God, the conqueror. The words that follow are also spoken by someone 'seated on the throne' (Revelation 21:5), who identifies himself as 'the Alpha and the Omega, the beginning and the end' (Revelation 21:6); and to remove any further doubt as to his identity, we read in the opening chapter of John's vision, '"I am the Alpha and the Omega," says the Lord God, "who is and who was and who is to come, the Almighty"' (Revelation 1:8). These titles combine to declare the eternal sovereignty of God, who created all reality out of nothing and is utterly in control of it. As its designer, architect and builder, God knows exactly what heaven is like; and he assures John that death, mourning, crying and pain will be absent. In the present life these are frequent experiences and at times all four combine with devastating force. Their total absence in heaven immediately tells us that life there is radically different.

The king is dead!

Firstly, there is no death in heaven. The American statesman Benjamin Franklin (1706–1790), one of the Founding Fathers of the United States, famously said that the only two things certain in life were death and taxes, but he was only fifty per cent right. Taxes of one kind or another can be legally avoided or illegally evaded, but there is no way to escape death. On 21 April 1992 Robert Alton Harris became the first man in twenty-five years to die in a Californian gas chamber. His lawyers had managed to delay the carrying out of the execution for over fourteen years, their last appeal failing only when Harris was already strapped into the death chair. His final act was to ask a prison official to make a note of his last words and to release them when the execution was over. They read, 'You can be a king or a street sweeper, but everybody dances with the Grim Reaper.'

The Austrian neurologist Sigmund Freud (1856–1939), the father of psychoanalysis, claimed, 'No one really believes in his own death.'[129] There may be an element of truth in this. People tend to shy away from the subject whenever they can, and prefer to talk of someone having 'passed away'. They even try to lighten things up by using a variety of expressions to describe death; they say that someone has 'kicked the bucket', 'snuffed it', 'bitten the dust', 'cashed in his chips', 'checked out', 'dropped off the twig', 'conked out' or 'given up the ghost'; but there is no escaping the simple fact that for all of us living is the process of dying. Death is an appointment we never make but are unable to cancel and the global death rate is awesome—nearly three people die every second, over a hundred every minute, over seven thousand every hour, nearly 170,000 every day and close to sixty million every year. Even with all the marvels of modern medicine at our disposal, we can never do more than delay the inevitable.

In his poem 'Do not go gentle into that good night', written for his dying father, the Welsh poet Dylan Thomas (1914–1953) urges, 'Rage, rage against the dying of the light'; and many do just that. Others believe that it will one day be scientifically possible to overcome death. In cryonics, blood is drained from the corpse immediately after death and the corpse is then filled with freezer fluid, encased in aluminium and suspended in a bath of liquid oxygen. The plan is that when a cure has been found for the disease that killed the person concerned—in hundreds or even thousands of years' time—the body can be thawed out, the disease cured and normal life resumed. The package is expensive, but for a cheaper version only the head is frozen, and when it is eventually thawed out a new body will be grown on to it, using the remaining supplies of DNA. Neither version comes with a guarantee!

Others claim that ageing can be suspended and that lifespans can be dramatically increased. In 2001, Marios Kyriazis, Chairman of the British Living Society, said that there were about ten people aged 110 in the world, but that there would soon be five hundred, then a thousand. He went on, 'Before long, it's reasonable to say that we will be living for 500 years.'[130] Convinced that ageing will eventually be defeated, Aubrey de Grey, founder of the Methuselah Association, told a *Daily Telegraph* reporter that he thought a lifespan of a thousand years is 'entirely possible,' adding, 'I don't see why after just a few years we die and become worms' intestines.'[131]

Such bizarre ideas contradict the Bible's teaching on death.

One of the psalmists asks the rhetorical question, 'What man can live and never see death? (Psalm 89:48). Someone defined as 'a wise woman' tells Israel's King David, 'We must all die; we are like water spilled on the ground, which cannot be gathered up again' (2 Samuel 14:14). An even wiser person writes, 'For everything there is a season, and a time for every matter under heaven: a time to be born, and a time to die' (Ecclesiastes 3:1–2), while a New Testament writer bluntly summarizes the simple truth: 'It is appointed for man to die once' (Hebrews 9:27). Even living for a thousand years or more would not alter the ultimate statistic: one out of one dies.

The British author Terry Pratchett—an outspoken atheist—was diagnosed with a rare form of early onset Alzheimer's disease in 2008. Speaking at a literary festival in June 2012 he told his audience, 'I can't be bothered with death. I have made him so popular that he owes me one.'[132] Yet however people bluster about death, the truth is that it baffles and bothers man, frustrates and frightens him. Many, including some with no serious religious convictions, find themselves fighting a stubborn instinct that after death they will have to give an account of their lives to God, and they fear the consequences. When the British racing driver Stirling Moss was at the height of a career in which he had a well-earned reputation for courage and daring, he told a newspaper reporter, 'I am frightened of death. I know it means going to meet one's Maker, and one shouldn't be frightened of that, but I am.'

For many others, the dread of death is a fear of the unknown. We prefer situations with which we are familiar, but by its very nature death is not in this category; none of us has any first-hand experience of dying. It is unknown territory, with no landmarks or signposts. This mysterious aspect of death is the kind of thing that drove the American film producer Woody Allen to say, 'I'm not afraid of dying. I just don't want to be there when it happens.'[133]

These reactions are understandable and it is easy to see why there are some who spend their lives enslaved 'through fear of death' (Hebrews 2:15); but Christians have no reason to find themselves in that position. In Volume Two of his *Works*, first published in 1648, John Owen points out why this is the case. In a powerful exposition of biblical teaching, he shows that for all those chosen in Christ before the foundation of the world Jesus 'abolished death and brought life and immortality to light through the gospel' (2 Timothy 1:10) by his resurrection from the dead. Christians still have to go through the process of dying, but as Paul reminds those in Corinth, 'The sting of death is sin, and the power of sin is the law. But thanks be to God, who gives us the victory through our Lord Jesus Christ' (1 Corinthians 15:56–57). It is not death that stings, but the sin that causes it; and sin's power lies in the law of God that condemns us all as sinners. Without law there would be no sin and without sin there would be no death, but Jesus destroyed the power of sin by his total obedience to the law and removed the sting of death by paying sin's penalty in full. His resurrection from the dead is a dynamic demonstration of the fact that he has conquered both sin and death, and Christians share in that victory from the moment they put their trust in him. Isaiah prophesied that Jesus the Messiah would 'swallow up death for ever' (Isaiah 25:8)—and he did.

Driving home with his daughter after the funeral of his wife Ruth, the American preacher Donald Grey Barnhouse (1895– 1960) stopped at traffic lights. As he did so, a large truck passed in front of them and just for a moment they were engulfed by its shadow. Turning to his daughter, he asked, 'Tell me, would you rather have been hit by the truck or by its shadow?' 'Why, by its shadow, of course,' came the reply. 'That's what happens to us Christians when we die,' Barnhouse commented. 'We are hit by the shadow of death, while those who do not know God are hit with the full force of death'.

One of Job's friends called death 'the king of terrors' (Job 18:14), but one of the greatest joys of heaven will be to know that this terrifying 'king' is dead; he is 'no more'. In 1852 John Owen's exposition of the subject was published separately under the title *The Death of Death in the Death of Christ*—a perfect title! Heaven has no funeral homes, coffins, cemeteries, graves, crematoriums, death certificates, wreaths, condolence cards, memorial services or obituaries. As my own pastor Dan Green told his Banstead congregation, 'In the new heaven and the new earth there will be no handkerchiefs, no hospitals and no hearses. There will be no crying, no cancer and no corpses.' This is a neat use of 'apt alliteration's artful aid' and he could have widened the subject and gone right through the alphabet listing what in this chapter I have called positive negatives—including no xeroderma, no xerophthalmia and no xenophobia—check them out!

Charles Wesley puts this glorious truth about the death of death in these triumphant words:

Our Lord is risen from the dead!
Our Jesus is gone up on high!
The powers of hell are captive led,
Dragged to the portals of the sky.

Who is this King of glory? Who?
The Lord that all our foes o'ercame,
The world, sin, death and hell o'erthrew;
And Jesus is the Conqueror's Name.

When a doctor visited the dying English clergyman Henry
Venn (1796–1873) in his Mortlake home he told his family, 'He
will not be here in the morning.' Venn overheard this and
realized what it meant: by morning he would be in heaven. The
more he thought about this, the better he felt—and he lived for
another two weeks! When Catherine Booth (1829–1890), wife of
William Booth, the founder of The Salvation Army, lay dying of
cancer she was heard to say, 'The waters are rising, but I am not
sinking!' When the American evangelist Dwight L. Moody
(1837–1899) was on his deathbed his son Will heard him cry out,
'Earth recedes, heaven opens before me!' As Will hurried to his
side his father went on, 'This is no dream, Will, this is beautiful
... If this is death, it is sweet. God is calling me and I must go.
Don't call me back!' Three days before he died, Martyn Lloyd-
Jones wrote on a scrap of paper for his wife Bethan and their
family, 'Do not pray for healing. Do not hold me back from the
glory.' All four of these believers had what we might call sneak
previews of the indescribable wonders of heaven in which God
the sovereign conqueror reigns, while King Death has passed
away!

Black need not be worn!

Secondly, there is no mourning in heaven. As death is by far the
greatest of the four 'absentees' from heaven we can look much
more briefly at the other three. We normally associate mourning
with deep grief and sorrow at the loss of a loved one, or someone

we knew well, an event that touches all of us at one time or
another. Yet we can experience sadness, regret and
disappointment at other times. An accident, serious illness, bad
news after a medical examination, the breakdown of a
relationship, falling into debt, losing a job and countless other
things can all cause sorrow.

The word 'mourning' translates the Greek *pénthos* and words
with the same root are sometimes used in the Bible in direct
association with death. Three examples in the Septuagint, the
first Greek translation of the Old Testament, express the
emotion well. When his wife Sarah died 'Abraham went in to
mourn for Sarah and to weep for her' (Genesis 23:2). When
Joseph's brothers tricked their father Jacob into believing that
Joseph had been killed by a wild animal, 'Jacob tore his
garments and put sackcloth on his loins and mourned for his
son for many days' (Genesis 37:34). Other uses of the word are
directly associated with sin. When the people of Israel came to
their senses and realized where their backsliding had got them
they cried out to God for forgiveness and confessed, 'The joy of
our hearts has ceased; our dancing has been turned to
mourning' (Lamentations 5:15). There are similar examples in
the New Testament. Concerned that it was apparently not
taking any action over a blatant case of sexual immorality, Paul
tells the church at Corinth, 'Ought you not rather to mourn?
Let him who has done this be removed from among you'
(1 Corinthians 5:2). In a second letter to the same church he tells
them that he 'may have to mourn over many who sinned earlier
and who have not repented' (2 Corinthians 12:21). James warns
careless sinners that they should realize their danger and
instead of laughing their way through life they should 'mourn
and weep' (James 4:9).

There is, however, a kind of mourning which the Bible commands and commends in this life. The Sermon on the Mount includes nine promises of God's blessing, including 'Blessed are those who mourn, for they shall be comforted' (Matthew 5:4). The word 'mourn' here is a present active participle, which means that we could translate Jesus' words 'Blessed are those who are continuing to mourn'. This blessing is not promised to those constantly crushed by a poor self-image or who are hard-wired pessimists, but to those who are genuinely repentant when the Holy Spirit convicts them of sin. Biblical mourning for sin is not self-centred but God-centred. God calls believers to mourn over sin in the assurance that if they do he will graciously respond in forgiveness and blessing. As David rejoices to claim when grieving for his appalling sins of adultery and arranging a murder, 'The sacrifices of God are a broken spirit; a broken and contrite heart, O God, you will not despise' (Psalm 51:17). Emphasizing that sorrow must be for the sin itself and not merely for its effects, Paul promises, 'Godly grief produces a repentance that leads to salvation without regret' (2 Corinthians 7:10). Genuine repentance leads to a closer walk with God in this life and eventually to heaven. Anticipating this, an Old Testament prophecy promises, 'And the ransomed of the Lord shall return and come to Zion with singing; everlasting joy shall be on their heads; they shall obtain gladness and joy, and sorrow and sighing shall flee away' (Isaiah 35:10). Nothing that can give rise to mourning will ever raise its head in heaven; like death itself, all mourning will have 'passed away'.

Dry eyes!
Thirdly, there will be no crying in heaven. I will never forget standing at the Vietnam War Memorial in Washington DC, a

massive black granite wall inscribed with the names of over 58,000 American service personnel (with an average age of twenty-three) who had lost their lives in that tragic conflict. As I stood there, a man with tears streaming down his face knelt in front of a particular name, clearly affected by the loss of someone he loved. As I watched him I reflected on the innumerable tears that have been shed on battlefields, in hospitals, at accident sites and at countless millions of funeral services and committals.

Yet a 'loud voice from heaven' assures John that in heaven crying will be 'no more'. Whoever coined the phrase 'a vale of tears' to describe the experience of living on earth was right to do so; the *Oxford English Dictionary* defines the phrase as 'the world regarded as a scene of trouble or sorrow'.[134] The Bible is being totally realistic when it admits that there is 'a time to weep' (Ecclesiastes 3:4), and it is natural to shed tears at times of death and mourning. When David heard of the deaths of Saul and Jonathan he and all those with him 'mourned and wept and fasted until evening' (2 Samuel 1:12). Surrounded by those mourning the death of a mutual friend, 'Jesus wept' (John 11:35). When Jesus rose from the dead and appeared to Mary Magdalene she went immediately to share the great news with his other friends 'as they mourned and wept' (Mark 16:10).

Tears are also shed at times other than those associated with death. When Job's friends first heard of the catastrophes that had hit him, 'they raised their voices and wept' (Job 2:12). Later, when he was under pressure, he told his friends, 'My face is red with weeping' (Job 16:16). Jeremiah confessed to the arrogant people of Judah who were rejecting his God-given message, 'If you will not listen, my soul will weep in secret for your pride' (Jeremiah 13:17). When Jesus had been arrested and Peter denied three times that he had been associated with him, Jesus had only to look at him and 'he broke down and wept' (Mark 14:72), another writer adding that he 'went out and wept bitterly' (Matthew 26:75).

It is not surprising when tears are shed at times of regret, sorrow, bitter disappointment, frustration or anger. When for some reason he was prevented from attending the temple in Jerusalem, a place set aside by God for the nation's worship, one of the psalmists cried out, 'My tears have been my food day and night' (Psalm 42:3). David was so distressed at one point that he confessed, 'I am weary with my moaning; every night I flood my bed with tears; I drench my couch with my weeping' (Psalm 6:6). Deeply concerned about serious problems in the early church at Corinth, the apostle Paul wrote to it 'out of much affliction and anguish of heart and with many tears' (2 Corinthians 2:4).

All of these examples find sad echoes today, and as long as we live in this world tears are as certain as breathing. On earth, our final tear is always in the future; in heaven, they will all be in the past, as in heaven all crying will have 'passed away'. Isaiah's prophecy anticipates this: 'The Lord GOD will wipe away tears from all faces, and the reproach of his people he will take away from all the earth' (Isaiah 25:8). C. H. Spurgeon used to say that the believer's resurrection body would not have any tear glands because they would not be necessary. His physiology may have been faulty, but his theology was flawless!

The pain-free zone
Fourthly, there is no pain in heaven. In some ways this is the most remarkable of the 'absentees' as it is the one with which we are most familiar. Pain is part and parcel of life here on earth, and one that affects us in countless ways. The British clergyman G.

Studdert Kennedy (1883-1929)—nicknamed 'Woodbine Willie' during World War 1 for giving out Woodbine cigarettes while ministering to wounded and dying soldiers—used to say that if anyone is not disturbed by the problem of pain it is for one of two reasons, hardening of the heart or softening of the brain.

Physical pain can be felt in every part of the human body and can have many different causes. I have a medical dictionary that runs to 1,200 pages and I sometimes hesitate to look up the possible cause of a pain I have in case my eyes are drawn to unrelated entries that might suggest other things that should concern me. Access to the internet raises infinitely more possibilities! Pain caused by accident, illness or disease can sometimes last for weeks, months or years; a friend of mine has rarely been free from pain for the last fifty years. There are times when undergoing a course of treatment or even recovering from surgery is painful. Even without the trauma of a serious accident, an illness or disease, everyday happenings can cause pain. Falling or twisting awkwardly, sustaining even a small cut, pulling a muscle and literally hundreds of other things can cause pain, which sometimes seems out of proportion to the cause. But in heaven there will be no pain of any kind, because (as we shall see later in this book) people in heaven will have changed bodies that are not only perfectly adapted for life in their new environment but are incapable of contracting illness or disease, sustaining injury, wearing out or breaking down.

There are many other causes of pain apart from those that are physical. Everyone can suffer chronic or acute emotional or psychological pain. Betrayal by someone who was trusted, a broken relationship, marriage breakdown, divorce, unemployment, redundancy, financial problems, shame, frustration, failure and disappointment all bring pain—as do anger, envy, jealousy and many other emotions. Yet there will be none of these in heaven.

There are also times when Christians suffer spiritual pain, which can take many forms. One is the guilt they feel when they become aware that they have grieved the Holy Spirit. God's love ensures that he always has their best interests at heart, wants them to avoid things that are harmful and longs for them to walk consistently in 'the path of the righteous' which is like 'the first gleam of day, shining ever brighter till the full light of day' (Proverbs 4:18, NIV). It can be painful when the Holy Spirit shows a Christian that he has strayed from that path—at one point David cries, 'My pain is ever before me. I confess my iniquity; I am sorry for my sin' (Psalm 38:17–18). But there will be no such pain in heaven as Christians will willingly think, say and do only those things that conform to 'the will of God', which is 'good and acceptable and perfect' (Romans 12:2).

Another form of pain occurs when God's hand of discipline is felt. Quoting various parts of the Old Testament, the writer of Hebrews touches on this: 'The Lord disciplines the one he loves, and chastises every son whom he receives' (Hebrews 12:6). He then adds that just as wise and loving fathers discipline their children, so God 'disciplines us for our good, that we may share his holiness' even though 'all discipline seems painful rather than pleasant' (Hebrews 12:10–11). When God punishes his enemies he is showing his wrath; when he disciplines his children he is showing his love. He loves them too much to allow them to go through life without their faith being tried, tested and strengthened—as Edgar Andrews says, he is 'the perfect parent',[135] patiently preparing his children for life in the new creation, when they will revel in the results. Visiting the Billy Graham Library near Charlotte, North Carolina, the item that made the biggest impression on me was the rough-hewn stone that marks the grave of the famous evangelist's wife, Ruth Bell Graham. She died on 14 June 2007, aged 87 and the stone bears the delightful inscription, 'End of Construction—Thank you for your patience'.

Death, mourning, crying and pain are among heaven's 'positive negatives', but the full list is almost literally endless. In heaven, God's people 'shall hunger no more, neither thirst any more; the sun shall not strike them, nor any scorching heat' (Revelation 7:16). There will be no stresses, no pressures, no failures, no baffling problems, no remorse, no guilt trips, no unsatisfied desires, and no lost causes. There will be none of the sad effects of separation and divorce, no breakdowns in families or society, no need to guard against anything being stolen, no business failures, no declining industries, no corrupt politics, no injustice, no deprivation of any kind, no sad or tragic news on the media. There will be nothing that will bring doubt, concern, unease or annoyance. There will be no let-downs and no complaints. There will be no unproductive days, sleepless nights or wasted time. Even the climate will be permanently perfect; there will be no bitter cold or stifling heat. Those who had lived in sub-zero temperatures and those who had lived in tropical heat will be equally at home.

Crowns

As God has conquered death and everything associated with it, nothing that bruises, scars or hurts the Christian in this life will be there in the life to come. In fact, the opposite is the case; while all these things are absent, other things will be present, and we can close this chapter by looking at some of them.

Four times in the New Testament we are told that Christians

will have crowns in heaven. To understand what these mean we need first to step back to read a remarkable prophecy. In the Old Testament God gives the prophet Daniel visions about the future history of the world, foretelling the rise and fall of many great kingdoms, including their final ruin. But Daniel also writes:

> I saw in the night visions, and behold, *with the clouds of heaven there came one like a son of man*, and he came to the Ancient of Days and was presented before him. And to him was given dominion and glory and a kingdom, that all peoples, nations and languages should serve him; his dominion is an everlasting dominion, which shall not pass away, and his kingdom one that shall not be destroyed (Daniel 7:13–14, emphasis added).

Some six hundred years later, when Jesus is challenged by Caiaphas the high priest as to whether he is 'the Christ, the Son of God' he replies, 'You have said so. But I tell you, from now on you will see the *Son of Man seated at the right hand of Power and coming on the clouds of heaven*' (Matthew 26:63–64, emphasis added). It is easy to see the connection between this and Daniel's prophecy. The title 'Son of Man' occurs over eighty times in the four Gospels and is one Jesus uses of himself more than any other. For instance, he uses it in explaining his purpose in coming into the world: 'The Son of Man came not to be served but to serve, and to give his life as a ransom for many' (Mark 10:45). This particular title obviously emphasizes his humanity but, as Daniel's prophecy and the claim Jesus made to Caiaphas show, there is more to it than that. Jesus, the Son of Man, is also seen to be the one whose kingdom is universal and everlasting.

This ties in perfectly with John's vision of heaven in which he sees, 'One like a son of man, with a golden crown on his head, and a sharp sickle in his hand' (Revelation 14:14). This is clearly Jesus. The crown and sickle are symbols of universal sovereignty and judgement. The only crown Jesus wore during his earthly life was when, after his arrest, Roman soldiers 'twisted together a crown of thorns and put it on his head' (John 19:2), but in heaven Jesus is 'crowned … with glory and honour' with 'everything in subjection under his feet' (Hebrews 2:7–8). This is the context in which the Bible speaks of Christians in heaven having crowns. These crowns are not to be taken literally and seen as some kind of heavenly headgear. C. S. Lewis warns, 'People who take these symbols literally might as well think that when Christ told us to be like doves, he meant that we were to lay eggs.'[136] The crowns are symbols of what it will mean for the Christian to be in heaven.

The crown of life

Of the four references to Christians being crowned in heaven, the first two can be looked at together, as the wording about crowns is identical in each. James tells his readers, 'Blessed is the man who remains steadfast under trial, for when he has stood the test he will receive *the crown of life*, which God has promised to those who love him' (James 1:12, emphasis added), while God promises members of the hard-pressed church in Smyrna, 'Be faithful unto death, and I will give you *the crown of life*' (Revelation 2:10, emphasis added).

The 'crown of life' promised in both of these passages goes beyond this present age and refers to the age to come. As we shall see when looking at each reference to a crown, its meaning is given in the words that immediately follow it. In James and Revelation the phrase is 'a crown of *life*'; in other words, 'life' is the crown the writers have in mind. Elsewhere, John tells his fellow Christians, 'God gave us eternal life, and this life is in his Son. Whoever has the Son has life' (1 John 5:11-12). The phrase 'eternal life' used here is nothing less than the life of God given to those he chooses to save and, as God is endless, so is the life that he gives. Yet 'eternal' refers not only to quantity but to quality. It is something entirely different from man's natural life. Nor does it begin when a believer goes to heaven. Christians already have a foretaste of this life while still on earth. Jesus said that he had come so that believers 'may have life and have it abundantly' (John 10:10) and that those who trusted him had already 'passed from death to life' (John 5:24). It may not mean a longer or wealthier life, but it does mean one lived in fellowship with God, knowing his presence, experiencing his power and reflecting something of his glory. The crown of life (we could call it the crowning of this present life) meant by James and John is eternal life in its fullest, most glorious sense—life on the renewed, glorified earth. It is the ultimate experience of the highest good for which man is made. The believers in Smyrna were promised this after they had been 'faithful unto death' (Revelation 2:10), but it was not something they had earned as a reward for being faithful. James makes it clear that the crown of life will be given not only to believers who had gone through persecution because of their faith, but to all who love God.

The crown of righteousness

In the third reference to Christians being crowned in heaven, Paul tells Timothy, 'Henceforth there is laid up for me the crown of righteousness, which the Lord, the righteous judge, will award to me on that Day, and not only to me but also to all who have loved his appearing' (2 Timothy 4:8). This crown is also defined by what immediately follows, which in this case is 'righteousness'. The key to its meaning lies in two statements in Paul's letter to the Corinthians.

In one of these we read the astonishing statement, 'For our sake [God] made [Jesus] to be sin who knew no sin, so that in him we might become the righteousness of God' (2 Corinthians 5:21). The central message of the entire Bible is packed into these few words and we will never in this world be able to do justice to them. In saying that God caused Jesus 'to be sin' Paul does not mean that Jesus was a sinner by nature, or that he ever committed sin; the Bible makes it clear that although he was 'tempted as we are' (Hebrews 4:15) he remained 'holy, innocent, unstained, separated from sinners' (Hebrews 7:26). Nor does it mean that those for whom he died are no longer sinners. Instead, it means that Jesus became the personification of the sins of others and bore in his own body and spirit God's righteous wrath which they deserved. God the Father did not force God the Son to undergo horrendous punishment, but both Father and Son agreed to provide a way of salvation for sinners who would otherwise be eternally condemned. In doing so they were fulfilling an Old Testament prophecy in which Isaiah gives this testimony on behalf of God's people: 'Surely he has borne our griefs and carried our sorrows; yet we esteemed him stricken, smitten by God, and afflicted. But he was wounded for our transgressions; he was crushed for our iniquities; upon him was the chastisement that brought us peace, and with his stripes we are healed' (Isaiah 53:4–5).

The purpose of such a sacrifice was so that sinners might become 'the righteousness of God' *in him*. In the death of Jesus two amazing transactions took place. All the sins of those in whose place Jesus died were transferred to him and all his perfect righteousness was transferred to them. Just as Jesus became sin personified, so in God's sight the sinners become righteousness personified and no longer subject to his terrifying punishment for sin.

The second of Paul's statements shows that Christ became to us 'wisdom from God, *righteousness* and sanctification and redemption' (1 Corinthians 1:30, emphasis added). Those putting their trust in Christ have not become sinless, but in terms of their salvation they are viewed by God as if they are as righteous as their Saviour. Paul claims that he is in a right relationship with God, 'not having a righteousness of my own ... but that which comes through faith in Christ, the righteousness from God that depends on faith' (Philippians 3:9).

In trusting Christ, believers have his righteousness *imputed to them*, but elsewhere Paul goes further and states that in heaven they will have Christ's righteousness *imparted to them*. He is so sure of this that (as we saw a moment ago) he writes, 'Henceforth there is laid up for me the crown of righteousness, which the Lord, the righteous judge, will award to me on that Day, *and not only to me but also to all who have loved his appearing*' (2 Timothy 4:8, emphasis added). The crown of righteousness is not a trophy given to those who have led outstandingly godly lives. It is God's gracious gift to all believers; in Alec Motyer's delightful phrase, 'The goal is reached not by the stairs but by the lift'![137] Believers' righteousness in heaven is the ultimate purpose for which Christ died on their behalf: 'Christ loved the church and gave himself up for her ... so that he might present the church to himself in splendour, *without spot or wrinkle or any such thing*' (Ephesians 5:25,27, emphasis added). As he himself promises, 'The righteous will shine like the sun in the kingdom of their Father' (Matthew 13:43).

John Calvin has a famous passage on this:

> This is the wonderful exchange which, out of his measureless
> benevolence, he has made with us; that, becoming Son of man
> with us, he has made us sons of God with him; that, by his descent
> to earth, he has prepared an ascent to heaven for us; that, by taking
> on our mortality, he has conferred his immortality upon us; that,
> accepting our weakness, he has strengthened us by his power; that,
> receiving our poverty unto himself, he has transferred his wealth to
> us; that, taking the weight of our iniquity upon himself (which
> oppressed us), he has clothed us with his righteousness.[138]

The more we reflect on such an amazing sacrifice, the more
astonishing it becomes. One of Job's friends, Bildad the Shuhite,
pessimistically asks, 'How then can man be in the right before
God?' when he is no more than 'a maggot' and 'a worm' (Job
25:4–6). The answer is simple but sublime: *the grace of God.*
Jonathan Edwards (1703–1758), rated by some as one of America's
greatest ever theologians and preachers, rightly comments, 'Even
the very best of men are, on earth, imperfect. But it is not so in
heaven. There shall be no pollution or deformity or offensive
defect of any kind seen in any person or thing; but everyone
shall be perfectly pure and perfectly lovely in heaven.'[139] Isobel
Kuhn claims that the most wonderful thing in heaven will be 'to
be with the Lord *with the root of sin gone.* To fellowship with him
without the lazy flesh dragging us back, or unwanted thoughts
or pride and self constantly straining us. To be finally rid of
corruption, to worship and enjoy him with heart purged into his
own purity, *that* will be an advance over anything that is possible
on earth.'[140]

The crown of glory

In the fourth reference to Christians being crowned in heaven, Peter addresses the elders among his readers, assuring them that 'when the chief Shepherd appears, you will receive the unfading crown of glory' (1 Peter 5:4).

Once again, this crown is defined by the word that follows—in this case 'glory'. It is a word we commonly use in our prayers and preaching, and it is often in Christian hymns and songs. It is also used in secular circles; one of the stands at White Hart Lane, the home of London's Tottenham Hotspur Football Club, has a huge sign reading, 'The game is about glory'. (Not to be outdone, a stand at Old Trafford, home of Manchester United Football Club, reads 'Manchester is my heaven'). The word 'glory' appears well over a hundred times in the New Testament—but what does it mean? It has a fascinating root, a verb basically used to express a favourable opinion about someone.[141] From there it came to mean the excellence, honour, splendour, radiance or renown that deserved a good opinion. Related Old Testament words appear over 350 times with the basic meaning of heavy or weighty. They are rarely used in this literal sense, but are often used of a person who is honourable, impressive, and worthy of respect. For example, Joseph tells his brothers, 'You must tell my father of all my *honour* in Egypt' (Genesis 45:13, emphasis added). Combining these two meanings together helps us to see why the Bible speaks so frequently about the glory of God. This is the totality of all the attributes that make him what he is by nature and there is nothing more 'weighty' (that is, more significant) than the awesome and infinite majesty, splendour, radiance, beauty and perfection of all that God is. After their deliverance from captivity in Egypt, the people of Israel sang, 'Who is like you, O LORD ... majestic in holiness, awesome in glorious deeds, doing wonders?' (Exodus 15:11). God is 'the King of glory' (Psalm 24:7) and the Bible is bursting with examples of its revelation. Even glancing at some of these will prepare us for what follows.

It is seen in creation; 'The heavens declare the glory of God' (Psalm 19:1). *It is seen in the salvation of his people*; he states that 'everyone who is called by my name' was 'created for my glory' (Isaiah 43:7). *It is seen in the defeat of their enemies*; he tells Moses that in defeating the Egyptians and allowing the people to escape, 'I will get glory over Pharaoh and all his host' (Exodus 14:17). *It is seen in his Word*; after receiving the Ten Commandments, Moses tells the people of Israel, 'The LORD our God has shown us his glory and greatness' (Deuteronomy 5:24). *It is seen in the earthly life of Christ*; 'The Word became flesh and dwelt among us, and we have seen his glory, glory as of the only Son from the Father, full of grace and truth' (John 1:14). *It is seen in his ascension*; when he ascended to heaven he was 'taken up in glory' (1 Timothy 3:16). *It will be seen in the final destruction of the wicked*; this will 'make known the riches of his glory' (Romans 9:23). *Finally, it will be seen in the new creation*; 'For the earth will be filled with the knowledge of the glory of the LORD as the waters cover the sea' (Habakkuk 2:14). As the American preacher Steven Lawson puts it, 'God's glory will fill and permeate the entire new heaven, and not just one centralized place. Thus, wherever we go in heaven, we will be in the immediate presence of the full glory of God. Wherever we go, we will enjoy the complete manifestation of God's presence. Throughout all eternity we will never be separated from direct, unhindered fellowship with God.'[142]

Christians here on earth are meant to live 'to the praise of his glory' (Ephesians 1:14) and to do even the most basic things 'to the glory of God' (1 Corinthians 10:31). They glorify God most when their behaviour reflects his character. There are signs of this as through the work of the Holy Spirit they are 'being transformed into [God's] image from one degree of glory to another' (2 Corinthians 3:18), but this is a gradual process and even at their very best they still continue to 'fall short of the glory of God' (Romans 3:23).

Now it gets exciting! Left to themselves, people have 'no hope' and are 'without God in the world' (Ephesians 2:12), but those who have responded to the call of God through the gospel will one day 'obtain the glory of our Lord Jesus Christ' (2 Thessalonians 2:14). They may struggle to reflect God's glory in this life, but they will be certain to do so in the life to come. They are 'vessels of mercy, which [God] has prepared beforehand for glory' (Romans 9:23) and who are 'called ... to [God's] eternal glory in Christ' (1 Peter 5:10). This is why Paul tells the Colossian Christians that 'Christ in you' is their 'hope of glory' (Colossians 1:27) and why he assures them that at the Second Coming they will 'appear with him in glory' (Colossians 3:4). The certainty of all of this is underlined in Paul's staggering statement that God's plan of salvation was 'decreed before the ages *for our glory*' (1 Corinthians 2:7, emphasis added). John Piper has coined a great phrase about the glory of God, which he defines as 'the going public of his infinite worth'. In the New Jerusalem all of God's people will be part of that 'going public' as they will be resplendent with 'the glory of God' (Revelation 21:11). The promise of an 'unfading crown of glory' will be fulfilled in every believer.

These four references to crowns that Christians will receive in heaven should cause every believer to rejoice—but something else can be added. In John's vision he sees that whenever the living creatures give glory and honour and thanks to him who is seated on the throne, who lives for ever and ever, the twenty-four elders fall down before him who is on the throne and worship him for ever and ever. *They cast their crowns before the throne*, saying, 'Worthy are you, our Lord and God, to receive glory and honour and power, for you created all things, and by your will they existed and were created' (Revelation 4:9–11, emphasis added).

Whoever these twenty-four elders are (and there is a case for saying that they represent the entire church), the important thing to notice is that they acknowledge the transcendent glory of God and submit to his supreme sovereignty. In 1903, London's *Daily News* carried the following piece the British clergyman Dean F. W. Farrar (1831–1903) had written about Queen Victoria:

> On one occasion, one of her chaplains, in preaching before her at Windsor, had made the second advent of Christ the subject of his discourse. After the service, the Queen, always a most attentive listener, spoke to him on the topic which he had chosen, and said: 'Oh, how I wish that the Lord might come during my lifetime!' 'Why,' asked the preacher, 'does your Majesty feel this very earnest desire?' The Queen replied with quivering lips, and her whole countenance lighted by deep emotion, 'I should so love to lay my crown at His feet.'

As with their other heavenly crowns, the believers' crown of glory is said to be 'unfading'. Paul emphasizes this by contrasting it with earthly honours. While athletes go into disciplined training 'to receive a perishable wreath', believers will receive one that is 'imperishable' (1 Corinthians 9:25). This wreath (the original Greek word is *stephanos*, the same as the one translated 'crowns' in the verses quoted in this chapter) was woven of leaves or flowers from plants or trees and given to winning athletes in the Isthmian Games. These wreaths eventually perished, but believers' heavenly crowns are 'imperishable', in contrast to all earthly honours which eventually fade, some of them very quickly.

Jonny Wilkinson is an iconic English rugby union player whose greatest claim to fame came in the final of the 2003 Rugby World Cup between England and Australia. The game was tied 17–17 as it moved into extra time. With only moments to go before the end of the game, Wilkinson kicked a magnificent drop goal to give England a 20–17 victory. He was voted the BBC Sports Personality of the Year and the 2003 International Rugby Board's International Player of the Year and was awarded an OBE (Order of the British Empire) in the 2004 Honours List. It is impossible to imagine the elation he felt at landing that trophy-winning drop goal, but six years later he made a significant confession to *The Times*:

> I had already begun to feel the elation slipping away from me during the lap of honour around the field. I couldn't believe that all the effort was losing its worth so soon. This was something I had fantasized about achieving since I was a child. In my head I had reached the peak of the mountain and now all that was left was to slowly descend on the other side. I'd just achieved my greatest ambition and it felt a bit empty.[143]

Heaven's glory could not be more different. Instead of years of dedication, discipline and concentrated effort producing glory that so easily slips away, God's redeemed people will have a crowning glory that will be theirs by the grace of God and that will never ebb, evaporate or end. They will also revel in an ever-deepening understanding of God's glory; as Jonathan Edwards says, there will never be a time when there 'is no more glory for the redeemed to discover and enjoy'.[144]

Time and motion

In *Here I Stand*, his excellent biography of Martin Luther, the British-born American church historian Roland Bainton (1894–1984) quotes from Luther's *Table Talk*, mealtime musings he led for students and others. One entry reads, "'I cannot think what we will do in heaven,"mused Luther. "No change, no work, no eating, no drinking, nothing to do." "Yes," said Melancthon [a fellow Reformer], "Lord, show us the Father, and it sufficeth us." "Why, of course," responded Luther, "That sight will give us quite enough to do."'[145]

Luther was right, and in the next chapter we will try to savour something of what this means; but people who know little or nothing of the Bible's teaching about heaven often assume that being there for ever will be utterly boring. The Irish playwright George Bernard Shaw (1856–1950) writes, 'Heaven, as conventionally conceived, is a place so inane, so dull, so useless, so miserable, that nobody has ever ventured to describe a whole day in heaven, though plenty of people have described a day at the seashore.'[146] In Mark Twain's *Captain Stormfield's Visit to Heaven* Sam Bartlett says, 'Why, Stormfield, a man like you, that had been active and stirring all his life, would go mad in six months in heaven where he hadn't anything to do!'[147] The Nobel Prize-winning English novelist William Golding (1911–1993), best known for his chart-topping novel *Lord of the Flies*, dreaded such a prospect, telling a fellow author, 'God exists outside time. He goes on for ever. But I don't have to. Good heavens! I'd die of boredom.'[148] This kind of thinking is reflected in an epitaph on a gravestone in a London cemetery:

Weep not for me, friend;
Though death us do sever.
I'm going to do nothing
For ever and ever.

People like these sometimes take another line: 'I can't bear the thought of spending eternity sitting on a cloud idly strumming a harp, or flying aimlessly around with nothing better to do.' This is a widely held picture, but the Bible gives not the slightest basis for believing this. There are at least three reasons why we can reject such misleading ideas.

Firstly, the idea of people sitting on clouds in heaven has no biblical basis. In scientific terms, clouds are masses of condensed watery vapour, and to picture them being used as armchairs or sofas is bizarre. The Bible does speak of clouds surrounding God—'Clouds and thick darkness are all round him' (Psalm 97:2)—but this is symbolic language pointing to God's infinite glory and his 'otherness' from creation. As Matthew Henry comments, 'Sometimes indeed clouds and darkness are round about him; his dispensations are altogether unaccountable; his way is in the sea and his path in the great waters. We are not aware of what he designs, what he drives at; nor is it fit that we should be let into the secrets of his government. There is a depth in his counsels, which we must not pretend to fathom.'[149]

Secondly, in the apostle John's God-given vision of heaven, there is only one picture of God's redeemed people playing harps, which they do while praising God with words beginning, 'Great and amazing are your deeds, O Lord God the Almighty' (Revelation 15:3). We should not try to build a doctrine about music in heaven on this, though we can be sure heaven's music will be so beautiful that it will make today's finest harmonies sound like a child's uncoordinated banging on a tin can. We can also be sure that the idea of everyone in heaven sitting on clouds and idly strumming harps for ever in self-indulgent or recreational ways is sentimental nonsense with no biblical basis.

Thirdly, although the Bible tells us that heavenly beings such as cherubim, seraphim and other angels have wings (see Isaiah 6:2, Ezekiel 10:16, Revelation 4:8), nowhere is this said to be true of human beings in heaven.

Details?

We have an insatiable thirst for information about things beyond our earthly experience, something reflected in NASA naming its 2012 Mars rover *Curiosity*. When we turn our attention to life in heaven our inbuilt curiosity produces an avalanche of questions. Websites teem with these and one blogger speaks for countless others when she writes, 'There are so many questions about heaven, I don't know where to start.' This chapter will focus on the supremely important truth about believers' activity in heaven. Over the centuries, preachers, teachers and others have tried to answer the questions people ask, and they do so either by developing hints they claim to have found in the Bible or by assuming that life in heaven will simply enhance all the things we presently do on earth. The danger is that in their enthusiasm to stimulate believers' anticipation of heaven they go too far and allow speculation to take the place of revelation.

A popular modern example of this is Randy Alcorn's book *Heaven*, first published in 2004, which the publishers say is 'thoroughly biblical'. It has hundreds of Bible quotations and Alcorn uses many of these to produce clear teaching, especially on death, resurrection and the distinction between heaven as it now is and heaven as it will be in the new creation. He uses the fine phrase 'redemptive continuity'[150] in showing that God will not annihilate his original creation, but redeem and restore it, and that life on earth at present will be perfected in the new creation. The book gives Alcorn's views on what new creation life will be like; and it is here that he goes 'off-piste' and allows his imagination to take over. Excluding the notes, bibliography and indexes, the book runs to 492 pages, giving him ample room to expound his ideas on what life on the new earth will be like; but in these pages I have counted nearly five hundred instances in which he uses words such as 'may', 'maybe', 'imagine', 'likely', 'seems', 'could be', 'possibly', 'perhaps', 'if', 'suggest', 'appears', 'assume', 'might', 'presumably' and 'think'. Here are a few examples of his unbiblical speculation:

We may not set foot on the new earth until 'the sixth day of the new creation' and perhaps 'watch God at work for another creative week'.[151] We may 'look back at the present Earth and conclude, creatively speaking, that God was just "warming up" and getting started'.[152] God may create 'new races of intelligent beings, either on Earth or on other planets spread across the new universe'.[153]

There may be 'talking animals' and 'intelligent non-human beings'.[154] Animals will be seen to have 'non-human souls'.[155] Confusingly, although 'Humans continue to exist after death' and this 'may not be the case for animals', God may have 'a future plan for animals as well'.[156] We will see 'more attributes of God in animals than we've ever thought about', especially 'God's playfulness'.[157] Extinct animals may all be brought back, and we can imagine 'riding a brontosaurus—or flying on the back of a pterodactyl'.[158]

Famous authors may 'challenge each other's ideas in what's still unknown to them' and 'bounce ideas' off Paul, Luther and Augustine.[159] Authors may go back and rewrite some of their books 'in the light of the perspective we'll gain'.[160] There will be large bodies of water on the earth, but instead of salt water it will be pure, and we could dive into it 'perhaps without tanks or masks' and 'effortlessly' hold our breath 'for hours'.[161] God may create 'far better substances' than meat but that would qualify as meat 'in every sense of taste and texture'.[162] 'Heaven will be full of children ... even if we look like adults'.[163] 'What will it be like to run beside God, laugh with God, discuss a book with God, sing and climb and swim and play catch with God?'[164] Although there will be no death in the new creation, 'there might be enough damage to require healing'.[165]

Other questions Alcorn addresses include, 'What languages will we speak?', 'Will our bodies shine?', 'Will we be male or female?', 'Will we have sex?', 'Will we wear clothes?', 'Will we get hungry?', 'How will food taste?', 'Will we have free will?', 'Will we know everything?', 'Will we have our own homes?' 'Will we ever disagree?', 'Will we have pets?', 'Will we dance?' and 'Will there be sports?'

This may be stimulating stuff, but towards the end of his book Alcorn makes the awkward admission that 'some of my hundreds of interpretations [of Scripture] are undoubtedly false,'[166] a confession that points us towards the fact that the only things about life in the new creation of which we can be absolutely certain are those which God has revealed to us in his Word. Scott Oliphint and Sinclair Ferguson have got it right: 'As in all biblical teaching, we need to recognize that the New Testament underlines the importance of prioritizing. The most essential things God wants us to know are the things he reveals most frequently and clearly. Some things are not essential for us to know, and other things are simply beyond our present ability to understand.'[167] We should settle for the fact that certain truths are 'secret things' that 'belong to the LORD our God' (Deuteronomy 29:29).

What is not a secret is that from beginning to end the Bible is saturated in the overall truth that people will live in his intimate and enjoyed presence for ever in 'new heavens and a new earth in which righteousness dwells' (2 Peter 3:13). As with many other subjects, the Bible does not tell us everything we want to know, but it does tell us everything we need to know, and leaving us with questions is not the same as leaving us in the dark. On the subject of heaven, what more do we *need* to know?

The banishment of boredom

There is nothing in the Bible to support the idea that believers spend eternity floating around like glorified ghosts, but even when the 'harps and clouds' idea has been set aside, sceptics have another question to ask: as the human spirit is so active, inquisitive and inventive, will worshipping God for ever eventually become boring? There are at least three very good reasons why we can answer this question with a resounding 'No!'

Firstly, because everyone in heaven will want to be there; it will be the fulfilment of the deepest longings of their hearts, which will be utterly and gladly in tune with God's. Paul tells the Corinthians that whether in the present life on earth or 'at home with the Lord' his aim is 'to please him' (2 Corinthians 5:8–9); in heaven, believers will rejoice in fulfilling that aim in everything they do. It has been said that there are three types of boredom and that these are related to times when we are prevented from engaging in some wanted activity, when we are forced to engage in some unwanted activity, or when we are simply unable, for no apparent reason, to maintain engagement in any activity. The Russian-born American historian and science fiction author Isaac Asimov (1920–1992) said, 'I don't believe in an afterlife, so I don't have to spend my whole life fearing hell, or fearing heaven even more. For whatever the tortures of hell, I think the boredom of heaven would be even worse.'[168] This skewed thinking could not be further from the truth. None of the factors leading to boredom exist in heaven, and believers will rejoice for ever at being in the presence of their God and Saviour.

For all King David's privileges and pleasures, he had one consuming passion: 'O God, you are my God; earnestly I seek you; my soul thirsts for you; my flesh faints for you, as in a dry and weary land where there is no water' (Psalm 63:1). On another occasion he cries, 'One thing have I asked of the LORD, that will I seek after; that I may dwell in the house of the LORD all the days of my life, to gaze upon the beauty of the LORD' (Psalm 27:4).

This does not mean that he had ambitions to become a Levitical priest and to spend his days in God's tabernacle. Instead, it spoke of his passionate longing for constant, unbroken communion with God, in which he would revel in all God's glorious attributes. This was the dominating burden of his prayer—'One thing have I asked of the Lord'. As one commentator put it, 'The Psalmist is determined to seek the abiding security and joy of God's presence.'[169] David had a heightened sense of God's presence from time to time, but there were also times when he knew little of its security or joy. Yet his faith was constantly strengthened by the assurance that 'goodness and mercy shall follow me all the days of my life, *and I shall dwell in the house of the LORD for ever*' (Psalm 23:6, emphasis added). It has been said that millions long for immortality yet don't know what to do with themselves on a rainy Sunday. A recent email from a friend confesses, 'Our tastes as earthly people have become so jaded and stunted that we can only imagine interesting (non-boring) pleasure in terms of self-indulgence, often in the common, the tawdry, the gross or the lascivious. We prefer spiritual fish and chips or a dollar hamburger to spiritual filet mignon.' This will not be an issue in heaven, as with transformed tastes and perspectives none of God's people will ever wish that they were somewhere else.

Secondly, they will enjoy the very life for which they were originally created. In one of the most stupendous verses in the Bible we are allowed to eavesdrop on a decision being made within the Godhead: 'Let us make man in our image, after our likeness' (Genesis 1:26). This does not mean that man was to be made in the size or shape of God, as 'God is spirit' (John 4:24) and has neither. Nor does it mean that God was lonely or in some way unfulfilled; he is 'from everlasting to everlasting' (Psalm 90:2), the only utterly independent reality that exists. Within the Godhead there has always been intimate, loving fellowship that far exceeds anything we can imagine. Jesus points to this when he speaks to the Father of 'the glory that I had with you before the world existed' (John 17:5) and rejoices that 'you loved me before the foundation of the world' (John 17:24).

God does not need mankind, or any other part of his creation. Jonathan Edwards was right to say, 'He chose to create the heavens and the earth so that his glory could come pouring out from himself in abundance. He brought a physical reality into existence in order that it might experience his glory and be filled with it and reflect it—every atom, every second, every part and moment of creation. He made human beings in his own image to reflect his glory, and he placed them in a perfect environment which also reflected it.'[170] The British preacher Peter Lewis adds the intimate touch that God did this 'ultimately to take us into the perfect circle of his life and fellowship for ever'.[171] In the Westminster Shorter Catechism, drawn up by English and Scottish divines in the 1640s, the first question is, 'What is the chief end of man?' and the answer is, 'To glorify God and to enjoy him for ever'. This is the glorious purpose for which we were brought into being, and it is important to see that it is one 'chief end', not two. All of God's creation was brought into being to glorify God. We have only to look up to see massive evidence for this, as 'The heavens declare the glory of God, and the sky above proclaims his handiwork' (Psalm 19:1). Without a word being spoken, every atom in the firmament joins in providing universal testimony. As C. H. Spurgeon points out, 'It is not merely glory that the heavens declare, but the "glory of God," for they deliver to us such unanswerable arguments for a conscious, intelligent, planning, controlling, and presiding Creator, that no unprejudiced person can remain unconvinced by them.'[172] In the new creation, God's people will have an even greater testimony as they fulfil the mandate originally given to Adam and in doing so glorify not only God's majesty, power and wisdom but his saving and enabling grace.

Man's purpose exceeds that of the rest of creation. His 'one chief end' is not only to glorify God but to *enjoy him*, and to do so for ever. He was not created merely so that God might enjoy him, but that he might enjoy God. He is so constituted that it is impossible for him to glorify God without enjoying him, or to enjoy him without glorifying him. The focus is entirely on God. John Piper captures this in coining a phrase which has been the driving force of his ministry for many years: 'God is most glorified in us when we are most satisfied in him.' In heaven the glory and the satisfaction will be beyond anything Christians can experience here and now, a truth that may be what led C. S. Lewis to call joy 'the serious business of heaven'.[173]

Thirdly, because in the new creation time will not affect God's people as it does now. Boredom is always related to time and the way in which it frustrates what we want to do—or stop doing. We become bored when things last too long or take too long to happen. All of our thinking in this life is immersed in time. We think only in terms of things taking place in sequence and our lives are filled with appointments and events, timetables and deadlines. We are so locked into this that even when thinking about heaven we find it difficult or impossible to shake off the shackles. Yet in his autobiographical book *A Severe Mercy*, the American author Sheldon Vanauken (1914–1996) points out an important difference in the way animals and humans relate to time. Animals seem totally unaware of its existence and act as if this time-and-space world is their natural environment, whereas human beings are in a constant fight against time. There always seems to be too little (or too much) of it. It dashes by or drags on and we never seem completely comfortable with it—as if this world was *not* the one for which we were created. As Vanauken comments, we seem to have 'a kind of appetite for eternity'.[174] The Bible explains why this is the case: God 'has put eternity into man's heart' (Ecclesiastes 3:11). Christians are presently creatures of time, yet there is something in them that transcends it. They have an inbuilt sense that there is something beyond the here and now; and have faith's assurance that what lies beyond is heaven.

Is there such a thing as time in heaven? Christian hymns have conflicting things to say on the subject. A verse added by someone else to the hymn 'Amazing Grace' by the British preacher John Newton (1725–1807) speaks about singing God's praise in heaven 'When we've been there ten thousand years'; but in his hymn 'When the roll is called up yonder' the American teacher James Milton Black (1856–1938) opens with the words, 'When the trumpet of the Lord shall sound, and time shall be no more'. One of the most exciting promises God makes in giving us a glimpse of the world to come is, 'Behold, I am making all things new' (Revelation 21:5) and there seems to be no reason why we should exclude time from this. There is a sense in which time has no concrete existence of its own. It is merely the way the distance between events is measured, always within a finite frame of reference. But in heaven, the only frame of reference is God, who is eternal, infinite and outside of time. One of the Bible's ways of describing the difference between creation's finite present and its infinite future is to call each of them an 'age'. Jesus gives a perfect example of this clear distinction when he speaks about 'this age' and 'the age to come' (Matthew 12:32).

Paul refers to 'the present evil age' (Galatians 1:4) and links 'the age to come' with 'eternal life' (Mark 10:30).

None of this suggests that in the new creation 'time shall be no more,' yet it seems that events we naturally think of as following one another will have an entirely different perspective. The main point of this chapter is to show that Christians will not be lying idly around but will be energetically engaged in fulfilling God's purposes as they go about their glorified lives in heaven, unaffected by time as activities on earth are. People in heaven will not get bored or tired. They will not get weaker or older, so getting to the point where there are certain things they can no longer do. They will be delivered from the tyranny of earthly time into what could be called the 'everlasting present' of heavenly time. The American author and radio host Joni Eareckson Tada shows, 'The only reason we find even the best things monotonous after a while is because of ... *a while*. In other words because of the passage of time. Eternity is not changelessness (which is boring) because changelessness means that time passes while everything stays the same. It's not like that in heaven at all. Eternity is not many millennia. It's not even a billion millennia or a trillion. Time doesn't pass in heaven—it just *is*.'[175] As the Dutch theologian Hendrikus Berkhof (1914–1995) puts it, 'The glorification of existence will not mean that we are taken out of time and delivered from time, but that time as the form of our glorified existence will also be fulfilled and glorified.'[176] Boredom will never be an issue!

New life

The idea that in heaven Christians will eventually become bored because there will be nothing much to do is so far removed from the truth that it does not even qualify as a caricature. Quite apart from what we have just seen, one statement alone sweeps it aside: 'Therefore they are before the throne of God, and *serve him day and night in his temple*' (Revelation 7:15, emphasis added). Augustus H. Strong suggests that on heaven's door are inscribed the words, 'No admission except on business.'[177] As we unpack John's words in Revelation we can begin to see something of what this means.

The significant word here is 'serve'—and there is much more to it than meets the eye. In the New Testament there are two major verbs related to service. The first is *douleia*, which is used in connection with slavery or some other kind of enforced service. It has been described as the state of a person 'in which he is prevented from freely possessing and enjoying his life, a state opposed to liberty.'[178] This is *not* the word John uses here! The second is *latreia*, which is not only repeatedly used in the New Testament of service to God but is intertwined with the idea of worship. When Paul tells the Christians at Rome, 'For God is my witness, whom I *serve* with my spirit in the gospel of his Son' (Romans 1:9, emphasis added) he uses the related word *latreuo*. He uses the same word when he tells Christians at Philippi that true believers '*worship* by the Spirit of God' (Philippians 3:3, emphasis added). In the English Standard Version of the Bible (which I am using in this book) the translators bring out the meaning of the word *latreuo* in the context of heaven by saying, 'The throne of God and of the Lamb will be in it, and his servants will *worship* him' (Revelation 22:3, emphasis added).

Writing to the Romans, Paul urges his readers, 'I appeal to you therefore, brothers, by the mercies of God, to present your bodies as a living sacrifice, holy and acceptable to God, which is your spiritual *worship*'(Romans12:1, emphasis added). The word 'worship' translates the word *latreia*; and in a culture in which animal sacrifices were common, Paul shows that the way believers are to worship God is to 'present your bodies as a living sacrifice, holy and acceptable to God'. Instead of *giving* a *dying* sacrifice they are to *be* a *living* one. This follows up something he had told them earlier: 'Do not present your members to sin as instruments for unrighteousness, but present yourselves to God as those who have been brought from death to life, and your members to God as instruments for righteousness' (Romans 6:13). In his letter to the Corinthians he includes in these members the foot, the hand, the ear, the eye and the head (see 1 Corinthians 12:12–26). To 'present' means that all of these are to be put at God's disposal. Paul's own longing is that 'Christ will be honoured in my body, whether by life or by death' (Philippians 1:20). Commenting on Paul's exhortations to the Romans, John Calvin says that Paul means 'not only our skin and bones but the totality of which we are composed'.[179]

Paul adds that this would be 'holy and acceptable to God' as 'spiritual worship'. At first glance, the word 'spiritual' seems a strange way to translate the Greek word *logikos*, which means something reasonable or rational. Christian worship is certainly an intelligent response to God's saving mercy, in stark contrast to the sacrificing of animals by Jews under the obsolete Old Testament rituals, or by pagans hoping to appease their idolatrous gods. Yet believers presenting themselves to God in thanksgiving for his saving grace are also doing an intensely spiritual thing. This utter commitment of themselves to God will powerfully influence every aspect of their daily lives, and Paul points the Corinthians in this direction when he urges them, 'Whether you eat or drink, or whatever you do, do all to the glory of God' (1 Corinthians 10:31).

This gives us a fuller picture of what John means when saying that believers before God's throne 'serve him day and night in his temple'. All of these down-to-earth activities will be carried out perfectly in heaven. The Bible's picture is not one of believers drifting aimlessly around, but one in which they pour all their infinite, joyful energies into serving and worshipping God without any of the stresses, pressures, distractions or disappointments that they so often find on earth. A. A. Hodge goes so far as to say this: 'Heaven, as the eternal home of the divine Man and of all the redeemed members of the human race, must necessarily be thoroughly human in its structure, conditions and activities. Its joys and its occupations must all be rational, moral, emotional, voluntary and active. There must be the exercise of all the faculties, the gratification of all tastes, the development of all latent capacities, the realization of all ideals. The reason, the intellectual curiosity, the imagination, the aesthetic instincts, the holy affections, the social affinities, the inexhaustible resources of strength and power native to the human soul, must all find in heaven exercise and satisfaction.'[180] Not all Bible students will agree with every word of that, but the overall picture hardly sounds boring! As Paul Wolfe points out, 'If the new creation is one in which the powers of our new bodies are not used to the uttermost but instead lie dormant, it would seem that God would have left us "all dressed up and nowhere to go."'[181] The exact opposite will be the case!

Elsewhere in Revelation John tells us two other things that are directly relevant to heavenly worship and service. The first is that 'night will be no more' (Revelation 22:5). At first glance, this seems to contradict the statement that in heaven believers serve God 'day and night' (Revelation 7:15); but this is not the case. The absence of night has to be linked to the earlier statement, 'And *the city* has no need of the sun or moon to shine on it, for the glory of God gives it light, and its lamp is the Lamb ... and there will be no night there' (Revelation 21:23,25, emphasis added). It is not the new creation, but the holy *city* (Revelation's description of God's redeemed people) that has no need of natural phenomena to reveal God's glory. The Bible does not say that in the new creation there will be no sun or moon, day or night, but that God's people will not need these in order to reveal anything about God.

Worshipping God day and night is the Bible's way of saying that worship will be uninterrupted and unending. It will also be utterly satisfying because, as we have just seen, the worshippers will be fulfilling to perfection the very purpose for which they were created. All of their renewed, sanctified, expanded, perfected, undying faculties will be endlessly and joyfully poured into worshipping and serving their Creator. Such a thing is possible only in heaven. Housing the capacities of glorified spirits in earthly bodies would be like harnessing an aircraft's jet engine to a bicycle, but glorified bodies will be the (literally) perfect vehicles for expressing worship without weariness of body or spirit.

The second thing John tells us about heavenly worship and service is this: 'And I saw no temple in the city, for its temple is the Lord God Almighty and the Lamb' (Revelation 21:22). In biblical times Jerusalem was known as 'the city of the LORD of hosts' (Psalm 48:8). Fifteen of the Psalms (120–134) are each headed 'A Song of Ascents', probably because they were meant to be sung as Jewish men went up (literally uphill) to Jerusalem for the special feasts of Passover, Pentecost and Tabernacles. These were all centred on the temple, chosen by God to be the place in which his presence was to be symbolized by the Ark of the Covenant.

But both the temple (and the tabernacle before the temple was built) were temporary shadows of God's eternal dwelling place. The first temple, built by Solomon, was destroyed by the Babylonians in 586 BC. Old Testament prophets expressed Israel's yearning for another one to be built in its place, but this one, built by Herod the Great and commonly called the Second Temple, was destroyed by the Romans in AD 70. Heaven renders any rebuilding plans redundant, and we are specifically told that in his vision of heaven John 'saw no temple in the city' (Revelation 21:22). In Jerusalem, the temple symbolized God's presence with his people; in heaven, the symbol is unnecessary. There will be no need for sacrificial lambs, as God's people will be in the immediate presence of *the Lamb!* They will never need to travel anywhere to be in his special presence, nor will they need to attend church in particular places and at fixed times. Instead, they will always be in God's immediate presence and everything they do will be worship. Serving God day and night in his temple means constantly serving God in his immediate and glorious presence! As one Bible Commentary has it, 'Means of grace shall cease when the end of grace is come. Church ordinances shall give place to the God of ordinances.'[182]

Heaven is not where God's people go to retire after finishing their work on earth. It is not a place of glorified inactivity or an everlasting 'holy huddle'. Nor will they float around on clouds, doing nothing more energetic than strumming harps. Instead, they will enthusiastically serve God in worship and worship him in service. They will never get tired, bored or distracted in doing so, nor will their lives be regulated by clocks or calendars. Commenting on one aspect of this, Leon Morris writes, 'Heaven is not so much a place where no work is done, as one where pain has ceased.'[183]

Reigning, ruling and rewards

We can now take things a little further. There are several other Bible passages that raise intriguing questions about what God's redeemed people will do in heaven. Some volumes of systematic theology say little or nothing about these passages, and it is interesting (and frustrating for preachers!) that many commentaries and study Bibles tend to gloss over them. This is not the place to go into a detailed analysis of the many ways in which these passages have been interpreted, but a few notes may help.

- A rich young man once asked Jesus what he needed to do to have eternal life. Knowing that his possessions were governing this man's thinking, Jesus challenged him to sell them all and to follow him. When the man refused, Jesus told his disciples that riches were often a stumbling block that prevented people entering the kingdom of God. Peter immediately reminded Jesus that he and the other disciples had 'left everything' to follow him, and asked, 'What then will we have?' (Matthew 19:27). In reply, Jesus told him that their reward would not be in this life, but in the world to come: 'Truly, I say to you, in the new world, when the Son of Man will sit on his glorious throne, you who have followed me will also sit on twelve thrones, *judging the twelve tribes of Israel*' (Matthew 19:28, emphasis added).

We need to look carefully at the words Jesus used. The phrase 'the new world' (the original Greek means 'the regeneration') refers to heaven in its final state—in other words, the new heavens and the new earth. As Albert Barnes puts it, 'It refers to that great revolution, that restoration of order in the universe; when the dead shall rise, and all human things shall be changed, and a new order of things shall start up out of the ruins of the old.'[184] The 'glorious throne' is not to be taken literally as meaning a dazzling item of heavenly furniture; it is symbolic language meaning the throne of God's glory and reflecting his majesty, dignity, honour and power as the Sovereign Lord of the new heavens and new earth. In the same way, promising the disciples that they would 'sit on twelve thrones' can hardly be taken literally. In chapter 3 we saw that 'the twelve tribes of Israel' is commonly used to mean the eternal ingathering of all of God's people. The word 'judging' may possibly refer to the particular honour to be given to these original disciples because of their unique role in laying the foundations of Christ's church. Pulling this together, we are not being asked to imagine the staggeringly huge new heavens and new earth, with its billions of God's redeemed people, being micro-managed by twelve disciples seated permanently on thrones. Treating this passage as being symbolic rather than literal in no way limits its authority. *Every promise Jesus made was absolutely true, but not all of them were meant to be taken literally.*

• Jesus said something very similar when he met with the disciples for a final meal and they were jostling for places at the table: 'A dispute also arose among them, as to which of them was to be regarded as the greatest' (Luke 22:24). Jesus interrupted their self-centred bickering by telling them that they ought not to behave like this, but instead should be glad to take a lower position. He then made them this promise: 'You are those who have stayed with me in my trials, and I assign to you, as my Father assigned to me, a kingdom, that you may eat and drink at my table in my kingdom and sit on thrones judging the twelve tribes of Israel (Luke 22:28–30). Ignoring their character defects, Jesus praised them for their faithfulness to him when the going had got tough, then promised that they would eat and drink at his table in the new world. Again, we are not to think in literal terms and to imagine a never-ending feast (or even a one-off private meal), but to see the eating and drinking as being symbolic of the everlasting joy that would be theirs in the new heavens and new earth. Linking this to any sacrifices that believers make to follow Christ, Matthew Henry comments that 'the glory and the dignity reserved for the saints in heaven ... will be an adequate recompense for the disgrace they suffered here in Christ's cause'.[185]

• In his vision of heaven, the apostle John is told to send a message to the church at Laodicea. In the course of this, Jesus promises, 'The one who conquers, I will grant him to sit with me on my throne, as I also conquered and sat down with my Father on his throne' (Revelation 3:21). What are we to make of this? Are we to be crudely literal and see God's throne as a two-seater occupied by Jesus and his Father? If so, would there also be room for the disciples? It seems clear that symbolic language is being used here; as Leon Morris explains, 'The "throne" signifies royal honour, and a place with Christ is the highest honour conceivable for a Christian'.[186] It is worth noticing that this promise is extended far beyond the twelve disciples to whom Jesus spoke in the Gospels of Matthew and Luke—and that it was given to believers who belonged to a church that was generally 'lukewarm, and neither hot nor cold (Revelation 3:16).

The next passage poses more questions than all the others, and may raise more eyebrows than almost any other statement in the New Testament. Scolding church members at Corinth for dragging fellow believers into secular law courts when they had a grievance against them, Paul asks, 'Do you not know that *the saints will judge the world?* And if the world is to be judged by you are you incompetent to try trivial cases? Do you not know that *we are to judge angels?*' (1 Corinthians 6:2–3, emphasis added). There have been wagon loads of interpretations of what this means, and I am not about to add to them here. Some suggest that this judging will reflect the roles of Israel's Old Testament judges and refers to governing rather than passing judicial sentences; the British scholar David Gooding goes further and writes of believers knowing 'the delight of close personal fellowship with [Christ] in his glory and active participation with him in government.'[187] Others say the meaning is that on the final day of judgement the redeemed will be so completely in tune with God that they will endorse all his pronouncements, including those on angels, and join him in enacting his judgements. Yet nowhere in the Bible is there any more information that would give us a crystal clear picture of what is meant. As with the passages we have just looked at, we must accept that *devout speculation is no substitute for divine revelation*. When the Bible is silent we ought to follow suit. It may not tell us everything we want to know, but it does tell us everything we need to know.

Rewards

The teaching in these four passages leads us into the subject of rewards in heaven, an issue that has also produced many different interpretations. For example, Jesus told several parables in which people were rewarded for their diligence and faithfulness and in one of them he pictured faithful servants rewarded by being given authority over certain numbers of cities.[188] These parables have been seen by some as predicting that God's redeemed people will enjoy different levels of reward in heaven. But when these and other related sections of Scripture are examined carefully, a case can also be made for saying that they refer either to the distinction already existing between believers and unbelievers, or to blessings granted to particular believers in this life, or to the great division that Jesus will make between believers and unbelievers on the day of final judgement. It is not crystal clear that they must always refer to the status of believers in heaven and tell us that they will spend eternity at different levels of comfort or convenience, rather like occupying First Class, Business Class or Economy seats on an aircraft.[189] I was once staying in the home of friends when I accidentally stained the front of a shirt I needed later that day. My hosts' cleaner soon had it in the washing machine and was about to iron it when the lady of the house offered to help her. 'No,' said the cleaner (an ardent Roman Catholic), 'There's going to be a reward in heaven for this, and I want it!' We dare not interpret the Bible's teaching on rewards in this crude kind of way and assume that there will be a heavenly Prize-Giving Day, with medals, diplomas and other honours being given out. When all the biblical evidence is carefully assessed, there is no reason to expect 'an everlasting hierarchy in heaven'.[190] As John Gilmore points out, 'Heaven's equality will combine distinctions without divisions, differences without disagreements, variations without vanity, individuality without jealousy, classes without clashes and unity without absorption. Whenever these elements are found on earth we are experiencing a foretaste of heaven ahead.'[191]

The Bible pays virtually no attention to the positions, possessions, preferences or places of believers in heaven, but instead focuses on God and his glory, and Eryl Davies is right to say, 'The lack of detail in the Bible concerning reward in heaven should make us very cautious in approaching the subject.'[192] So is the British theologian Paul Helm when he states, 'Whatever the position turns out to be about rewards in heaven, the dominant fact is the fact of salvation through divine grace, of mercy enjoyed *on account of what another has done*' (emphasis added).[193] The emphasis in the Bible's teaching on heaven is on God and his grace, not on man and his merits or medals. All the redeemed are equally redeemed. In some of the last words written by the seventeenth-century British preacher Samuel Rutherford, 'The Lamb is all the glory of Immanuel's land.'[194]

That last point needs to be emphasized. Having listed many passages of Scripture that he suggests can be taken to teach or imply degrees of reward in heaven, Wayne Grudem makes such a helpful comment that it is worth quoting in full:

> Even though there will be degrees of reward in heaven, the joy of each person will be full and complete for eternity. If we ask how this can be when there are different degrees of reward, it simply shows that our perception of happiness is based on the assumption that happiness depends on what we possess or the status or power we have. In actuality, however, our true happiness consists in delighting in God and rejoicing in the status and recognition that

he has given us. The foolishness of thinking that only those who have been highly rewarded and given great status will be fully happy in heaven is seen when we realize that no matter how great reward we are given, there will always be those with greater rewards, or who have higher status or authority, including the apostles, the heavenly creatures, and Jesus Christ and God himself. Therefore if the highest status were essential for people to be fully happy, no one but God would be fully happy in heaven, which is certainly an incorrect idea. Moreover, those with greater reward and honour in heaven, those nearest the throne of God, delight not in their status, but only in the privilege of falling down before God's throne to worship him.[195]

He is right. In heaven nobody will be proud of their status or envious of anyone else's. There will be no sense of being superior or inferior. Instead, there will be constant and unending gratitude for the grace of God that brought them into his heavenly home. In the vision of heaven given to the apostle John, he saw that angelic beings 'fell on their faces before the throne and worshipped God, saying, "Amen! Blessing and glory and wisdom and thanksgiving and honour and power and might be to our God for ever and ever! Amen."' (Revelation 7:11–12). This theme will be part of the spiritual DNA of all God's people in heaven and will rule out any possibility of there being anything but deeply felt satisfaction with what and where they are. They will have everything they desire, desire everything they have, and rejoice in knowing that they are fulfilling the purpose for which they were created.

One other important point needs to be made. At one stage in Old Testament history, four foreign kings invaded the Dead Sea area, routed five local kings, made off with plundered property and kidnapped Lot, Abram's nephew. When he got the news, Abram took 318 trained troops, pursued the foreign armies for over 140 miles, recovered the stolen goods and rescued Lot and the other captives. When Abram returned in triumph, the godless king of Sodom offered him all the recovered goods, but Abram refused to take a single thing—'I would not take a thread or a sandal strap or anything that is yours' (Genesis 14:23). Soon afterwards, God appeared to him in a vision and put worldly possessions into perfect perspective: 'Do not be afraid, Abram. I am your shield, your very great reward' (Genesis 15:1, NIV). Believers' reward in heaven is not to be thought of in terms of status. Ultimately, their reward is *God himself*, revealed, understood, enjoyed, loved, adored and worshipped in ways infinitely superior to anything they experienced in the present life.

Devolved dominion

Man is in some ways inferior to many other creatures. Fish can breathe under water, birds can fly without mechanical help, many animals can run much faster, tortoises live much longer, eagles have keener eyesight, dogs have a better sense of smell and some monkeys have bigger brains in relation to the size of their bodies. Yet when God created man he gave him 'dominion over the fish of the sea and over the birds of the heavens and over every living thing that moves on the earth' (Genesis 1:28), a cultural mandate conferring on man the authority and responsibility for governing earthly life. That mandate has never been withdrawn *and will remain in place in the world to come*. To have God-given dominion in the new heavens and the new earth and to be fulfilling to sinless perfection God's original intention for humanity is surely to be reigning with him. As the American preacher William Barcley writes, 'The hope that the saint will reign with Christ in the age to come is a great encouragement to God's people, especially to those who suffer persecution and oppression under the hands of godless rulers.'[196] If we needed to know the practical details of exactly what that will entail, God would have told us in his Word. Instead, we should settle for the glorious glimpses he has given us, and rejoice that in his baffling grace he has qualified us 'to share in the inheritance of the saints in light' (Colossians 1:12).

God also made man 'a little lower than the heavenly beings' (Psalm 8:5), in that for the time being he lives in a temporal world of time and space. Yet as Matthew Henry quaintly puts it, 'He is but for a little while lower than the angels while his great soul is cooped up in a house of clay, but the children of the resurrection shall be ... no longer lower than they.'[197] Even in his present state man is 'crowned ... with glory and honour' (Psalm 8:5). In the world to come, when all creation will witness 'the revealing of the sons of God' (Romans 8:19) this will be seen to be true of redeemed humanity in ways utterly beyond our imagination. The British worship leader and songwriter Kristyn Getty puts it well:

There is a higher throne
Than all this world has known,
Where faithful ones from ev'ry tongue
Will one day come.
Before the Son we'll stand,
Made faultless through the Lamb;
Believing hearts find promised grace—
Salvation comes.

Hear heaven's voices sing;
Their thund'rous anthem rings
Through em'rald courts and sapphire skies.
Their praises rise.
All glory, wisdom, pow'r,
Strength, thanks, and honour are
To God our King, who reigns on high
Forevermore.

And there we'll find our home,
Our life before the throne;
We'll honour Him in perfect song
Where we belong.
He'll wipe each tear-stained eye
As thirst and hunger die.
The Lamb becomes our Shepherd King;
We'll reign with Him.[198]

9

Unimaginable certainties

This *Hitch-hiker's Guide to Heaven* has given only a glimpse of the subject, but even if we were to study everything the Bible reveals about heaven we should still have only a vague idea of what it will mean. In Alec Motyer's words, 'The Bible bends to us in our limitations. God knows that we cannot unloose ourselves from space and time, whether in action or in thought. With perfect grace, therefore, he allows us to think of heaven as a place, and life there as endless time. The reality, of course, will be super-aboundingly, overwhelmingly greater, but here we live with entrancing snapshots.[199]

Visiting a college one day, I noticed that its motto was 'Beyond the best there is a better'. This was no doubt intended to spur its students on to greater things, but it also reminded me of what heaven is like, something infinitely better than the very best we have here on earth. Paul is crystal clear as to why this will be the case; he longs 'to depart and be with Christ, for that is far better' (Philippians 1:23). The phrase 'far better' hardly does justice to the original Greek, in which Paul pulls out all the stops to make his point. He uses a triple adverb which literally translates as 'much rather better', so can be read as 'by far the best'. He has no way of describing exactly what this will mean, and writing to the Corinthians he admits 'For now we see in a mirror dimly, but then face to face. Now I know in part; then I shall know fully, even as I have been fully known' (1 Corinthians 13:12).

Studying what the Bible says about heaven does not leave us knowing nothing about it, but the more I read in Scripture the more I realize that while God has stooped to our weakness and painted us pictures of heaven in earthly language, the reality lies far beyond our present reach and is infinitely greater than anything our finite imagination can conjure up from what we read. We need to bear this in mind as we address one of the most fundamental questions Christians ask about heaven: 'What will we be like when we are there?' The question is understandable, but the answer to it is utterly beyond our ability to grasp. As we will see in a moment, it lies in a staggering statement made by the apostle John.

In Shakespeare's *As you like it* the melancholy Jaques delivers a monologue that has become known as 'The Seven Ages of Man'. It begins, 'All the world's a stage, and all the men and women merely players'. It has some great phrases, such as 'The infant, mewling and puking in the nurse's arms', and 'the whining schoolboy ... creeping like snail unwillingly to school', before adding that man's 'strange, eventful history' ends in 'mere oblivion, sans teeth, sans eyes, sans taste, sans everything'.[200]

There is enough truth in Shakespeare's words to get our attention. Not even regular exercise, good eating habits, a steady intake of vitamins and other food supplements, constant medical supervision and a carefully monitored lifestyle can paper over the cracks. As the years tick by we gradually lose the 'zip' we once had, we tire more easily, our eyesight and hearing deteriorate, aches and pains increase, we walk where once we ran, we sit where once we stood, and at times we completely forget what we once remembered easily. Some reach what has been called 'The Metallic Age—silver in the hair, gold in the teeth and lead in the boots'. When I quoted this to a friend recently he added with some feeling, 'And titanium in the hips'! We have access to a vast array of medicines and can call on a growing number of increasingly effective surgical procedures, yet none of these can do more than delay the inevitable. We may not come to the end of life feebly ticking all of Shakespeare's boxes, but eventually we are reduced to being 'sans everything', at which point our lifeless bodies are disposed of.

The British philosopher Bertrand Russell (1872–1970) could offer nothing more on this than, 'When I die I shall rot.'[201] This reflects his atheistic worldview but ignores the fact that the body's degradation is not its final state, any more than the sowing of a seed marks the end of its story. The Bible teaches that death means separation, *but never termination*, and we saw in chapter 4 that beyond the grave Christians have an eternal future in which they will be gloriously transformed.

Writing to first-century Christians about the life to come, the apostle John begins one section of his letter by telling them that as members of God's redeemed family they are all 'children of God'. He underlines this by adding 'and so we are', then repeats himself by saying, 'Beloved, we are God's children *now*' (1 John 3:1–2, emphasis added). He wants to drive home the truth that even while here on earth Christians can be certain that they are God's children and that nothing can change their status. John wants his readers to be absolutely sure of this, and to do so he makes one of the Bible's greatest statements, one so astonishing that it deserves to be set out from the rest of the text on this page:

> What we will be has not yet appeared; but we know that when he appears we shall be like him, because we shall see him as he is (1 John 3:2).

This staggering promise naturally falls into three parts, each one of which needs our close attention.

The agnostic apostle
John begins with a word of caution by admitting that there are issues about the future life of believers on which he is uncertain: 'What we will be has not yet appeared'. He is not confessing any lack of faith or suggesting that we are totally in the dark as to what lies beyond the grave. He is simply confirming that God has not chosen to tell us everything about our future destiny. Christians should always maintain a healthy agnosticism about certain aspects of heaven, as its full glory is infinitely beyond anything we can ever imagine. Even the apostle Paul tells his readers, 'For now we see in a mirror dimly, but then face to face. Now I know in part, then I shall know fully, even as I have been fully known' (1 Corinthians 13:12). In Paul's day Corinth was famous for its manufacture of mirrors, which were made of highly polished metal and would not give the perfect reflection we see in modern mirrors. The word 'dimly' translates the Greek *ainigma*, the basis of our English word 'enigma', which refers to 'a person or thing that is mysterious or difficult to understand.'[202] Paul is making it clear that our earthly understanding of heaven

is always unclear. There are glimpses, glimmers and tantalizing cameos, but most of the pieces are missing.

Anyone posing as an expert on the precise outworking of prophecy or on a detailed explanation of what heaven will be like is mixing revelation with speculation, but anything not clearly stated or soundly inferred from what the Bible says can be safely ignored. Just as there is no way in which a new born baby can grasp what it is to be one-year-old or a teenager, let alone an adult, so there is no way in which our finite minds can understand the infinite, and so no way in which we can sense, feel or know exactly what it will be like to live in heaven. As Robert Dabney (1820–1898) puts it, 'Far be it from us to presume to be wise above that which is written; let us modestly collect those traits of the saints' everlasting rest which the Bible, in its great reserve on this subject, has seen fit to reveal.'[203]

We can now look at the two positive parts of John's statement: 'But we know that when he appears we shall be like him, because we shall see him as he is' (1 John 3:2). Martyn Lloyd-Jones claims that it is 'surely the most amazing thing that has ever been said to man',[204] and it is difficult to disagree. In these twenty words (even fewer in the original Greek) there are two truths beyond our understanding and infinitely greater than we could ever imagine, yet conveyed by God to the apostle John as facts in which every Christian can have complete confidence. This is why I have called them 'unimaginable certainties'. We shall look at the second one first.

Seeing the Saviour

On 2 June 1953 I was one of three million people who crowded London's streets to celebrate the Coronation of Queen Elizabeth II. As a representative of a national youth organization, I was allocated a place on the steps surrounding the Victoria Memorial, directly in front of the gates of Buckingham Palace. I can still remember the excitement that swept through the crowds as the Gold State Coach left the palace forecourt and turned into The Mall on its way to Westminster Abbey. That was when I caught a first glimpse of my Queen, who had acceded to the throne on 6 February 1952 on the death of her father King George VI. Some three hours after that first sighting the excitement was even greater as she returned to the palace, this time formally crowned as sovereign. It was my supreme 'Kodak moment' and from then on my tiny black and white photographs, taken with a primitive box camera, became treasured reminders of something I could never forget—*I had seen the Queen!*

Although I have never seen her since, my memory of 2 June 1953 is indelible. Yet I can join every other Christian in being certain of an experience infinitely more wonderful—seeing our Saviour! In a fascinating Old Testament incident, Moses asks God, 'Please show me your glory' (Exodus 33:18). In reply, God promises him tokens of his goodness, grace and mercy, then adds, 'But you cannot see my face, for man shall not see me and live' (Exodus 33:20). A little earlier we are told, 'The LORD used to speak to Moses face to face, as a man speaks to his friend' (Exodus 33:11); but there is no contradiction here, nor in the Bible's later testimony that Moses was someone 'whom the LORD knew face to face' (Deuteronomy 34:10). The phrase 'face to face' is an idiom about intimacy, not physical vision. The Bible tells us that God 'dwells in unapproachable light' and is one 'whom no one has ever seen or can see' (1 Timothy 6:16). It is impossible for human beings on earth to see God, as our sinful nature has blinded us to God's character and essence, but when that barrier has been removed we shall be able to gaze without restriction on his indescribable beauty.

Yet God has revealed something of his nature in titles given in the Bible, by his actions in history and supremely in the person of his eternal Son, the Lord Jesus Christ. John tells us this by saying that while 'No one has ever seen God', in coming to earth Jesus, the second Person in the Godhead, 'has made him known' (John 1:18). In his incarnation Jesus assumed our humanity without losing any of his deity, so that when one of his disciples said, 'Lord, show us the Father and it is enough for us,' Jesus had no hesitation in replying, 'Whoever has seen me has seen the Father' (John 14:8-9). In Charles Wesley's memorable phrase, Jesus was deity 'veiled in flesh'.[205] Yet his entire life was a dazzling visual aid of God's essential nature, revealing more of his love, holiness, grace and power than we can see anywhere else. In the person of Jesus Christ, God brings the visible and the invisible together.

In the 'unimaginable certainties' we are exploring, John promises that in heaven believers will see even more than the disciples who lived in close company with Jesus for three years. There is a glimmer of this where we are told in the Old Testament, 'The path of the righteous is like the light of dawn, which shines brighter and brighter until full day (Proverbs 4:18). A double-barrelled promise God gave to Isaiah points in the same direction: 'Your eyes will behold the king in his beauty' (Isaiah 33:17). The immediate reference is to the miraculous liberation of Jerusalem from its Assyrian enemies and the celebration of the godly Hezekiah as king, but it also anticipates the coming of Jesus Christ, the Messiah, who is 'the King of kings and Lord of lords' (1 Timothy 6:15). David goes even further and in a passionate prayer calls out to God, 'As for me, I shall behold your face in righteousness; when I awake, I shall be satisfied with your likeness' (Psalm 17:15).

At a time when he was grieving the loss of his ten children and his entire livestock in a single day, Job gives the greatest prophetic testimony on the subject in the entire Bible. He sees beyond all his indescribable agony and cries, 'For I know that my Redeemer lives, and at the last he will stand upon the earth. And after my skin has thus been destroyed, yet in my flesh I shall see God, whom I shall see for myself, and my eyes shall behold, and not another' (Job 19:25–27).

John makes it clear that the prospect of seeing the God-man Jesus Christ in heaven is not limited to prophets, church leaders, or people of exceptional faith or outstanding Christian service. *All believers*, regardless of their standing, reputation or achievements here on earth, are included in the God-given promise, 'We shall see him as he is.' John repeats this elsewhere, when in his vision of heaven he says of God's people, 'They will see his face' (Revelation 22:4). Will this 'seeing' be simply with the naked eye of the resurrection body, or in some other way? There is no way in which we can fathom the answer. As Martyn Lloyd-Jones puts it, 'We just do not know. The very Being of God is so transcendent and eternal that all our efforts to arrive at an understanding are doomed to failure ... All we know is that, in some way or other, the pure in heart shall see God.'[206]

The apostle Peter says the same thing when writing to Christians who were 'grieved by various trials' (1 Peter 1:6). He promises them that although the going is tough their resolute faith will one day be seen to result in 'praise and glory and honour at the revelation of Jesus Christ' (1 Peter 1:7). He then adds, 'Though you do not now see him, you believe in him and rejoice with joy that is inexpressible and filled with glory,

obtaining the outcome of your faith, the salvation of your souls'
(1 Peter 1:8–9). There was something other-worldly about their
joy in the midst of pressures and problems. It was 'inexpressible'
and inexplicable, yet the reason for it was that they were already
experiencing something of the final outcome of their faith, the
fullness of their salvation in heaven. They now saw Jesus only
with the eye of faith, but that faith brought an assurance that
one day they would live in his presence in a world of surpassing
glory for ever. Even the joy they knew when Peter wrote to them
would be overwhelmingly exceeded in heaven. The Old
Testament prophet Isaiah anticipates this by declaring that
when God has finally overcome all their enemies, God's people
will 'come to Zion with singing; everlasting joy shall be upon
their heads; they shall obtain gladness and joy, and sorrow and
sighing shall flee away' (Isaiah 35:10).

A few months before he died, the British preacher John Donne
(1572–1631) commissioned a portrait of himself in his shroud as
he expected to appear when he rose from the grave at the
Second Coming, then hung it in his study as a reminder of the
transience of the present life. A sermon he preached in 1620
included this moving passage about his certainty of seeing God
in heaven: '"No man ever saw God and lived." And yet, I shall not
live till I see God; and when I have seen him I shall never die ...
When we shall see God, we shall see all things as they are. We
shall be no more deluded with outward appearances ... there will
be no delusory thing to be seen.'

People often carry around photographs of their loved ones
that from time to time they can look at and be reminded of all
that the people concerned mean to them. Whenever they do this
they look forward to the much greater pleasure of seeing them
face to face. Here on earth we can see only 'photographs' of Jesus

as we read of him in Scripture. These bring us great joy as we revel in the glory of his deity, the beauty of his character, the depth of his love and the wonder of his grace in rescuing us from the fate our sin deserved, but Wilbur Smith points us to a greater joy to come:

> How glorious it will be to look upon the face of him who loved us and gave himself for us, who has lived to make intercession for us, the one who fought many battles and won them all, in whose life there has never been one single moment of sin of any kind, in word or deed or thought, whose face will be radiant with unbroken victory, with unquenchable love and with perfect obedience to the perfect will of God.[207]

I began writing these paragraphs in Milan, Italy. Earlier today I visited its massive cathedral. The front of this imposing building is full of religious images, several depicting Jesus. On one of these, part of the surface has been worn away by countless thousands of people who have touched his hands, then kissed theirs in the hope that through this ritual they would receive a blessing. What a tragic contrast to the promise that those who truly put their trust in Jesus will one day 'see him as he is'! As Thomas Boston writes, 'They will behold that glorious, blessed body, which is personally united to the divine nature, and exalted above all principalities and powers and every name that is named. There we shall see, with our eyes, that very body which was born of Mary at Bethlehem and crucified at Jerusalem between two thieves; the blessed head that was crowned with thorns; the hands and feet that were nailed to the cross; all shining with inconceivable glory.'[208]

My good friend Peter Jackson was blinded by measles when he

was just eighteen months old. In his book *Heaven in Sight*, he tells of his experiences as a piano tuner, an evangelist, a pastor and a gospel pianist. At one point he writes,

> I have forgotten the last person I ever saw. It might have been my Mum, the nurse or the surgeon in the white coat, I don't know. I have no recollection whatsoever, but of course, all things being equal, the very next person I shall see will be the Lord Jesus Christ, and until that day, written across my eyes are the words "reserved for him". I know that I shall recognize him![209]

From seeing to being

If seeing God is one 'unimaginable certainty', so is the phrase that comes before it: 'We shall be like him.' This statement is so stunning that it breaks through our ability to grasp its full meaning. We have what Edward Donnelly calls 'a delicious incompleteness of knowledge'.[210] The story is told of a missionary working with a native convert on translating this part of the New Testament. When they came to the phrase 'we shall be like him' the native laid down his pen and cried, 'No! This is too much; let us write, "we shall kiss his feet."' His attitude is understandable, but we dare not edit what God tells us in his Word. Instead, we must unpack each word carefully—and the phrase John uses seems to me to gather pace if we begin at the end and work backwards, emphasizing each key word in turn.

Firstly, we will be like *him*. It is just possible that by 'him' John means God the Father, but as believers will have this wonderful experience 'when he appears' it seems more natural to see this event as the Second Coming and to think of 'him' as meaning God the Son. Even if we link the promise only to his earthly life it is truly astonishing. Although 'in every respect' he was 'tempted as we are', he was 'without sin' (Hebrews 4:15). His speech was such that people 'marvelled at the gracious words that were coming from his mouth' (Luke 4:22). He mixed with many people who were driven by their egos, yet the Bible speaks of 'the meekness and gentleness of Christ' (2 Corinthians 10:1) and he himself said, 'I am gentle and lowly in heart' (Matthew 11:29). He showed great composure under pressure; 'when he was reviled, he did not revile in return; when he suffered, he did not threaten, but continued entrusting himself to him who judges justly' (1 Peter 2:23). He had a finely-tuned social conscience; when he saw people in need 'he had compassion on them' (Mark 6:34) and said that he had come into the world 'not to be served but to serve' (Matthew 20:28). Above all, his obedience to his heavenly Father was such that he was able to say, I *always* do the things that are pleasing to him' (John 8:29, emphasis added).

Yet when we have trawled through the New Testament for examples of the perfect character of Jesus, we have only brushed against what John is saying, because the one who throughout his earthly life was 'holy, innocent, unstained, separated from sinners' is now 'exalted above the heavens' (Hebrews 7:26) and John's promise is that believers will be like him. The picture John is holding before us is not Jesus in his earth-bound humanity, perfect though that was, but in *his glorified humanity*. In his high priestly prayer Jesus assures God the Father, 'The glory that you have given me I have given to them' (John 17:22); and what believers know in some measure here on earth they will know in all its fullness in heaven. This does not mean that in heaven they will share the essential glory of Jesus as a member of the Godhead; they will not become divine. Yet they will share in the glory given to Jesus Christ as the Saviour of sinners. This is why Paul calls Jesus 'the firstborn among many brothers' (Romans 8:29). All the glory that was poured upon Jesus in his role as Saviour he accepted not merely for himself but also for the benefit of all who would put their trust in him.

This is what Christians will share with Jesus in heaven as 'heirs of God and fellow heirs with Christ' (Romans 8:17). As with every part of John's astonishing statement, this truth staggers the imagination. As the eternal Son of God, Jesus is heir by nature, whereas Christians are heirs of God by adoption. Nevertheless they *are* heirs, with a share in God's promised inheritance. Paul tells Christians at Colosse that they should give thanks to God 'who has qualified you to share in the inheritance of the saints in light' (Colossians 1:12). The word 'qualified' carries no hint of merit. Nobody earns an inheritance; they receive it as a free gift. In the same way (though to an infinitely greater degree), it is by God's sovereign grace alone that a Christian becomes 'qualified' to receive the inheritance, yet the Bible states that all who by grace come to put their trust in Jesus are given 'the right to become children of God' (John 1:12). The word 'right' translates the Greek *exousia*, which means authority. For a Christian to claim to be a child of God and an authorized heir of his eternal kingdom is not arrogance—and to doubt it is to question the truth of God's Word.

Nor dare we limit what is included in this inheritance. Jesus is 'Lord of all' (Acts 10:36) and as such claims, 'All that the Father has is mine' (John 16:15). We are also told that Jesus is 'the heir of all things' (Hebrews 1:2). To hold this alongside the statement that Christians are 'fellow heirs with Christ' is truly marvellous. In his vision of a new heaven and a new earth John hears God say, 'I am making all things new' (Revelation 21:5), then promise that all who conquer (that is, by God's saving grace overcome Satan, sin and death) 'will have *this heritage*' (Revelation 21:7, emphasis added). There are times when an earthly beneficiary has no idea what he will inherit until he receives it. Christians will not fully know the glory of their heavenly inheritance until they are enjoying it in their divine benefactor's presence.

Secondly, we shall be *like* him. In chapter 4 we saw that at the Second Coming believers' bodies will be changed. Writing to the Philippians, Paul takes us further and promises that Jesus will 'transform our lowly body to be like his glorious body' (Philippians 3:21). The Bible does not give us a detailed explanation of this, but the key word is 'transform', which comes from the Greek root *schema*, meaning the outward form or appearance. Paul uses a similar word in the previous chapter when he points out that while Jesus retained his divinity he came to earth 'in human *form*' (Philippians 2:8, emphasis added). Elsewhere he uses similar language to tell the Corinthians that 'the present *form* of this world is passing away' (1 Corinthians 7:31, emphasis added). We have already seen that the present world will not be annihilated, but transformed. The same will be true of believers' bodies at the resurrection. Just as the body Jesus now has is no longer subject to earthly restrictions, so the body a believer has in heaven will no longer be subject to the limitations of time and space. It will never be subject to wear and tear, injury, illness or disease. Nor will it ever grow old or deteriorate in any way, This explains why Paul confesses that while living on earth Christians 'groan inwardly as we wait eagerly for adoption as sons, the redemption of our bodies' (Romans 8:23).

Many Greeks in New Testament times did not believe that the body would be raised, but thought of the body as a prison from which the spirit would escape at death, while the Sadducees, a Jewish religious group, bluntly claimed 'there is no resurrection' (Matthew22:23). Paul makes it clear that both ideas are wrong, and uses a horticultural analogy to illustrate this, comparing death and resurrection to the sowing of a seed and its subsequent growth: 'What is sown is perishable; what is raised is imperishable. It is sown in dishonour; it is raised in glory. It is sown in weakness; it is raised in power. It is sown a natural body; it is raised a spiritual body' (1 Corinthians 15:42–44). As a human body is lowered into the grave it is already a decaying corpse, but when Jesus returns to the earth the bodies of believers will leave the grave and be transformed into glorious, living bodies adapted for eternal life 'by the power that enables [the Lord Jesus Christ] even to subject all things to himself' (Philippians 3:21). As we saw in chapter 4, this will include the resurrection and re-integration of all bodies that were not buried but were destroyed in some other way.

In *Four Books of Sentences*, which in its time became a standard textbook of theology, the Italian theologian Peter Lombard (c.1096–1160) saw the resurrected bodies of believers as a reconstitution of their true humanity: 'Nothing of the substance of the flesh from which humanity is created will be lost; rather, the natural substance of the body will be reintegrated by the collection of all the particles that were previously dispersed. The bodies of the saints will thus rise without any defect, shining like the sun, all their deformities having been excised.'[211]

This statement should thrill every Christian, and for some it will have a special significance. Joni Eareckson Tada is a moving example. She became a total quadriplegic after diving into Chesapeake Bay, Maryland in 1967, and in 2010 was diagnosed with breast cancer. At some stage after the accident her

Christian faith was severely tested, but she came through that phase and her radiant testimony has been the foundation of a ministry that has blessed countless people all over the world. This is Joni's perspective on the transformation of her body: 'I can still hardly believe it. I, with shrivelled, bent fingers, atrophied muscles, gnarled knees, and no feeling from the shoulders down, will one day have a new body, light, bright and clothed in righteousness—powerful and dazzling. Can you imagine the hope this gives someone spinal-cord injured like me? Or someone who is cerebral palsied, brain-injured, or who has multiple sclerosis? Imagine the hope this gives someone who is manic-depressive. No other religion, no other philosophy promises new bodies, hearts and minds. Only in the gospel of Christ do hurting people find such incredible hope.'[212]

I once heard a self-styled British prophet claim that when he got to heaven his body would then be as if he were a little over thirty years old, as that was the age Jesus was when he rose from the dead and ascended into heaven. Some of his hearers were stunned, but he was saying nothing new. The medieval theologian Thomas Aquinas (1225–1274) believed the same thing, based on his mistaken understanding of the Bible's statement that God planned for believers to attain to 'mature manhood, to the measure of the stature of the fullness of Christ' (Ephesians 4:13). Aquinas taught that at the resurrection human nature will be brought back 'to the state of youth, toward which the movement of growth is terminated, and from which the movement of degeneration begins'.[213] In this scenario those who died at a younger or older age would have a radical makeover, resulting in all of them giving the appearance of being in their early thirties. This is a fascinating idea, but it owes more to sentimental speculation than to scriptural revelation, as the

Bible gives no hint that this will be the case. It speaks of the
body's transformation, but nowhere does it give us a basis for
believing that those who arrive in heaven younger than in their
early thirties will have their bodies 'upgraded', or that the bodies
of those who are older will somehow revert to a lower default
age that will be the same for all of heaven's human residents.
The Bible does not address the issue. As we have seen in
previous chapters, it merely states that all believers (those who
died before the Second Coming and those still living at the time)
will be physically transformed. Their bodies will be permanently
and eternally perfect. As John MacArthur points out, 'You will
never look in a mirror and notice wrinkles or a receding hairline.
You will never have a day of sickness. You won't be susceptible to
injury or disease or allergies. There will be none of those things
in heaven. There will only be absolute, imperishable
perfection.'[214]

Wayne Gruden puts this well:

> Our resurrection bodies will not only be free from disease and
> aging, they will also be given fullness of strength and power—not
> infinite power like God, of course, and probably not what we
> would think of as 'superhuman power' in the sense possessed by
> the 'superheroes' of modern fictional children's writing, for
> example, but nonetheless full and complete human power and
> strength, the strength that God intended human beings to have in
> their bodies when he created them. *It will therefore be strength that
> is sufficient to do all that we desire to do in conformity with the will of
> God* (emphasis added).[215]

Being like Jesus will mean not only physical transformation
but spiritual consummation, the ultimate fulfilment of God's

plan for his people that they should be 'conformed to the image of his Son' (Romans 8:29). When new parents and other family members first see a new-born baby, they often look for physical features that reflect their own. It is a genetic certainty that all children bear a resemblance to their parents, even if the resemblance is very slight and not immediately obvious. It is equally certain that in heaven all Christians will not only have bodies that have the same qualities as the body of their Saviour, but will be spiritually transformed in such a way that in this sense, too, they will be 'like him'.

We need not speculate about this, as John goes on to tell us three specific things about Jesus 'as he is'. Firstly, 'he is pure' (1 John 3:3), that is, he is morally perfect, without contamination or defilement of any kind. Secondly, in him 'there is no sin' (1 John 3:5), which in the context of the promise we are examining is the basis of a breathtaking prospect. He has not the slightest sympathy with sin, no inclination towards it and no affection for it. Finally, 'he is righteous' (1 John 3:7). The word 'righteous' is related to God's law. It carries meanings such as rightness, integrity, justice, truthfulness, faithfulness and consistent conformity to God's nature and will. John sums up the character of the glorified Jesus as being pure, sinless and righteous, then assures all believers that they will be 'like him'! Everything that can be said now about the character of Jesus will be true of believers in heaven. They will be as pure, sinless and righteous then as he is now. They will not be his equals, but neither will they feel out of place in his presence!

Thirdly, 'we *shall* be like him'. If John had written that being like Jesus for ever was a possibility (say as a reward for exceptional Christian living or outstanding service during a person's lifetime) it should still leave us amazed, as this would far exceed anything that had been done to deserve it. But John goes infinitely further and promises that 'we *shall* be like him'—and does not allow a shadow of doubt to fall across the prospect. Can the believer really be sure of this, or is John letting his imagination run away with him? Is there any confirmation of this staggering promise elsewhere in the New Testament? Yes, there is! Peter writes, 'When the Chief Shepherd appears, you will receive the unfading crown of glory' (1 Peter 5:4). Paul assures the Colossians that 'Christ in you' is 'the hope [the word means absolute certainty] of glory' (Colossians 1:27), then comes even closer to John's language when he goes on to tell them, 'When Christ who is your life appears, then you will also appear with him in glory' (Colossians 3:4).

The strongest confirmation of all is one we looked at in a previous chapter. This is Paul's statement that all Christian believers are 'predestined to be conformed to the image of [God's] Son' (Romans 8:29). The word 'predestination' comes from the Latin words *prae* ('before' or 'in advance') and *destinare* ('appoint', 'determine' or 'establish'). Before time began, God determined that everyone he chose would spend eternity in heaven and be conformed to the likeness of Jesus. Predestination is about the believer's destination, which is so utterly secure that Paul can add, 'For I am sure that neither death nor life, nor angels nor rulers, nor things present nor things to come, nor powers, nor height nor death, nor anything else in all creation, will be able to separate us from the love of God in Christ Jesus our Lord' (Romans 8:38–39).

Finally, 'we shall be like him'. Everything John has said has been amazing: we shall be like *him*; we shall be *like* him; and we *shall* be like him. Yet the crowning glory is that *we* shall be like him. When our first parents fell into sin they dragged all of their descendants with them, so that every human being is subject to deterioration, decay, disease and death. The whole world is a hospital and everybody in it is a terminal patient. To make matters worse, man's original sin has left all of humanity spiritually wrecked. Nobody is godly by nature or starts life with a clean sheet. Assuming it has been carried to term, a child has been a sinner for nine months before it is born. Israel's King David eventually became a man after God's own heart (see Acts 13:22), but confesses, 'I was brought forth in iniquity, and in sin did my mother conceive me' (Psalm 51:5). Jesus makes it clear that every sin comes 'from within, out of the heart of man' (Mark 7:21). Even at the peak of his ministry Paul admits, 'I know that nothing good dwells in me, that is, in my flesh' (Romans 7:18). He was not saying that his physical body was evil; the word 'flesh' here means his sinful nature. It was what William Hendriksen calls 'that wicked squatter'[216] that caused him to sin—and it does the same to all believers.

All Christians are also 'by nature children of wrath, like the rest of mankind' (Ephesians 2:3). They were born exposed to God's righteous wrath and under his justified death sentence, so that left to themselves they are destined to 'go away into eternal punishment' (Matthew 25:46). This makes the promise that Christians will spend eternity in heaven with Jesus and will there be 'like him' so astonishing. In spite of the fact that 'the intention of man's heart is evil from his youth' (Genesis 8:21) and of everything that may have stained their lives, believers will all be transformed into the likeness of our glorified Saviour. C. H. Spurgeon once received a copy of a commentary on Leviticus by the Scottish preacher Andrew Bonar (1858–1923). He enjoyed it so much that he sent it to Bonar, asking if he would sign it and also send him a photograph of himself. Bonar replied: 'Dear

Spurgeon, here is the book with my autograph and photograph. If you had been willing to wait a short season you could have had a better likeness, for I shall be like him: I shall see him as he is.'

In his vision of heaven, John saw that God's people there had the name of Jesus and of his Father 'written on their foreheads' (Revelation 14:1). This is generally thought to speak of believers' ownership by God, and this is borne out when John hears 'a loud voice from the throne' saying, 'Behold, the dwelling place of God is with man. He will dwell with them, *and they will be his people*, and God himself will be with them as their God' (Revelation 21:3, emphasis added). But is there another meaning here? In the Bible a person's name often reflects his or her nature, revealing what that person is like. For example, because of their dynamic nature, Jesus calls James and his brother John 'Boanerges, that is, Sons of Thunder' (Mark 3:17). When God sees his people in heaven—'a great multitude that no one could number, from every nation, from all tribes and peoples and languages' (Revelation 7:9)—with his name written on their foreheads, is this not one way of expressing the incredible truth that he sees his own nature reflected in every one of them?

Christians are often taken up with anticipating the joy that will be theirs when they see their Saviour in heaven, but give little or no thought to the joy that will be *his* in their being there. The German hymn writer Gerhardt Tersteegen (1697–1769) expresses this beautifully:

> He who in His hour of sorrow
> Bore the curse alone;
> I who through the lonely desert
> Trod where He had gone;

He and I, in that bright glory,
One deep joy shall share—
Mine, to be forever with Him;
His, that I am there.[217]

The psalmist says, 'Precious in the sight of the LORD is the death of his saints' (Psalm 116:15) and Isaiah prophesies that the slain, risen and glorified Messiah will see the result of 'the anguish of his soul' and 'be satisfied' (Isaiah 53:11). This is such a stunning statement that any Christian reading these words should be overwhelmed—and pause to reflect on the enormity of what is being said. *Their* redemption is the result of *his* anguish—and he is satisfied that it was all worthwhile!

Before leaving John's staggering statement 'But we know that when he appears we shall be like him, because we shall see him as he is' we need to focus on the important word 'because'. This tells us that the first part of the sentence, 'we shall be like him', depends on the second part, 'we shall see him as he is'. This ties in perfectly with something Paul writes to the Christians at Corinth. He tells them that when unconverted Jews read the Old Testament and failed to see that the old covenant was not an end in itself but was meant to draw them to Christ it was because 'a veil lies over their hearts' (2 Corinthians 3:15). He then adds that for Christians the Holy Spirit has torn the veil away, with the result that 'we all, with unveiled face, beholding the glory of the Lord, *are being transformed from one degree of glory to another*' (2 Corinthians 3:18, emphasis added).

Christians now see God's glory in some measure as they read his Word and meditate on all it tells them about him, including his perfection, power, wisdom, faithfulness, mercy and grace, especially as seen in the Lord Jesus Christ. Martin Luther calls

Jesus 'the centre and circumference of the Bible' and says that, 'As we go to the cradle only in order to find the baby, so we go to the Scriptures only to find Christ.' Paul's word 'beholding' is in a present continuous tense—it is something Christians are to be in the habit of doing—and if they do so honestly and openly, earnestly asking God to apply its truth to their lives, they will find, as we have just seen, that by the Holy Spirit's enabling they are 'being transformed from one degree of glory to another'.

The phrase 'being transformed' underlines the fact that this is not a sudden, once-for-all crisis, but a gradual, cumulative process. Yet as all believers know only too well, they sometimes take one step forward and two steps back. There are times when they feel discouraged and ashamed that their progress is so painfully slow and erratic, especially when they find themselves repeating the kind of sin that 'clings so closely' (Hebrews 12:1). There are times when they are so disgusted with themselves that they are even tempted to think that they may never have been truly converted. Nevertheless, the more the Holy Spirit applies the relevance of what they see of Jesus Christ in the Bible with the eye of faith, the more they are transformed, until that marvellous moment—that 'unimaginable certainty'—when they 'see him face to face' and immediately become 'like him'.

Just as Christ is 'the exact imprint of [God's] nature' (Hebrews 1:3), so in heaven Christians will be the exact imprint of Christ's nature—pure, sinless and righteous. Charles Wesley captures the truth perfectly:

Changed from glory into glory
Till in heaven we take our place,
Till we lay our crowns before you,
Lost in wonder, love and praise.[218]

Destination:
heaven

On an American radio programme, a number of famous people were asked what they thought heaven would be like. All of them said they believed in heaven and assumed they would go there, but when asked to describe it not one of them mentioned that God would be there! Their entire focus was on *their presence* and what this would mean for them, ignoring the fact that it is *God's presence* alone that makes heaven what it is. Their thinking was seriously skewed, as the Bible's emphasis is not on believers going to a place but on being with a Person.

Popular ideas of heaven sometimes picture it as being primarily a place of physical pleasure, where all the things that were enjoyed most on earth will be even more fully enjoyed, but this kind of thinking entirely misses the point that *God is the centrepiece of heaven's glory*. The American theologian Millard J. Erickson is exactly right: 'Since glory is of the very nature of

God, heaven will be a place of great glory.'[219] God is 'the Lord of heaven' (Daniel 5:23). It is 'his holy temple' (Psalm 11:4), his 'holy habitation' (Deuteronomy 26:15) and his 'dwelling place' (1 Kings 8:30), and he calls it 'my throne' (Isaiah 66:1). It is because God lives and reigns in heaven that everything there is as it is. It is God's presence that guarantees the absence of all the negative things that plague our lives here—but this is only part of the picture, what we might call the flip side of the coin. The final chapter of the British preacher Brian Edwards' superb book *Grace—Amazing grace* is called 'Ultimate Grace'. Introducing the subject of heaven, he writes, 'We are about to describe the indescribable, explain the inexplicable and keep a steady eye on the invisible—that doesn't look too hopeful as a final chapter in a book.'[220] I can identify with that!—but something he writes two pages later points me in the right direction: 'All that God is, heaven is ... Heaven, therefore, is not to be described by what we are like, still less by what we like, but by what God is like. All that God is will be enjoyed by all that we become.'[221] It is impossible to think of any admirable quality that is not true of God to an infinite degree, and all of these are enjoyed in heaven by all who are there. God created mankind in his own image (Genesis 1:26), and in heaven that image, ruined for so long by human sin, is perfectly and permanently restored.

I have been engaged in an itinerant ministry for over fifty years, preaching on six continents, in scores of countries and in many hundreds of cities, towns and villages, yet there is only one place where I truly feel, 'This is where I belong.' It is the tiny Channel Island of Guernsey, where I was born. Yet the analogy breaks down. The longer I live, the more tenuous my felt links with the island become. The house in which I was born has been demolished, my ancestors are all dead, and the family has never owned any property there. The best I can do is to stand at the top of New Street in St Peter Port and look up at a third-floor flat my parents once rented—and even that has been redesigned almost beyond recognition. Paul assures believers that 'our citizenship is in heaven' (Philippians 3:20); the contrast could hardly be greater!

Jonathan Edwards writes, 'God is the highest good of the reasonable creature, and the enjoyment of him is the only happiness with which our souls can be satisfied. To go to heaven fully to enjoy God is *infinitely* better than the most pleasant accommodations here. Fathers and mothers, husbands, wives, children, or the company of earthly friends, are but shadows. But the enjoyment of God is the substance. These are but scattered beams, but God is the sun. These are but streams, but God is the fountain. These are but drops, but God is the ocean.'[222] Even if the Bible were to give a list (and it would be an exceptionally long one) of all the privileges, joys, thrills and blessings that Christians will experience in heaven, it would not add up to a thousandth part of the greatest experience of all: *God himself*. In the new creation every one of God's redeemed people will have direct, unclouded, uninterrupted, intimate and personal fellowship with him. R. C. Sproul is right to say, 'There's nothing more glorious about heaven than to be bathed in the radiance of the unveiled presence of God.'[223]

Read that again! It points to an experience that is infinitely beyond our imagination. Christians enjoy spiritual 'mountaintop experiences' in their lives, but these are tantalizingly elusive and pass so quickly. Writing in his journal on 27 April 1742, David Brainerd (1718–1747), the American missionary to the native Indians, was clearly on a spiritual high: 'My soul never enjoyed so much of heaven before; it was the most refined and most spiritual season of communion with God I ever yet felt.' But we find a very different entry less than nine months later, when on 14 January 1743 he writes, 'My spiritual conflicts today were unspeakably dreadful, heavier than the mountains and overflowing floods. I was deprived of all sense of God, even of the being of a God; and that was my misery.' If they are honest, Christians can all point to the same highs and lows in their spiritual condition and emotions—but there will be no such fluctuations in heaven. There, the full, conscious enjoyment of their God and Saviour will never change or come to an end. They will see God without distortion, praise him without diversion, love him without division, enjoy him without dilution and serve him without distraction.

Wayne Grudem puts it well: 'More important than all the physical beauty of the heavenly city, more important than the fellowship we will enjoy eternally with all God's people from all nations and all periods in history, more important than our freedom from pain and sorrow and physical suffering, and more important than reigning over God's kingdom—more important by far than any of these will be the fact that we will be in the presence of God and enjoying unhindered fellowship with him.'[224] The British theologian Bruce Milne agrees: 'We may be confident that the crowning wonder of our experience in the heavenly realm will be the endless exploration of that unutterable beauty, majesty, love, holiness, power, joy and grace which is God himself.'[225] Commenting on the suggestion that men and women use only about two per cent of their brain capacity, the British educator Chris Gray writes, 'I have a theory—and this is my opinion and you must see it as such and not take it as anything other than speculation—that we use only two per cent of our brains [here on earth] because when we get to heaven we'll need the remaining ninety-eight per cent to take in the sheer wonder of God, his creation, his plan of salvation and the whole of the universe.'[226] He may not be too wide of the mark! What is certain is that *heaven is first and foremost the presence of God.*

The jewels

As we saw a few pages ago, Christians' anticipation of heaven will be all the greater if they think about what their presence there will mean to God. In an Old Testament prophecy that has both a temporal and an eternal meaning, God tells his people, 'You shall be a crown of beauty in the hand of the LORD, and a royal diadem in the hand of your God' (Isaiah 62:3). In another prophecy he says of them, 'They shall be mine … in the day when I make up my treasured possession' (Malachi 3:17). Elsewhere he promises that 'like the jewels of a crown they shall shine on his land' (Zechariah 9:16).

An estimation of the value of things can often be judged by what people are prepared to pay for them, and some estimations are bizarre. A tooth lost in the nineteen-sixties by John Lennon, best known as a founder member of the English rock band The Beatles, was sold at Omega Auction House, Stockport on 4 November 2011. Admitting that it was 'rather gruesome, yellowy and browny with a cavity', Omega's Karen Fairweather said before the sale, 'It is a truly unique item and it is really difficult to put a value on it.' She settled for a listed reserve price of £10,000, and it was eventually bought by the Canadian dentist Michael Zuk for £19,500. He was said to be 'buzzing' after his successful bid and planned to take it on a 'tooth tour' to other dental practices and schools. At another level of extravagance, almost exactly a year earlier billionaire jeweller Laurence Graff broke the world record for a jewel bought at auction when he paid £29 million for a 24.78 carat pink diamond ring at Sotheby's Geneva saleroom.

These prices are mind-boggling, but the value of God's people to him is infinitely greater and should constantly amaze them. Just think about it! We live on a relatively small planet orbiting the sun, which is one million times its size, in what the British physicist Stephen Hawking calls 'the outer suburbs of an ordinary spiral galaxy'. This is the Milky Way, which has 100,000 million stars and is one of 100,000 million galaxies in the known universe. Even without knowing these details, David asks God, 'When I look at your heavens, the work of your fingers, the moon and the stars, which you have set in place, what is man that you are mindful of him, and the son of man that you care for him?' (Psalm 8:3–4). Job is equally bewildered: 'What is man, that you make so much of him, and that you set your heart on him?' (Job 7:17).

Well might they ask! Left to himself, man is a rebel against God's authority, exposed to God's righteous anger and doomed to be shut out for ever from his loving presence in heaven; and not only a castaway but a captive, what Jesus calls 'a slave to sin' (John 8:34). But Jesus 'came into the world to save sinners' (1 Timothy 1:15), and he did so at a cost that goes far beyond anything that can be measured in financial terms; he gave *his life* 'as a ransom for many' (Mark 10:45). Peter tells his readers, 'You were ransomed ... not with perishable things such as silver or gold, but with the precious blood of Christ, like that of a lamb without blemish or spot' (1 Peter 1:18–19). While Old Testament Israelites killed a lamb at the annual Passover feast to commemorate the way God had rescued them from captivity in Egypt, Jesus came to earth as 'the Lamb of God, who takes away the sin of the world' (John 1:29). He did this not by offering a sacrifice, but by *being* the sacrifice. He gave his own sinless life as a ransom price to satisfy divine justice, with the result that those in whose place he died are released from sin's captivity.

God tells his people, 'You are precious in my eyes, and honoured, and I love you' (Isaiah 43:4). Peter confirms that 'in the sight of God' believers are 'chosen and precious' (1 Peter 2:4). They are his jewels—and there are no semi-precious stones in his collection! They are 'a chosen race, a royal priesthood, a holy nation, a people for his own possession' (1 Peter 2:9). When God sweeps his eyes over all of creation, taking in the unspeakable glories of heaven, the staggering immensity of space with its millions of galaxies, planets and stars, and the subatomic marvels of creation beyond the reach of the most advanced microscopes, he can find nothing more precious than a sinner redeemed by the blood of Christ.

Christians can also treasure the truth that in heaven they will rejoice in the fullest experience of God's love. The 1980 film *The Elephant Man* was based on the true story of Joseph Merrick (called John Merrick in the film), a nineteenth-century Englishman who was horribly disfigured by the worst recorded case of Proteus syndrome, an abnormal and incurable growth of bones, skin and other systems. After spending years as a side-show freak he was rescued by a Victorian surgeon who found a permanent home for him. At one point during his rehabilitation Merrick cried out, 'My life is full because I know I am loved.' In heaven, believers will have found 'a permanent home', precious proof of the fact that God loves them 'with an everlasting love' (Jeremiah 31:3). On a gravestone in Epsom Cemetery I recently saw the words, 'If love could have saved you, you would have lived for ever.' God's people will spend eternity with him in heaven because his love did!

Home!

We are all familiar with the phrases, 'There's no place like home' and 'Home Sweet Home'. I believe I could outshout most people in endorsing them! In the course of my ministry people have sometimes booked me into hotels far above my pay scale, or arranged for me to stay in homes that made mine look decidedly down-market. Yet I always looked forward to the day when I could return to Banstead, especially when I was working overseas. When I arrived I was often faced with a practical problem of some kind—a leaking gutter, a missing roof tile, an electrical fault, or a piece of equipment that had broken down. My wife Joyce had continued to tend the garden, but there were always 'man things' that still needed to be done. My desk was routinely piled high with paperwork and when the electronic age arrived my Inbox had dozens (sometimes hundreds) of unanswered messages. Yet all of these responsibilities and problems were outweighed by the great joy of knowing that I was back home and in the company of the one I loved more than anyone else in the world. There were times when on arrival I felt like shouting, 'Hallelujah!'—though British reserve would have made me wait until I was inside the house!

This is not even a pale reflection of what it will mean for Christians to go to heaven, a word that is used in the New Testament over 250 times as the name of the dwelling place of God and the future eternal home of his people. Of all that is said about it, nothing is greater for believers than this: 'The dwelling place of God is with man. He will dwell with them, and they will be his people, and God himself will be with them as their God'

(Revelation 21:3). This mirrors God's Old Testament promise, 'My dwelling place will be with them, and I will be their God, and they shall be my people' (Ezekiel 37:27). Christians have a foretaste of this from the moment of their conversion. In his high priestly prayer Jesus tells his heavenly Father, 'This is eternal life, *that they know you* the only true God, and Jesus Christ whom you have sent' (John 17:3, emphasis added). Yet in this life those who know him and have a living relationship with him are in the minority. Although 'the world was made through him', when Jesus came to earth 'the world did not know him. He came to his own and his own people did not receive him' (John 1:10–11). His own people were the Jews, but most of them rejected him. What is more, even when he was thirty years of age, 'not even his brothers believed in him' (John 7:5).

Things will be very different in heaven. Everybody there will know God in a more intimate and immediate way than even the finest believers in history did on earth. The phrase 'He will dwell with them, and they will be his people, and God himself will be with them as their God' (Revelation 21:3) almost sounds needlessly repetitive, but surely the wording is as it is in order to underline the glorious reality *and supreme importance* of this promise. For Christians to tie themselves in knots puzzling over details about which God has revealed nothing—What kind of clothes will we wear? Will there be television? What language will we speak? Will we play sports? Will my dog be there?—is not only a waste of time, it takes their eyes off the one glorious certainty that governs everything: *they will be with the Lord!* Endless discussions about matters weightier than the five examples I have given, but about which the Bible is silent, run the same risk and sometimes generate more heat than light. It is often said that nobody knows what the future holds, but this is not strictly true. The last words my wife Joyce heard me say to her just before she died were, 'Surely goodness and mercy shall follow me all the days of my life, and I shall dwell in the house of the LORD for ever' (Psalm 23:6). She had proved the truth of the first part of that testimony for many years; immediately after her death she was enjoying the second part.

The climax to Jesus' high priestly prayer was his passionate longing that those the Father had given him to save 'may be *with me* where I am' (John 17:24, emphasis added). As we saw in an earlier chapter, Paul tells the Thessalonians that Christians who are living on earth at the Second Coming will hear a cry of command, the voice of an archangel and the sound of the trumpet of God, at which the dead in Christ will rise and those still living on earth will be caught up together with them in the air. Yet he packs the result of all this indescribable activity into just eight words: 'so we will always be with the Lord' (1 Thessalonians 4:17). *This is the transcendent truth about heaven!* As Leon Morris comments, 'There are doubtless many points on which we should like further information; but when Paul comes to that great fact, which includes everything else, and makes everything else unimportant, he ceases. There is nothing to add to it.[227]

Heaven as a world in which all the pleasures enjoyed on earth are intensified is a caricature. The all-important, overwhelming thing is being in God's presence. It would no doubt be fascinating to know here and now everything that believers will experience there and then, but we dare not go beyond what God reveals in his Word. Worshipping in Grove Chapel, Camberwell, in South London one day I saw on an inner wall a memorial tablet that puts the emphasis where it should be. It commemorates Samuel Carter, one of the twelve founders of the chapel, who contributed nearly half of the cost of the building and laid its foundation stone on 15 March 1819. Carter died on 1 February 1827 'having lived a life of extensive usefulness' (an epitaph to be envied!). At the bottom of the memorial tablet are these words:

> He lov'd to hear within this sacred place
> Of God's electing love and sovereign grace.
> He liv'd and died by faith in Jesus' blood,
> And now he lives for ever with his God.

When his disciples were distressed because Jesus was soon to leave them, he made this wonderful promise: 'Let not your hearts be troubled. Believe in God; believe also in me. In my Father's house are many rooms. If it were not so, would I have told you that I go to prepare a place for you? And if I go and prepare a place for you, I will come again and *will take you to myself, that where I am you may be also*' (John 14:1–3, emphasis added). This would have been a great comfort to those dejected disciples—and should be to all believers—as it points to his presence as being the all-embracing truth about heaven. Older English versions of the Bible have 'many mansions' instead of 'many rooms', but this misleading translation has led to speculation about the relative size and quality of individual believers' houses in heaven. 'Rooms' is a far better translation of a word based on the Greek *mone*, which means 'remain, abide, dwell, live'.[228] When people invite me to stay with them overnight and say, 'We have enough room', they are not referring to the quality of their home, but merely letting me know that it has enough space to accommodate me. As the Scottish preacher Gordon Keddie notes, 'That is precisely Jesus' point here. The

Father's house has many rooms. In other words, *there is no shortage of living space in heaven*. It is a large place with rooms for all the Lord's people.'[229]

This points to the important fact that in the New Testament there is no reference to an individual being there. All references to believers in heaven are corporate. All of God's redeemed people, 'a great multitude that no one could number, from every nation, from all tribes and peoples and languages' (Revelation 7:9) will be there. So will all the unfallen angels. The German theologian Albert the Great (ca.1193/1206–1280) calculated that there are 399,920,004 of these, but we can settle for 'innumerable angels' (Hebrews 12:22), including cherubim, seraphim and archangels, beings who have never sinned, but who have been praising and serving God in glorious and harmonious unity since the moment of their creation. All believers will join them in doing so. The British songwriter Stuart Townend expresses his longing for heaven like this:

> There is a hope that stands the test of time,
> That lifts my eyes beyond the beckoning grave
> To see the matchless beauty of a day divine
> When I behold his face!
> When sufferings cease and sorrows die,
> And every longing satisfied.
> Then joy unspeakable will flood my soul,
> For I am truly home.[230]

The family

Reflecting on heaven as home raises many questions about relationships, and especially that of marriage. When Sadducees ask Jesus a trick question about this (it was hypocritical, as they denied that there was such a thing as resurrection) he replies, 'You are wrong, because you know neither the Scriptures nor the power of God. For in the resurrection they neither marry nor are given in marriage, but are like angels in heaven' (Matthew 22:29–30). The Old Testament (which the Sadducees had) clearly teaches the resurrection of the body, and the New Testament speaks of '[God's] great might that he worked in Christ when he raised him from the dead' (Ephesians 1:19–20). On the issue of marriage Jesus could not have been clearer: his redeemed people will be 'like angels', who neither marry nor die.

After creating Adam, the first human being, God said, 'It is not good that the man should be alone; I will make a helper fit for him' (Genesis 2:18). He then created the first woman, who became Adam's intimate companion, making them 'one flesh' (Genesis 2:24). God then told them, 'Be fruitful and multiply' (Genesis 1:28); and the final book in the Old Testament endorses this primary purpose for marriage by saying of a man and wife, 'Did he not make them one, with a portion of the Spirit in their union? And what was the one God seeking? Godly offspring' (Malachi 2:15). This gives the ideal earthly pattern, but as there will be no death in heaven there will be no need for children to be born. God's redeemed family will be complete; nobody will be subtracted from it or added to it. As the procreation of children will be unnecessary, so will the sexual intimacy needed to bring this about. Yet every good thing experienced in this life will be richer, better and fuller in the life to come. This means that relationships with spouses and other members of contemporary earthly families will be at a depth and degree far beyond anything known in this life. There will be no one-to-one marriages in heaven—*but there will be one marriage*, with Jesus as the Bridegroom and his redeemed people as the bride. As we saw in chapter 3, one of the descriptions of heaven is reflected in the cry, 'Hallelujah! For the Lord our God the Almighty reigns. Let us rejoice and exult and give him the glory, for the marriage of the Lamb has come, and his Bride has made herself ready' (Revelation 19:6–7). In that glorious marriage, what believers had on earth is replaced with something of infinitely greater value.

As the disciples were able to recognize Moses and Elijah when Jesus was transfigured (see Matthew 17:1–8), it seems clear that believers will be individually identifiable and recognizable in heaven. Joni Eareckson Tada puts it well: 'Somewhere in my broken, paralyzed body is the seed of what I shall become. The paralysis makes what I am to become all the more grand when you contrast atrophied, useless legs against splendorous resurrected legs. I'm convinced that if there are mirrors in heaven (and why not?) the image I see will be unmistakably Joni.'[231] In their perfected state close friends will be even closer and best friends even better. It is said that when an old Welsh preacher, John Evans, was asked by his wife, 'Do you think we shall know each other in heaven?' he replied, 'To be sure we shall. Do you think we will be greater fools there than we are here?'! Paul seems to point towards the recognition of treasured friends in heaven when he asks converts in Thessalonica, 'For what is our hope or joy or crown of boasting before our Lord Jesus at his coming? Is it not you? For you are our glory and joy' (1 Thessalonians 2:19–20). On earth, believers are 'no longer strangers and aliens' but 'fellow citizens with the saints and members of the household of God' (Ephesians 2:19). They are 'one body in Christ, and individually members one of another' (Romans 12:5). They are also spiritually united to those already 'enrolled in heaven' and described as 'the spirits of the righteous made perfect' (Hebrews 12:23). In the new creation their union with those already in heaven will be perfected as they share the joy of being 'at home with the Lord' (2 Corinthians 5:8).

In over fifty years of full-time Christian ministry I have gathered a widening circle of Christian friends and acquaintances all around the world, yet inevitably the wider the circle has become the less often I see many of them, and many times I hear of someone's death and grieve that I will see them no more in this life. Yet in heaven I will be with them all—and for ever. Even believers found somewhat hard to like here will be found easy to love there; as the American authors Dan Barber and Robert Peterson point out, 'Christ died that we might be reconciled not only to God, but also to each other.'[232] Heaven will be the biggest and best family reunion ever! Here on earth family members or close friends sometimes live a long way from each other and are not often able to meet; this will never be the case in heaven, where there will be meetings but no partings.

Some years ago, my wife and I returned to Guernsey for a few days of special events. Without telling her, I arranged for many of the friends we had left behind on the island some forty years earlier to meet with us one evening. Our hosts were in on the plan and on the chosen day announced that they were taking us out for an evening meal. Feigning ignorance, I said that Joyce and I would be happy to accept, and we made our way to Les Cotils Conference Centre. When someone opened the door to one of the meeting rooms I ushered Joyce in, and her face was a picture of perfect joy as we were greeted by dozens of friends, some of whom we had not seen for many years. The delightful hours that followed gave a tiny glimpse of what it will be like to be in heaven.

Richard Baxter pictures heaven as 'a corporation of perfected saints ... the communion of saints completed ... Not only our old acquaintances, but all the saints of all ages, whose faces in the flesh we never saw, we shall there both know and comfortably enjoy.'[233] It is amazing to think that every believer will know every other believer in history, not merely as an acquaintance, but as a brother or sister in the same family. Just to think of all the famous believers in history, going back through the centuries to New Testament days, then further back into Old Testament times to include prophets, priests and kings, then even further back to Noah (and even Adam and Eve if they were saved) sends the imagination into overdrive. Yet this would still be only dipping a toe into the ocean of the truth about heaven as every believer will have a family relationship with all the others, including all of those whose names have never hit the headlines but who belong to 'the household of faith' (Galatians 6:10). Edward Donnelly claims, 'In our heavenly family we will have tens of thousands of fulfilling relationships.'[234] Philip Ryken elaborates: 'In the celestial city of God, all our relationships and activities will gather to be what they were always intended to become ... In the new heavens and the new earth we will live in perfect harmony, peace and justice as the new family of God.'[235]

It is exhilarating to know that there will be no fighting (literally or metaphorically) about the theological differences that over the centuries have caused such difficulty and distress in the Christian church. Everybody will be of one mind as to the meaning of even the most difficult or complicated Bible passages, including those in apocalyptic books. According to the Center for the Study of Global Christianity at Gordon-Conwell Theological Seminary, there are currently some 41,000 Christian denominations in the world (though this does include some overlapping because of cultural distinctions). In heaven there will be none. Nor will there be any of the divisions or dissensions that have caused or characterized denominational distinctions. Taking this even further, my good friend and fellow preacher Peter Anderson suggests, 'It will be one of the glories of heaven that Christians will never misunderstand each other.' There will be no personality clashes, criticism, misrepresentation, false motives, manoeuvring or power struggles. David writes, 'Behold, how good and pleasant it is when brothers dwell in unity ... For there the LORD has commanded the blessing, life for evermore' (Psalm 133:1,3). He may be referring directly to times when the people gathered in Jerusalem for special religious feasts, but the principle extends much further. True, complete and uninterrupted unity among God's people is impossible in the present life; in heaven, it is the eternal norm.

In heaven's family nobody will feel neglected, marginalized, badly treated, offended or discriminated against, inferior or ignored, nor will anybody be lost in the crowd. On the other hand there will be no 'loners', or people so selfishly protective of their privacy that they will want to say with Bart in the animated television sitcom *The Simpsons*, 'My bubble, my space'. Nobody will feel alone, lonely or out of place. C. S. Lewis goes so far as to say, 'Your place in heaven will seem to be made for you and for you alone, because you were made for it—made for it stitch by stitch as a glove is made for a hand.'[236] Nor will relationships have any of the nuances that affect them here. As Jonathan Edwards points out,

> There shall be no such thing as flattery or insincerity in heaven, but there perfect sincerity shall reign through all in all. Everyone will be just what he seems to be, and will really have all the love that he seems to have. It will not be so in this world, where comparatively few things are what they seem to be, and where

professions are often made lightly and without meaning. But there, every expression of love shall come from the bottom of the heart, and all that is professed shall be really and truly felt.[237]

Another world

During a week of preaching at the Cayman Keswick Convention on the Caribbean island of Grand Cayman I was invited to go snorkelling, something I had never done before. I jumped at the opportunity and one morning was taken out in a small boat. Putting on the diving mask, snorkel and flippers was not a problem, though I did hesitate when told to throw myself backwards over the side of the boat! Moments later, I could hardly believe my eyes. Everywhere I looked there were brilliantly-coloured anemones, sea stars, stingrays, tarpon, yellowtail and blue tangs, green turtles, sea urchins, coral morphs, juvenile fish and many other marvels I had never seen before. I was overwhelmed by it all and it took a lot of persuasion to get me back into the boat in time to be ready to preach at that day's lunchtime convention service. I was in another world!

Even in its present state the world is remarkable. Modern science is producing growing evidence that the rest of the known universe is in some way fine-tuned to produce intelligent life on our planet. The British theoretical physicist Paul Davies claims, 'Through my scientific work I have come to believe more and more strongly that the physical universe is put together with an ingenuity so astonishing that I cannot accept it merely as brute fact ... We humans are built into the scheme of things in a very basic way ...We are truly meant to be here.'[238] This alone should cause Christians to marvel at the amazingly precise creative wisdom that ensured man's unique location and role in

God's purposes. They should marvel even more at his patience in allowing so many blessings to be theirs in spite of the fact that human sin has dislocated the entire universe, which is now 'in bondage to corruption' and 'groaning together in the pains of childbirth' (Romans 8:21–22). This is why there are natural upheavals, many becoming natural disasters that result in widespread loss of life and property.

However, the new creation will truly be 'another world'. There will be no such upheavals and disasters, as the entire cosmos will have been renewed and brought to a state of unshakeable perfection. There will be no tsunamis, tornadoes, hurricanes, cyclones, avalanches or earthquakes. Nor will there be any floods, droughts, heat waves or other events causing damage, distress or death. The eighteenth-century British theologian John Gill put it like this: 'The new heavens will be clear of all unhealthy fog, mists, storms of hail, storms of snow, blustering tempests, peals of thunder—nothing of this kind will be heard or seen but a pure, serene and tranquil air quite suited to the bodies of raised saints.'[239]

Nature will no longer be 'red in tooth and claw'[240] and there will be no violence or destruction in the animal kingdom. In a beautifully-worded prophecy, the Bible symbolizes the restoration of perfect harmony among all created beings:

> The wolf shall dwell with the lamb, and the leopard shall lie down with the young goat, and the calf and the lion and the fatted calf together; and a little child shall lead them. The cow and the bear shall graze; their young shall lie down together; and the lion shall eat straw like the ox. The nursing child shall play over the hole of the cobra, and the weaned child shall put his hand on the adder's den. They shall not hurt or destroy in all my holy

mountain; for the earth shall be full of the knowledge of the LORD as the waters cover the sea (Isaiah 11:6–9).

Perhaps the most telling phrase in this passage is the one that pictures a defenceless child perfectly safe in the presence of a serpent. It is impossible to miss the contrast with the enmity imposed by God between humans and the serpent that in Genesis 3:15 represents Satan and symbolizes sin, death and the power of evil; as Alec Motyer says of heaven, 'The enmity between the woman's seed and the serpent is gone.'[241] In the new creation God will reverse the curse!

In heaven the very atmosphere will be the result of God's promise to make 'all things new' (Revelation 21:5). There will be no suspended particulates, bacteria, gases or other pollutants that can cause such widespread (and sometimes deadly) havoc in the present life. An official investigation into the UK's 1956 Clean Air Act, conducted years later, concluded that the Act 'did contribute, albeit partially, to the increase in air quality in the UK over the last thirty years'.[242] God's 'Clean Air Act' will illustrate his cosmic sovereignty and ensure heaven's flawless atmosphere for ever.

Wear and tear will not plague the new creation, nor will the risk of losing any personal possessions. In the Sermon on the Mount Jesus urges us, 'Do not lay up for yourselves treasures on earth, where moth and rust destroy and where thieves break in and steal,' adding that heaven is a place where 'neither moth nor rust destroys and where thieves do not break in and steal' (Matthew 6:19–20). Over the years, moths have had many a mouthful from sweaters of mine, rust has sometimes eaten away at water pipes, and thieves have broken into my home and ransacked it three times, so a home that is moth proof, rust proof and thief proof has particular appeal to me!

There will be no wars in the new creation. War has been a horrific scourge throughout human history. It has been estimated that in the past three thousand years there have been fewer than four hundred without a major war. It has been wryly suggested that peace merely gives men an opportunity to reload. The history of the twentieth century was dominated by two World Wars, which between them accounted for over 75 million deaths. In the ultimate fulfilment of this Old Testament prophecy, the trumpet call at Christ's return will sound war's 'Last Post': 'They shall beat their swords into ploughshares, and their spears into pruning-hooks; nation shall not lift up sword against nation, neither shall they learn war any more ... and no one shall make them afraid, for the mouth of the LORD of hosts has spoken ... we will walk in the name of the LORD our God for ever and ever' (Micah 4:3–5).

There will be no crime in the new creation. Every civilized society on earth has laws, rules and regulations to govern its people and to maintain order—and the list is growing. The UK government alone brought in over three thousand new offences between 1997 and 2006. In heaven no judicial system will be needed as no crime will ever be committed. There will be judges, magistrates, policemen, prison officers and probation officers in heaven, but they will have abandoned their day jobs.

There will be no sickness, diseases or injuries in heaven, nor will there be anything that causes pain of any kind, physical, emotional or spiritual. In the present life, pain has great physical value, as it warns us that something is wrong and there are times when it helps us to survive by alerting us to a serious medical condition. Spiritual pain has even greater value as God can use it to draw believers to confession, repentance and restitution. But, as we saw elsewhere, heaven is a place where pain will be no more, but will have 'passed away' (Revelation 21:4). There will be surgeons, doctors, anaesthetists, nurses, dentists, opticians, pharmacists, psychiatrists, psychologists and countless others in health-related professions, but none of their professional services will be needed.

There will be no regrets in heaven. There will be no burdens to bear, no guilt to grieve over, no unanswered questions, no humiliating ignorance and no unsatisfied desires. Nothing that has stained and scarred life on earth will be there. There will be no remorse, no disappointments and no lost causes.

The promise of perfection

One statement alone enables us to be sure of all that has been said about heaven in the last eight paragraphs: 'Nothing unclean will ever enter it' (Revelation 21:27). God calls heaven 'the high and holy place' (Isaiah 57:15). Nothing there will prevent perfection and everything will contribute to it. This is endorsed by at least three biblical promises.

Firstly, God himself is unutterably holy. Repeating an adjective was a common Jewish form of emphasis, but there are only two places in the Bible in which we find the same word repeated twice, and both are in the context of heaven. We saw these in an earlier chapter, but can repeat them here. In Isaiah's vision of heaven he saw God 'sitting upon a throne, high and lifted up', surrounded by angels crying, 'Holy, holy, holy is the LORD of hosts; the whole earth is full of his glory' (Isaiah 6:1,3). In John's vision he saw celestial beings surrounding God's throne and crying out, 'Holy, holy, holy, is the Lord God Almighty; who was and is and is to come!' (Revelation 4:8). The Bible tells us, 'God is light, and in him there is 'no darkness at all' (1 John 1:5). The statement that 'God is light' speaks not only of his majesty and glory, but also of his moral perfection, underlined by the statement that 'in him is no darkness at all'. In Bruce Milne's words, 'His very being is the outshining and outpouring of purity, truth, righteousness, justice, goodness and every moral perfection.'[243] As God is 'of purer eyes than to see evil and cannot look at wrong' (Habakkuk 1:13), we know that in heaven there is no sin of any kind, only absolute perfection.

Secondly, there will be no place in heaven for Satan, the embodiment of sin. He is described as 'the god of *this* world' (2 Corinthians 4:4, emphasis added), that is to say, the present age, *but he is not the god of the age to come.* Jesus came into the world to destroy sin, that is 'the works of the devil' (1 John 3:8) and the crucial blow was struck at Calvary, Jesus bore in his own body and spirit the ultimate penalty for the sins of those for whom he died, releasing them from their fatal effects. All who put their trust in Christ are 'delivered ... from the domain of darkness and transferred ... to the kingdom of his beloved Son' (Colossians 1:13). While on earth they are still within Satan's reach and he can cause them a great deal of havoc and heartache. Yet he is under God's control and powerless to prevent the universal spread of the gospel; he is not able to 'deceive the nations any longer' (Revelation 20:3). The final blow will come when he is 'thrown into the lake of fire and sulphur' where he will be 'tormented day and night for ever and ever' (Revelation 20:10). It will be impossible for him, directly or indirectly, to have any access to heaven, where God's people will be eternally out of his reach.

Thirdly, believers' natures will have been transformed so that they are constantly and completely in tune with God's. Paul testifies, 'I delight in the law of God' (Romans 7:22), yet confesses to being frustrated to find that time and again 'another law' (his sinful nature) drags him down, so that he is forced to admit, 'I have the desire to do what is right, but not the ability to carry it out' (Romans 7:18). Things will be very different in the new creation. The evidence for the radical difference between this life and the next could not be clearer. The Bible speaks of 'the law of sin and death' (Romans 8:2), which is a law of cause and effect; elsewhere it makes it clear that 'the wages of sin is death' (Romans 6:23). Sin always leads to death and death is the inevitable result of sin, but as there is no such thing as death in heaven—it is one of the things that is 'no more' and has 'passed away' (Revelation 21:4)—we can be sure that heaven is totally free from sin of any kind, even 'invisible' sins such as envy, pride, lust, deceitfulness, jealousy, greed and hatred. Paul Helm writes about the believer in heaven: 'He is so constituted or reconstituted that he *cannot* sin. He does not want to sin, and he does not want to want to sin.'[244] We can take this even further and say that the believer in heaven *cannot* want to sin, as his nature has been transformed into one that is perfectly and unchangeably holy. At creation, man was able not to sin; in the new creation he will not be able to sin.

Joy!

Throughout this book we have put God first in order to get a biblical perspective on heaven, yet the Bible excites expectation by describing how believers will feel when they are there, and its overwhelming emphasis is on one particular emotion: *joy*. In the light of what we have read in previous chapters this should hardly surprise us; but in trying to move things towards a conclusion I have been struck by the number of times the Bible underlines the fact that every part of life in heaven will be filled with joy—and that it will be directly related to God's joy.

Referring to the new heavens and the new earth, God tells the prophet Isaiah, 'Be glad and rejoice for ever in that which I create; for behold, I create Jerusalem to be a joy, and her people to be a gladness. I will rejoice in Jerusalem, and be glad in my people' (Isaiah 65:18–19). When man fell into sin and God saw that 'the wickedness of man was great in the earth' it 'grieved him to his heart' (Genesis 6:5–6). When he sees the new creation, God will 'rejoice ... and be glad'. He will be overjoyed at seeing all his redeemed people securely in heaven, forming the holy city, the new Jerusalem. Alec Motyer goes so far as to say of God's joy then, 'By comparison even the "very good" of Genesis 1:31 seems cool!'[245] Small wonder that God's people are urged to 'be glad and rejoice for ever'! God uses two verbs ('be glad' and 'rejoice') which essentially mean the same thing, as if to make sure believers get the message that there will be no limit to their joy as they revel in the glories of heaven.

Even here on earth the joy of believers is to be focused on God. David calls God 'my exceeding joy' (Psalm 43:4) and Paul says, 'Rejoice in the Lord always' (Philippians 4:4). Their changing circumstances are sometimes far from joyful, yet they can always find joy as they lean on the unchangeable love, power, faithfulness and grace of God. In heaven, God's people will constantly rejoice at knowing these wonderful attributes in all their fullness. As I was writing this paragraph I received a letter from a friend telling me that her husband died on 25 December. In it, she wrote, 'I know he was rejoicing and singing with the angels in heaven on Christmas morning.' All believers will eventually join him!

Messianic passages in the Old Testament often look forward to the joy of heaven. One of the psalmists speaks of 'the city of our God' as 'the joy of all the earth' (Psalm 48:1,2). The immediate reference is to Jerusalem, the centre of the nation's worship, but the fuller meaning points to heaven. The Scottish preacher David Dickson (1583–1662) sees the present church as being the joy of all the earth 'by holding out to all the light of saving doctrine, and showing the authority, power, wisdom and grace of Christ'.[246] In heaven all of the new creation will share in that joy. Isaiah links the return of the Israelites from captivity in Babylon with the greater joy of God's people in heaven: 'And the ransomed of the LORD shall return and come to Zion with singing; everlasting joy shall be upon their heads; they shall obtain gladness and joy, and sorrow and sighing shall flee away' (Isaiah 51:11).

Elsewhere, David sums up the truth about the joy of God's people in heaven by saying, 'In your presence there is fullness of joy; at your right hand are pleasures for evermore' (Psalm 16:11). In his classic work *Human Nature in its Fourfold State* Thomas Boston writes,

> Joy shall not only enter into us, but we shall enter into it, and swim for ever in an ocean of joy, where we shall see nothing but joy wherever we turn our eyes. The presence and enjoyment of God and the Lamb will satisfy us with pleasures for evermore. And the glory of our souls and bodies, arising from thence, will afford us everlasting delight.[247]

This does not mean that every moment of life in heaven will be taken up with ecstatic exhibitions of happiness, but with joy that cannot be any deeper or more fulfilling. The Hebrew root of 'fullness' is the same as the one David uses when, looking forward to heaven, he tells God, 'I shall behold your face in righteousness; when I awake, I shall be *satisfied* with your likeness' (Psalm 17:15, emphasis added). In the present life, truly fulfilling joy tends to be temporary and believers find themselves saying, 'I wish this could last for ever.' Heaven's joys will!

In my home I have hung a picture of the Grand Canyon, and whenever I look at it I remember what it was to be there, marvelling at its sheer size and breathtaking beauty. When people admire the picture I always tell them it can never compare with the real thing, and then urge them to go there if they possibly can. Earthly joys are great, but they can never compare with the real thing because heavenly joys are infinitely greater. In heaven God's redeemed people will enjoy him for ever as he brings to everlasting perfection the very purpose for which he brought them into existence. Heaven is a prepared place for a prepared people.

So
what ...?

In this book we have seen something of the truly indescribable future God has prepared for his people. Living for ever in a place designed by God and filled with his holy presence and awesome glory is beyond our earth-bound imagination. There is much about heaven that has not yet been revealed to us and that we will only know when we are there, but in the previous chapters we have looked at some of the glorious glimpses the Bible gives us.

By the grace of God, Christians have been rescued from 'following the course of this world' (Ephesians 2:2) and been brought to put their trust in the Lord Jesus Christ, who is 'the way, and the truth, and the life' (John 14:6). From the moment they did so they became 'hitch-hikers' on the way to heaven and can know that their eternal destination is secure. Wonderful as this is, there is always the temptation to 'sit back and relax', pinning their security to the moment when they 'got on board'. Doing this will have special meaning to those whose conversion involved dramatic deliverance from a particularly godless background, yet the Bible urges believers to check the reality of their conversion by taking an honest look at their lives. Towards the end of his second letter to believers in Corinth Paul tells them: 'Examine yourselves, to see whether you are in the faith. Test yourselves' (2 Corinthians 13:5).

The key verbs, 'examine' and 'test' are both along the same lines. The first has the aim of discovering what a person's strengths and weaknesses are, and the second 'has the notion of proving a thing whether it is worthy or not'.[248] Importantly, both are in the present tense, meaning that they are not boxes that can be ticked once before moving on. They point to the need for careful, constant self-examination, aiming to 'renounce ungodliness and worldly passions, and to live self-controlled, upright, and godly lives in the present age, waiting for our blessed hope, the appearing of the glory of our great God and Saviour Jesus Christ, who gave himself for us to redeem us from all lawlessness and to purify for himself a people for his own possession who are zealous for good works' (Titus 2:12–14). In these last two chapters I want to get up close and personal and draw your attention to a number of ways in which the Bible will help you to take a reality check on your own life.

Once a hitch-hiker is safely on board there is little else for him to do except sit back and enjoy the ride. He may chat with the driver and at the end of the ride give him something by way of thanking him, but he has no responsibilities or duties. Hitch-hikers to heaven are in a very different position, and the Bible is packed with 'travel directions'. These are not things they need to do to be sure they get to heaven, as their salvation, which is certain and secure, is 'the gift of God, not as a result of works, so that no one may boast' (Ephesians 2:8–9). Instead, the Bible's 'travel directions' are meant to show them how to live on the way there.

On his ninetieth birthday George Bernard Shaw said, 'Our conduct is influenced not so much by our experience as by our expectations.' As he was an atheist, heaven would not have occurred to him, yet there is some truth in what he said and the prospect of heaven should radically affect every Christian's thinking and behaviour. Every direction the Bible gives, every warning it issues and every promise it makes is relevant, but even a brief look at these would take volumes rather than a few pages. However, many of the Bible's 'travel directions' are linked to the subject of this book, either directly or by example, and we shall look at some of them here. If you truly are a Christian, they should help you make every day count on your homeward journey.

Set your mind!

'If then you have been raised with Christ, seek the things that are above, where Christ is, seated at the right hand of God. Set your minds on things that are above, not on things that are on the earth' (Colossians 3:1–2).

This is a hugely important, double-barrelled 'travel direction', with positive and negative aspects. The negative one warns Christian hitch-hikers not to set their minds 'on things that are on the earth'. It is impossible to shut ourselves away from everything that surrounds us, nor does the Bible say that we should even try to do this. For example, we are stewards of the planet on which God has placed us and we are to treat it in a way that recognizes this. Also, as God gives us 'life and breath and everything' (Acts 17:25) and 'richly provides us with everything to enjoy' (1 Timothy 6:17), we should treasure these gifts, not trivialize them. Everything we properly possess is a gift from 'the Father of lights' (James 1:17) and we are to be grateful for each one of them and use them to benefit others as well as ourselves. Other 'things that are on the earth' include our responsibilities to governments, to society in general and to our families in particular, and we are to give careful attention to all of these.

Nowhere in the Bible are we told to become hermits and then imagine that this makes us more spiritual and pleasing to God. If we did this we would never be able to share the gospel with others—and in any case we would still not be able to escape the downward drag of our own sinful nature. Speaking of his followers, Jesus tells his heavenly Father, 'I do not ask that you take them out of the world, but that you keep them from the evil one. They are not of the world, just as I am not of the world ... As you sent me into the world, so I have sent them into the world' (John 17:15–16, 18). We are to be occupied with 'the things of the earth' *but we are not to be preoccupied with them.* We are to get them in perspective and not treat them as if they are the only things that matter.

Preaching a sermon he called 'The Weight of Glory' in the Church of St Mary the Virgin, Oxford, C. S. Lewis put this in a way that perhaps only he could:

When our involvement in them is so intense that they begin to dull our moral senses, lessen our spiritual appetite or push the prospect of heaven into the background we need to beware. At present we are on the outside of the world, the wrong side of the door. We discern the freshness and purity of morning, but they do not make us fresh and pure. We cannot mingle with the splendours we see. But all the leaves of the New Testament are rustling with the rumour that it will not always be so. Some day, God willing, we shall get in.[249]

What a glorious prospect for Christians!

'You are what you eat' is a popular slogan for those promoting physical health. 'You are what you think' is even more relevant for spiritual health, as what we allow to fill our minds will have a powerful effect on our lives. As an old saying goes, 'Sow a thought, reap an action; sow an action, reap a habit; sow a habit, reap a character; sow a character, reap a destiny.' 'GIGO' is a well-known acronym in computer science and information technology. It stands for 'Garbage in, garbage out' and tells us that computers can respond only to the information fed into them. In the same way, people become what they choose to feed into their minds and those who fill their minds with moral garbage, or even trivialities, will find that their behaviour reflects this.

What is involved here is the battle for the mind, a massively important issue for the Christian hitch-hiker. In this life-shaping battle the influences involved have never been stronger or more pervasive. One of the great weaknesses of dieters is allowing themselves to see forbidden foods which they then find themselves unable to resist. For Christians, the same principle has much wider ramifications. The mass media, including books, magazines, films and television, pours out godless material that can have devastating effects on a person's thinking and behaviour. The same kind of material is easily accessible on the internet and on smartphones and through social media, all adding to the challenge facing Christians called by God to 'be holy, for I am holy' (Leviticus 11:44).

Paul warns those who have their minds 'set on earthly things' that 'their end is destruction' (Philippians 3:19). When explaining why people commit certain sins Jesus explained that, 'What comes out of the mouth proceeds from the heart, and this defiles a person' (Matthew 15:18). This is why the Bible urges, 'Keep your heart with all vigilance, for from it flow the springs of life' (Proverbs 4:23). The safest prescription for Christian hitch-hikers is to replace the negative with the positive and to set our minds on 'things that are above', developing a taste for the world to come; in Paul's words, 'Do not be conformed to this world, but be transformed by the renewal of your mind' (Romans 12:2).

The clue as to how this is to be done lies in the word 'set', which means having a mindset that 'involves the will, affections and conscience'.[250] The Amplified Bible captures the tense of the verb by expanding the phrase to read 'set your minds and keep them set ...' Whenever I am due to cross time zones when flying back to England I set my watch to UK time the moment the plane's wheels leave the ground and keep it there. This 'travel direction' in Colossians says that when Christians begin the journey to heaven they should set their minds on things in the country to which they are going, not on things in the one through which they are travelling. We should put last things first!

The trigger for making this life-changing commitment is clear: 'If then you have been raised with Christ ...' This is one of those cases where 'if' assumes that something has happened; Paul is saying, '*Since* then you have been raised with Christ ...' In chapter 5 we saw that Jesus' death and resurrection were federal acts, things he did on behalf of all who put their trust in him.

His resurrection is dynamic evidence that in his death he paid in full the penalty for our sins. What is more, we now share in all the benefits of his resurrection: 'You were also raised with him through faith in the powerful working of God, who raised him from the dead' (Colossians 2:12). Christians should therefore have a new set of values. We should see that giving is more important than getting, serving others more important than being served, and being pure more important than being popular—and in every case Jesus is the perfect example. We should have a top-down perspective on life, seeing our possessions, positions, relationships, responsibilities, interests and priorities through a heavenly lens. Paul writes, 'We fix our eyes not on what is seen, but on what is unseen. For what is seen is temporary, but what is unseen is eternal' (2 Corinthians 4:18, NIV). Think about that last sentence!

This does not mean that we should try to get into some kind of trance so as to find out what 'things that are above' might be. Trying to have an open mind is not the way forward, as this leaves it open to anything. Instead, the Bible is very down to earth about what to do on the way to heaven: 'Whatever is true, whatever is honourable, whatever is just, whatever is pure, whatever is lovely, whatever is commendable, if there is any excellence, if there is anything worthy of praise, *think about these things*' (Philippians 4:8, emphasis added). Philip Arthur is right to say, 'People will never change their behaviour patterns until they change the way they think.'[251] The key to overcoming the power of sub-Christian thinking is to replace it with thinking that is biblically based—and centred on Jesus Christ. Ancient Greek philosophers such as Aristotle and Plato taught that Earth sat fixed at the centre of the entire universe, with all the other heavenly bodies circling around it. This idea was endorsed by the influential astronomer and geographer Claudius Ptolemy (c. AD 90–168) and was not seriously questioned for another 1,400 years, when the Polish astronomer and mathematician Nicolaus Copernicus (1473–1543) shocked the world by insisting that within an even vaster universe the sun was at the centre of a massive planetary system of which Earth was merely a part. Make the Son the centre of your thinking! Pray that the Holy Spirit will give you 'the mind of Christ' (1 Corinthians 2:16) and you will be moving in the right direction!

Dare to be different!

'Beloved, I urge you as sojourners and exiles to abstain from the passions of the flesh, which wage war against your soul. Keep your conduct among the Gentiles honourable, so that when they speak against you as evildoers, they may see your good deeds and glorify God on the day of visitation' (1 Peter 2:11–12).

The 'passions of the flesh' include all the sinful desires of our fallen human nature, and the Bible has several lists of these. The one in Galatians 5:16–21 singles out those relating to sex ('immorality, impurity, sensuality'), religion ('idolatry, sorcery'), personal relationships ('enmity, strife, jealousy, fits of anger, rivalries, dissensions, divisions, envy') and alcohol ('drunkenness, orgies'). This is not a complete list, as Paul adds the phrase 'and things like these' before going on to say that 'those who do such things will not inherit the kingdom of God'. As John Stott points out, the tense of the verb 'do' means 'habitual practice rather than an isolated lapse'.[252] People whose lives are characterized by things like these show that they have never been transformed by the grace of God and that they are still on the road 'that leads to destruction' (Matthew 7:13). Peter is urging Christian hitch-hikers to abstain from 'passions of the flesh' as a timely reminder to us that we are not immune from temptation in these areas and must resolutely resist the devil's efforts to make us yield.

The word 'honourable' translates the Greek word *kalos*, used in everyday language to mean something good, praiseworthy, honest or true. The 'travel direction' here calls for Christians to make sure that in a sceptical and antagonistic culture their thinking and their behaviour match their beliefs. This means daring to be different. Time and again we are told that to make an impact in the world Christianity should copy its culture. As the American preacher Voddie Baucham explains, we are told,

> We must walk like, talk like, dress like, live like and love like the world in order to win the world. However, exactly the opposite is true. It is, in fact, the straight and narrow path to the Celestial City that conforms us to the image of Christ. The path is where we learn the very truth to which we bear witness. And our desire is to have others join us on the path, not distract us from it.[253]

Forensic science has proved that every physical contact a person makes leaves an identifiable trace. The same is true spiritually. Paul tells us that through the lives of believers God 'spreads the fragrance of the knowledge of him everywhere' (2 Corinthians 2:14). What a brilliant picture! As Christians we should live in such a way that our words and actions leave the aroma of the gospel in the minds of those with whom we mix. Consistently godly living is a powerful evangelistic tool and has often proved the clinching argument in persuading unbelievers that they need to take Christianity seriously and get to grips with the claims of Christ on their lives.

However, we need to be aware that godly living can also produce opposition. Paul goes so far as to say, 'All who desire to live a godly life in Christ Jesus will be persecuted' (2 Timothy 3:12), and in chapter 6 we saw some of the ways in which Christians are made to suffer for their faith. Peter warns that there will be times when because of bitter prejudice unbelievers will even accuse Christians of being 'evildoers'. As Christian hitch-hikers our response should not be to fight back, but to live in such a way that we 'overcome evil with good' (Romans 12:21). Jesus sets us the perfect example: 'When he was reviled, he did not revile in return; when he suffered, he did not threaten, but continued entrusting himself to him who judges justly' (1 Peter 2:23).

Peter's words on which this section is based pick up a saying in the Sermon on the Mount: 'Let your light shine before others, so that they may see your good works and give glory to your Father who is in heaven' (Matthew 5:16), though Peter adds the interesting phrase 'on the day of visitation'. In the Old Testament God is often said to visit people in judgement for their sin, the Bible calling it 'the day of punishment' (Isaiah 10:3). Jesus warns the people of Jerusalem of a coming disaster because they rejected him in 'the time of your visitation' (Luke 19:44). At other times God's 'day of visitation' is a time of blessing. God promises that though the people of Israel were to be taken captive to Babylon they would be released on 'the day when I visit them' (Jeremiah 27:22). Filled with the Holy Spirit, John the Baptist's father, Zechariah, recognizes the infant Jesus as Messiah and cries, 'Blessed be the Lord God of Israel, for he has visited and redeemed his people' (Luke 1:68).

What Peter is saying may reflect the themes of both judgement and blessing. The final, great 'day of visitation', the Second Coming, will usher in the last judgement, after which even those condemned to eternal punishment will 'confess that Jesus Christ is Lord, to the glory of God the Father' (Philippians 2:11). As they do so, many will realize (too late) that the 'good works' of Christians they knew were a testimony to the truth and they will be forced to give God the glory that he alone deserves. The other meaning should be a great encouragement to Christian hitch-hikers. It pictures people being so impressed by the lives of believers that by the grace of God they begin to realize their own spiritual need and then to seek him for themselves. Should God graciously 'visit' them by irresistibly calling them to himself, they will glorify God by responding in repentance and saving faith. They will then put two and two together and see that the lives of Christians were key factors in opening their eyes to the truth. What an exhilarating incentive to live the kind of life that shows others the way to heaven!

Stay in the Word!

'And behold, I am coming soon. Blessed is the one who keeps the words of the prophecy of this book' (Revelation 22:7).

The context here is the Second Coming, and although this particular 'travel direction' is inferred rather than given directly it is reinforced by statements like this: 'Let the word of Christ dwell in you richly' (Colossians 3:16). The word 'dwell' is the same as that used about the Holy Spirit living within us (see Romans 8:11) and pictures the Bible taking root in the believer's life. The word 'richly' means 'abundantly', and is also used of the

Holy Spirit, who is said to have been 'poured out on us richly through Jesus Christ our Saviour' (Titus 3:6). The Amplified Bible pulls these meanings together very well: 'Let the word ... have its home (in your hearts and minds) and dwell in you in [all its] richness.' This is essential if we are to have the mind of Christ and to grow in grace along the journey.

This points to much more than going through a routine of reading a Bible passage every day. God has little or nothing to say to the formal or casual reader. Hit-and-run Bible reading tends to become hit and miss. We should be able to share the testimony of the psalmist, who tells God, 'Your word is a lamp to my feet and a light to my path' (Psalm 119:105); but many pay this truth no more than lip service. Psalms point us in a much better direction: 'Blessed is the man [whose] delight is in the law of the LORD, and on his law he meditates day and night' (Psalm 1:2); 'I have stored up your word in my heart, that I might not sin against you' (Psalm 119:11); 'I will meditate on your precepts and fix my eyes on your ways. I will delight in your statutes and will not forget your word' (Psalm 119:15–16); 'Oh how I love your law! It is my meditation all the day' (Psalm 119:97).

C. H. Spurgeon said of John Bunyan, 'Cut him anywhere and you will find that his blood is Bibline. The very essence of the Bible flows from him ... his soul is full of the Word of God.' This testimony was true only because Bunyan was able to claim, 'I was never out of my Bible.' We should aim just as high. This does not mean spending hours a day trying to cover huge amounts of text; Spurgeon used to say that he would rather soak his soul in a few verses every day than rinse his hand in several chapters! The secret is not 'how much?' but 'how?' Read it carefully to get the facts, study it seriously to get the meaning, and meditate on it slowly to get the benefit. In an age of blogging, tweeting and texting, meditation is in danger of becoming a lost art, but here are several reasons why you dare not miss out:

> The law of the LORD is perfect, reviving the soul; the testimony of the LORD is sure, making wise the simple; the precepts of the LORD are right, rejoicing the heart; the commandment of the LORD is pure, enlightening the eyes; the fear of the LORD is clean, enduring for ever; the rules of the LORD are true, and righteous altogether ... *in keeping them there is great reward* (Psalm 19: 7–9, 11, emphasis added).

Read those verses again! Wisdom, joy, enlightenment, holiness, truth and righteousness are surely things all Christian hitch-hikers need on such a challenging journey. Make sure you stay logged on to their source! Yet even the Bible, for all its magnificence, is not an end in itself. Appearing to two of his disciples after his resurrection, Jesus explains to them that all the Old Testament Scriptures were 'things concerning himself' (Luke 24:27), while in many Bibles the books that follow are called 'The New Testament of our Lord and Saviour Jesus Christ'. Answering critics who knew their Old Testament but refused to believe that he was divine, Jesus tells them, '[the Scriptures] bear witness about me' (John 5:39). As you come to the Bible, always seek to get beyond the page to the Person. Never be satisfied with merely gaining knowledge, storing information, analysing truth or remembering facts. The Word of God in print is meant to lead you to the Word of God in person. Martin Luther asks, 'Take Christ out of the Scriptures and what will you find remaining in them?',[254] and elsewhere claims, 'In the whole Scripture there is nothing but Christ, either in plain words or involved words.'[255] The prophet Hosea's cry to the people of Israel was not only, 'Let us know', but 'Let us press on to know the LORD' (Hosea 6:3). Make this your aim whenever you open your Bible!

Keep your eyes on the prize!

'One thing I do: forgetting what lies behind and straining forward to what lies ahead, I press on towards the goal for the prize of the upward call of God in Christ Jesus' (Philippians 3:13–14).

This 'travel direction' is embedded in Paul's example, which throbs with passionate commitment. The words 'I do' have been added by translators to make for better grammar in English, but they are not in the original Greek. Paul simply poured his passion into the phrase 'One thing.' Jesus warned about those whose spiritual lives had shrivelled because of 'desires for other things' (Mark 4:19), but Paul's life was geared to just 'one thing': 'I press on towards the goal for the prize of the upward call of God in Christ Jesus.' The word 'goal' translates the Greek *skopos*, which was the pillar or mark in a stadium towards which athletes would run. From the first moment of a race this is what filled their minds, and they would allow nothing to divert their thinking. Paul is using this kind of picture to make his point.

The American preacher Larry McCall tells of the time when his ninety-year-old grandfather, a farmer, told him the secret of how to plough a straight furrow with a horse-drawn plough: 'You must first set your eyes on a tree on the far side of the field. Once your eyes are fixed on that distant object, you must then put your hand to the plough and advance across the field, all the time keeping that tree sighted directly between the horse's ears.'

Two thousand years earlier Paul followed the same principle with his eyes set on a heavenly prize.

In Paul's day winning athletes were not crowned on the track. Instead, they were called to mount steps to the throne of a king or some other dignitary to receive their prize, and Paul adapts the picture perfectly. He too had an 'upward call' from the King of kings from whose hand he would receive the 'unfading crown of glory' (1 Peter 5:4). Elsewhere Paul reminds his readers that in athletic races 'all the runners run, but only one receives the prize', then adds, 'So run that you may obtain it' (1 Corinthians 9:24). He is not suggesting that only Christian 'winners' get to heaven, but urging his readers to run the Christian race with the dedication and commitment shown by winning athletes.

This involves two things. The first is 'forgetting what lies behind'. The word 'forgetting' is particularly strong in the original Greek and means forgetting completely. Just as a winning athlete refuses to get distracted by thoughts of the times when in training or in previous races he ran badly or failed to meet his targets, so Christians should refuse to be slowed down by mulling over past failures and disappointments. The devil has many ways of reminding us of these, but when he does we should refuse to be diverted by them. Instead, we should recognize that if truly confessed they are completely forgiven and have no power to influence the present or the future unless we let them do so.

The second is 'straining forward', which translates the dynamic Greek word *epekteinomenos*, exactly the word that would be used about an athlete coming towards the end of a race, straining every sinew to get to the finishing line. Yet 'straining forward' is in the present continuous tense, which tells us that this was Paul's *constant* approach. In a long-distance race, a runner will try to conserve his energy before choosing the right moment to 'kick' towards the tape. The picture in the spiritual race is completely different, as no believer knows how long his particular race will last (that is, how long he will live). Whether you read these words as a young person, someone in middle age or someone who was 'born earlier' (a delightful euphemism I heard years ago in Czechoslovakia!), you cannot be certain when your race will end and you receive 'the prize of the upward call'. There should be no place in your life for coasting, compromising or holding back. You should never be on 'cruise control'. On a recent visit to the Czech Republic I was delighted to renew a link with Eva Titeraova, someone I first met many years earlier. Still actively committed to her local church, her Christian service includes translating articles from other languages for use in a Czech Christian magazine and teaching Czech to German and French students. She is a widow and when we met again she was within days of being ninety years of age.

You may not feel as gifted as her. Neither do I, but 'each has his own gift from God, one of one kind and one of another' (1 Corinthians 7:7). These are not given to be hoarded, but to be used. The personal strapline on my newsletter is, 'As much as I can, as well as I can, for as long as I can.' People often tell me they are impressed by this; but surely this is how every Christian should respond to God's saving grace and to the promise of a future home in heaven. This is what John Stott said at an Inter-Varsity Mission Convention in Urbana, Illinois in 1976:

'Lift up your eyes! You are certainly a creature of time, but you are also a child of eternity. You are a citizen of heaven, and an alien and exile on earth, a pilgrim travelling to the celestial city. I read some years ago of a young man who found a five-dollar bill on the

street and who "from that time on never lifted his eyes when
walking. In the course of years he accumulated 29,516 buttons,
54,172 pins, 12 cents, a bent back and a miserly disposition." But
think what he lost. He couldn't see the radiance of the sunlight,
and sheen of the stars, the smile on the face of his friends, or the
blossoms of springtime, for his eyes were in the gutter. There are
too many Christians like that. We have important duties on earth,
but we must never allow them to preoccupy us in such a way that
we forget who we are or where we are going."[256]

Keeping your eyes on the prize will be a powerful incentive to
godly living and dedicated service.

Onwards and upwards

As we press on towards 'the goal for the prize of the upward call of God in Christ Jesus' there are four other 'travel directions' we need to follow very carefully if we are to respond to God's provision for us in the way he intends. The first is in some ways the most important of all, and we should give it close attention. It takes us back to chapter 3, where we caught a glimpse of the completed church as the bride of Christ, consisting of all God's people since the dawn of time. This complete church will not meet together until the great day when Christ returns, but in the meantime there is a visible church here on earth, made up of believers all over the world, worshipping and serving God in many different ways and places.

God cares for his people so much that he loves to 'settle the solitary in a home' (Psalm 68:6) and sees them as one 'family of believers' (Galatians 6:10, NIV). This points to them meeting together for corporate worship and service as part of their relationship with God and with each other, not as an option but as a vitally important factor in their spiritual development.

Cherish your church!

'And let us consider how to stir up one another to love and good works, not neglecting to meet together, as is the habit of some, but encouraging one another, and all the more as you see the Day drawing near' (Hebrews 10:24–25).

The key phrase here is 'not neglecting to meet together' and the word 'neglecting' tells us how serious it is to be casual about church attendance. It has the same root as in Paul's accusation, 'Demas, in love with this present world, has *deserted* me' (2 Timothy 4:10, emphasis added). Demas had been the apostle's close friend and colleague, but had left him in the lurch because he was 'in love with this present world'. Professing Christians who are not seriously committed to their local church have a heart problem—other things are more important or attractive to them. There are a number of reasons why meeting together as a church should not be neglected or treated as an unimportant option.

- *Because cherishing your church shows that you love the Lord Jesus, the Head of the church.* Describing how he felt in his college at Oxford University shortly before his conversion, C. S. Lewis writes, 'You must picture me alone in that room at Magdalen, night after night, feeling, whenever my mind lifted even for a second from my work, the steady unrelenting approach of Him who *I so earnestly desired not to meet*' (emphasis added).[257] As Sunday approaches you should feel exactly the opposite, because Jesus promises, 'For where two or three are gathered in my name, there am I among them' (Matthew 18:20). This led Vance Havner to tell one congregation, 'If I could get one church full of folks that actually believed that verse I don't know when we'd get out of here tonight!' If you truly love the Lord, he will surely be someone you *earnestly desire to meet* in the special way that he has promised and ordained. When you go to church, check your pulse!

Do you have that earnest desire? In 2012 Brian Ellis, a British missionary to the Philippines, wrote a piece in *Evangelical Times* about the great lengths some of his church members go to in order to attend services. 'One lady in her late sixties travels for two hours on public transport to attend the adult Bible Class and Sunday services. She begins on a tricycle, then takes a bus for the next part of her journey before completing it on a jeepney (a small public utility vehicle). She has been doing this for about twenty years. A married couple also take two hours to get to church, and in the monsoon season (June-October) have to walk for over thirty minutes on a muddy track from their farm before reaching a main road to catch a jeepney.'[258] Here are people who long to meet with other believers—and for whom desire shortens the distance! Does this challenge you?

When someone you love promises to be somewhere at a certain time, would you deliberately choose not to be there? The Christian life consists of relationships with Christ and other believers, and we should do all we can to deepen these. There is no biblical rule about churches holding two services on Sundays; but if your church has two services, Jesus is at both. Are you? If not, why not? Do you choose to turn the

Lord's Day into the Lord's Half-Day? Is your love for him so half-hearted and your hope of heaven so dim that you can settle for standing him up as often as you choose to meet him? One of the psalmists cries, 'O God ... a day in your courts is better than a thousand elsewhere' (Psalm 84:9–10). Another urges, 'Sing to the LORD a new song, his praise in the assembly of the godly!' and adds, 'For the LORD takes pleasure in his people' (Psalm 149:1, 4). If the Lord takes pleasure in the company of his people, we should surely do the same in his. The American preacher Don Fortner goes so far as to say, 'Public worship is the single most important aspect of the believer's life.'[259] Once this has been given its rightful place, there are other profitable things that can be done on this special day, and as Stuart Olyott points out, 'In areas of conscience, no believer is answerable to another.'[260]

- *Because Jesus himself has given you a perfect example.* After his brutal encounter with the devil during forty days in the desert, '[Jesus] came to Nazareth, where he had been brought up. *And as was his custom*, he went to the synagogue on the Sabbath day' (Luke 4:16, emphasis added). J. C. Ryle makes such a telling comment on this that I can do no better than quote it in full:

> In the days when our Lord was on earth, the Scribes and the Pharisees were the chief teachers of the Jews. We can hardly suppose that a Jewish synagogue enjoyed much of the Spirit's presence and blessing under such teaching. Yet even then we find our Lord visiting a synagogue, and reading and preaching. It was the place where his Father's day and word were publicly recognized, and, as such, he thought it good to do it honour.

We need not doubt that there is a practical lesson for us in this part of our Lord's conduct. He would have us know that we are not lightly to forsake any assembly of worshippers which profess to respect the name, the day and the book of God. There may be many things in such an assembly which might be done better. There may be a want of fullness, clearness and distinctness in the doctrine preached. There may be a lack of unction and devoutness in the manner in which the worship is conducted. But so long as no positive error is taught, and there is no choice between worshipping with such an assembly and having no public worship at all, it becomes a Christian to think much before he stays away. If there be but two or three in the congregation who meet in the name of Jesus, there is a special blessing promised. But there is no like blessing to him who tarries at home.[261]

- *Because there is nothing else like it.* Preaching in London's Metropolitan Tabernacle in 1891, C. H. Spurgeon said,

Imperfect as it is, it is the dearest place on earth to us ... All who have first given themselves to the Lord should, as speedily as possible, also give themselves to the Lord's people. How else is there to be a Church on the earth? If it is right for anyone to refrain from membership in the Church, it is right for everyone, and then the testimony for God would be lost to the world! As I have already said, the Church is faulty, but that is no excuse for your not joining it if you are the Lord's. Nor need your own faults keep you back, for the Church is not an institution for perfect people, but a sanctuary for sinners saved by grace, who, though they are saved, are still sinners and need all the help they can derive from the sympathy and guidance of their fellow believers. The Church is the nursery for God's weak children where they are nourished and grow strong. It is the fold for Christ's sheep—the home for Christ's family.[262]

No church on earth is perfect, and people can sometimes feel irritated or uncomfortable because of noisy children, poor singing, music that is too loud, hymns that are too modern (or too 'ancient'), preaching that is too long (or too short), or by a long list of other things. Sadly, Vance Havner may have been right to say, 'Too many churches start at eleven o'clock sharp, and end at twelve o'clock dull', but that is not God's design or desire; and whatever its weaknesses no other gathering of people comes close to the special place that the local church has in his eyes. When the Bible refers to Christians 'addressing one another in psalms and hymns and spiritual songs, singing and making melody to the Lord with all your heart' (Ephesians 5:19), God's people gathering together to worship him is clearly what is meant.

- *Because it is a 'heavenly' thing to do.* In a phrase that seems to jump off the page, Paul Wolfe dedicates his book *Setting our Sights on Heaven* to the members of his congregation in Fairfax, Virginia, 'with whom I share the privilege of going to heaven every Sunday morning at 9.30'. When he wrote this, the church met in the unlikely setting of a fire station, yet he explains his striking dedication: 'We go to heaven when we worship in the sense that we enjoy a foretaste of heavenly experience ... the church's worship on earth partakes of heavenly realities.'[263] The English preacher John Eliot (1604–1690), a missionary to American Indians in New England, used to say that Christians who had a passion for the Lord's Day would know they were in heaven when they got there as they would have spent at least one-seventh of their lives in heaven while living on the earth. Millard Erickson makes a good point: 'Our worship and praise here and now are preparation and practice for future employment of our hearts and voices.'[264]

One of the psalmists testified, 'I was glad when they said to me, "Let us go to the house of the LORD!"' (Psalm 122:1). Preaching on this, and assuming (perhaps wrongly) that David wrote the Psalm, C. H. Spurgeon said,

David's heart was in the worship of God, and he was delighted when he found others inviting him to go where his desires had already gone ... Nothing better can happen to men and their friends than to love the place where God's honour dwells ... He pricked up his ears at the very mention of his Father's house.'[265]

Do you do the same? Or has church-going become little more than a ritual? Another psalmist confesses, 'My soul longs, yes, faints for the courts of the LORD', where he could 'sing for joy to the living God' (Psalm 84:2). Does the very thought of joining with others to worship God excite you? If you are truly on your way to heaven with them it should!

- *Because gathering with God's people is one way of giving thanks to God for his goodness to you.* In the fourth of the Ten Commandments God sets one day in seven and commands us to 'keep it holy' (Exodus 20:8). The word 'holy' does not mean that we are to make a special effort to be free from sin on that day, as this would imply that we need not do this on the other six. The root meaning of 'holy' tells us that one day in seven is to be *different*. In his great kindness, God has ordained one day a week in which we can lay aside the burdens of daily work and use it to recharge our physical batteries. History shows that nations ignoring this have found their policy counter-productive, as we were created with this pattern in mind. In obedience to God's law, Jews in Old Testament times observed the seventh day of the week (the Sabbath) as a special day of both rest and worship; but after Jesus had fulfilled Old Testament law in his life, death and resurrection the early Christians (who were almost all devout Jews) switched their special day to Sunday, 'the first day of the week' (Acts 20:7) to commemorate the resurrection of Jesus Christ. For two thousand years the church has seen this special day as a precious gift from God, enabling Christians not only to rest from daily chores but to benefit from all the blessings that flow from true worship and genuine fellowship. As hitch-hikers to heaven we should treasure this gift, not toy with it. We should take every opportunity to respond to the Bible's exhortation, 'Enter his gates with thanksgiving, and his courts with praise!' (Psalm 100:4).

• *Because Christians thrive on encouragement.* Encouragement has been called 'oxygen for the soul' and we all know what a boost it gives us. The need for encouragement is so important that the writer of Hebrews charges, 'Exhort one another every day, as long as it is called "today", that none of you may be hardened by the deceitfulness of sin' (Hebrews 3:13). When Job was in deep trouble his friend Eliphaz the Temanite could still pay him this tribute: 'Your words have upheld him who was stumbling, and you have made firm the feeble knees' (Job 4:4). There is so much going on (and going wrong) in the world today that many Christians are stumbling around on 'feeble knees' and in need of encouragement, even if they do not openly give that impression.

The text on which this section is based links 'encouraging one another' with times when Christians 'meet together' and *just being there* can be an encouragement to others. The presence of young people is an encouragement to much older Christians as they see in them hope for the church's future. The presence of people in their sixties or seventies and beyond is an encouragement to young people as they see in them living evidence of God's faithfulness down the years. Christians of all ages are of equal standing in the body of Christ, and as the American preacher Tom Ascol rightly points out, 'A ten-year-old Christian has more in common with an eighty-year-old Christian than with ten-year-old unbelievers.'[266]

The presence of young, old and all of those in between is a constant encouragement to the pastor; it is exactly the opposite if your place is empty at half of the services. Apart from anything else, this would mean that fifty per cent of the time your pastor spends in prayerful study and preparation every week is wasted as far as you are concerned. It is an even greater encouragement to pastors when church members are at Bible studies or prayer meetings during the week. Are you missing out on these other opportunities to encourage others—*and to be encouraged?* If so, why?

It is difficult to exaggerate the importance of Christians encouraging one another as they battle against the pressures of a secular world. The word translated 'encourage' in Hebrews has the sense of coming alongside someone else to help, and it has the same root as the one used about the Holy Spirit, who is called 'another Helper' (John 14:16). Christians who are prepared to get alongside other believers, helping, guiding, comforting, strengthening or sympathizing with them as they have need are serving God—and can expect his help to do so. Not only are Christians 'members of [Christ's] body' (Ephesians 5:30), they are also 'members one of another' (Ephesians 4:25) and that unity is dynamically demonstrated when they meet together. Peter Lewis goes so far as to say, '[God] meets us in one another in public worship and ministers to us by one another in church life.'[267] The closer we come to 'the Day', the more faithful we should be in ensuring that we meet with God's people as often as we can so that we may be 'mutually encouraged by each other's faith' (Romans 1:12). Members of the congregation who are lonely, discouraged, confused, bereaved or in pain, or who have some other need, may be hugely encouraged by a warm greeting, a friendly smile, a firm handshake or a willingness to spend even a few moments with them. C. S. Lewis says, 'I must keep alive in myself the desire for my true country, which I shall not find until death; I must never let it get snowed under or turned aside. I must make it the main object of my life to press on to that other country *and to help others to do the same* (emphasis added).[268] Church gatherings are ideal times for us to do this!

- *Because we all need to make every possible use of the means of grace that God provides.* Strictly speaking, all the things freely given by God for his glory and for our good are means of grace. Within the fellowship of the church the preaching and teaching of the Word, the sacraments of baptism and the Lord's Supper—specifically said to be provided for us 'until he comes' (1 Corinthians 11:26)—praise, prayer and fellowship with other believers can be called the primary

means of grace for God's people, *and we all need all of them.*
When we meet together as his people, God ministers to us in
unique ways that are vital to our development as individuals
and as a church. No Christians know the Bible so well, are so
well grounded in doctrine, and so well informed about how
to counter a secular culture that they have no need for well-
prepared teaching by a man set apart to 'shepherd the flock
of God' (1 Peter 5:2). We honour God when our ears and
hearts are open to receive the teaching of his Word—and we
dishonour him when we treat it lightly. No Christians are so
far advanced in holiness and pray so fully and perfectly at
home that they have no need of the means of grace that God
provides in the context of a local gathering of his people. No
Christians can make the progress God intends for them if
they choose to isolate themselves from other believers.

Looking back to early church history, the Scottish
theologian James Moffatt (1870–1944) comments, 'Any early
Christian who attempted to live like a pious particle without
the support of the community ran serious risks in an age
when there was no public opinion to support him. His
isolation, whatever the motive ... exposed him to the risk of
losing his faith altogether.'[269] We can see this reflected in a
key verse about those early believers: 'And they devoted
themselves to the apostles' teaching and fellowship, to the
breaking of bread and the prayers' (Acts 2:42). In a world
swamped by secularism and scepticism, Christianity today
cannot expect any support from public opinion, but within a
fellowship of God's people the means of grace will help us to
'grow in the grace and knowledge of our Lord and Saviour
Jesus Christ' (2 Peter 3:18). Make the best use of them!

• *Because it says something significant to an unbelieving world.* In his unusual and challenging book, *Beware of Living too Long!*, a collection of weekly letters to what was then his congregation in Cornwall, the American pastor John Gillespie tells how while on holiday in Norfolk he decided not to go to church one Sunday 'because I didn't feel like going'. Before the morning was over he realised that his decision, 'born of conceit' (the sermon might not be very good; he might not like the music), had taught him a lesson in humility. Reflecting on this, the next letter to his church family was called 'A Meditation On Missing Church'. In urging them never to belittle the value of believers gathering together on the Lord's Day, he gave this as one reason for unbroken attendance: 'Each local church, as it gathers, shouts a defiant 'NO' to the Christ-defying culture around it.'[270] He is right! When your neighbours see you going regularly to church while they are cleaning the car, working or relaxing in the garden, or doing something else around the house, you will be bearing clear witness to the fact that you have found something more important than any of these responsibilities or pleasures.

Of course, if you are not a friendly and helpful person to have next door, your Sunday witness may be cancelled out by the other six days of the week and become another barrier against your neighbours coming to faith. The same is true of unconverted family members; your behaviour at home and in their company elsewhere should confirm the significance of your church attendance, not contradict it. Jesus said, 'Whoever does not gather with me scatters' (Matthew 12:30). Make sure that your daily life endorses the message other people get by seeing how you use the Lord's Day. Aim to live in such a way as to 'make the teaching about God our Saviour attractive' (Titus 2:10, NIV).

Invest in eternity!

'Make friends for yourselves by means of unrighteous wealth, so that when it fails they may receive you into the eternal dwellings' (Luke 16:9).

Jesus has just told a parable about the dishonest manager of a rich man's estate. Threatened with dismissal, this man had told his master's debtors that they could write off part of their debts, his thinking being that in return they would help him out when he lost his job. His master must have been furious when he found out what had been done, but in spite of this he 'commended the dishonest manager for his shrewdness' (Luke 16:8). The word 'shrewdness' translates a Greek word used about someone acting prudently, sensibly and pragmatically, and Jesus takes up this point in teaching his disciples about giving. An expanded paraphrase of what he tells his disciples may be a good way of explaining a statement that has been found difficult to interpret: 'Make good use of your money (which is often used by others for unrighteous purposes) by investing in the kingdom of God, so that when all your worldly possessions come to an end (as they will when you die) those who have been reached with the gospel because of the gifts you have made, and have become Christians as a result, will welcome you into heaven.' What a powerful incentive to support your church and other Christian causes!

The Bible has a surprising amount to say about material possessions. It has been calculated that while it has fewer than five hundred verses on faith and about five hundred on prayer it has over two thousand on money, which is the subject in sixteen of Jesus' parables. Yet nowhere does it condemn money or the possession of wealth; its great concern is how it is used. Few things test a person's spirituality more than the stewardship of their material possessions, whether these are many or few. Christian giving is not a matter of finance, but of faith. There is a kind of madness in materialism. We gather possessions that we think will add to our sense of security, but the more we cling to them in order to be secure, the less secure we feel, especially when we lose any of them.

As I have explained in more detail elsewhere,[271] the Bible has guidance on regular and proportionate giving (see 1 Corinthians 16:2) and calls Christians to give freely and willingly (see 2 Corinthians 9:7). Students, those out of work or unable to work, believers limited to state pensions and others who are under constant financial pressure are obviously not expected to give as much as those who are in a more favourable position, and the Bible takes this into account by saying, 'If the readiness is there, it is acceptable according to what a person has, not according to what he does not have' (2 Corinthians 8:12).

By the grace of God we are making our way to an eternal future when there will be no financial worries, but we are presently living in a world in which there are many such pressures, including those within our Christian communities. The cost of running a church, paying a pastor's salary, maintaining or expanding the building, and keeping it heated and safe is enormous, yet so often the church has inadequate income from its members. Missionary causes are having to cut back through lack of funds, pastors and other full-time Christian workers are underpaid, Christian publishers are financially crippled, Bible translation work is on hold, church-planting projects have had to be shelved or abandoned, and countless other Christian causes are stifled through lack of funds. This scenario reflects the situation in Jerusalem around 500 BC, when the rebuilding of the temple ground to a halt because people were concentrating on building or developing their own properties. God tackles them head-on and asks, 'Is it a time for you yourselves to dwell in your panelled houses, while this house lies in ruins?' before urging them to complete work on the temple, 'that I may take pleasure in it and that I may be glorified' (Haggai 1:4, 8).

Christian hitch-hikers should regularly reflect on their giving to God's work and seek his guidance as to what they should be doing. For example, there are Christians who have retired, paid off their mortgage, and enjoy a comfortable lifestyle that includes at least one good holiday a year. They have savings and income they think should see them through the rest of life and still leave their children decent legacies. They give to their local church and to other Christian causes—but could they give more? Some Christians in good full-time employment enjoy an annual salary review—could they increase their giving to reflect this? Some give to their local church by a bank standing order—should they not review this annually to meet rising costs? These are only some of the situations that may call for action.

The American missionary Jim Elliot (1927–1956), who was killed by Auca Indians he was trying to reach with the gospel in Ecuador, has a journal entry that reads, 'He is no fool who gives what he cannot keep to gain that which he cannot lose.'[272] The question every Christian hitch-hiker should be asking is this: *am I giving God what is right?—or what is left?*

Tell the world!

*'All authority in heaven and on earth has been given to me. Go
therefore and make disciples of all nations ... And behold I am with you
always, to the end of the age'* (Matthew 28:18–20).

According to Matthew's Gospel, these were the last words
Jesus spoke to his disciples before he ascended to heaven. As his
ministry had developed, Jesus had revealed more and more of his
authority. Now, having triumphed over death, he rightly claims
universal authority and on this basis sends his followers to
preach the gospel and to urge men to accept its offer of salvation
and to submit to him as Lord of their lives. His words have
become known as 'The Great Commission' and they call for a
response from all Christians. These are our marching orders!

At one point in Old Testament history the city of Samaria was
under siege by the Syrian army, which intended to starve it into
submission. Outside the entrance to the city were four lepers,
who had been thrown out because of their deadly and
contagious disease. Starving to death, they decided to take their
chances with the Syrians; but when they reached the Syrian
camp they found it deserted. God had miraculously convinced
the army that a much stronger one was about to attack them,
and they had run for their lives, leaving everything behind.

The lepers quickly went from tent to tent and soon found that
they now had more food than they could eat, and more clothing
and money than they would ever need. Suddenly, they said to
one another, 'We are not doing right. This day is a day of good
news ... let us go and tell the king's household' (2 Kings 7:9). At
first, the king thought the lepers were part of a plot, but when
scouts confirmed that the Syrians had gone the remaining

Samaritans (many had already starved to death) poured into the soldiers' camp and were saved.

Do you see the parallel? As a Christian hitch-hiker you have been saved from a fate worse than physical death. God has graciously delivered you from 'the domain of darkness' and transferred you to 'the kingdom of his beloved Son', in whom you have 'redemption, the forgiveness of sins' (Colossians 1:13, 14). Although you deserved eternal punishment, you have been given 'the free gift of God ... eternal life in Jesus Christ our Lord' (Romans 6:23). You are a member of 'the household of God' (Ephesians 2:19). You have access to 'the immeasurable riches of [God's] kindness' (Ephesians 2:7). You have been 'raised with Christ ... your life is hidden with Christ in God ... when Christ who is your life appears, then you will also appear with him in glory' (Colossians 3:1, 3–4). You are assured of 'the promised eternal inheritance' (Hebrews 9:15). In the new creation you will 'shine like the brightness of the sky above' and 'like the stars for ever and ever' (Daniel 12:3).

Yet you are surrounded by those who are not only spiritually blind (unable to see gospel truth) and spiritually deaf (unable to hear it) but spiritually *dead*. They may be socially acceptable and live what they would claim to be decent lives, but like all other people they are 'by nature children of wrath' (Ephesians 2:3). What is more, they have 'no hope' (Ephesians 2:12), because as they are not trusting Christ for salvation they are 'storing up wrath' for themselves—an appalling fate 'on the day of wrath when God's righteous judgement will be revealed' (Romans 2:5). Are you not concerned that while you are on your way to heaven they are on their way to hell unless God breaks into their lives and rescues them?

When persecution broke out against the early church at

Jerusalem, the leaders stayed behind but the other believers 'were all scattered throughout the regions of Judea and Samaria' (Acts 8:1). We then read, 'Now those who were scattered went about preaching the word' (Acts 8:4). They were not church leaders who compiled sermons and spoke to congregations. They were ordinary men and women who shared the gospel with people they met in the course of their daily lives. Ask God to help you to follow their example. As well as using your own initiative in personal witnessing, keep alert to opportunities provided by your church and make sure that you play your part in fulfilling the 'Great Commission'.

Make friends with death

'For to me to live is Christ, and to die is gain' (Philippians 1:21).

This 'travel direction' is given indirectly, by way of Paul's testimony. As we saw in chapter 4, he was hard pressed as to whether he preferred to go on serving Christ here on earth or to die and go to be with him in heaven. Although the two things were evenly balanced, if it were left to him his 'desire' was to 'be with Christ' (Philippians 1:23). The word 'desire' expresses a passionate longing. We could even say that Paul was so overwhelmed by all that heaven would mean that he had a death wish! He was not longing for the act of dying (tradition suggests that he was beheaded by the Roman Emperor Nero) but for the joy of being in his Saviour's immediate presence. Death is commonly spoken about in terms of loss, but Christians should not think of it in this way. Paul saw it as gain, and the clearer the picture we have of the Bible's teaching about heaven the more certain we shall be that he was right.

The German pastor Dietrich Bonhoeffer (1906–1945) expresses this so well: 'Death is only dreadful for those who live in dread and fear of it. Death is not wild and terrible, if only we can be still and hold fast to God's Word. Death is not bitter if we have not become bitter ourselves. Death is grace, the greatest gift of grace that God gives to people who believe in him. Death is mild, death is sweet and gentle, it beckons us with heavenly power, if only we realize that it is the gateway to our homeland, the tabernacle of joy, the everlasting kingdom of peace.'[273] Bonhoeffer was persecuted by the Gestapo, sentenced to death at a mockery of a trial in a concentration camp, and hanged the following day. The camp doctor who witnessed the execution writes of the way in which Bonhoeffer knelt and prayed 'and then climbed the few steps to the gallows, brave and composed. In the almost fifty years that I worked as a doctor, I have hardly ever seen a man die so entirely submissive to the will of God.'[274] However our lives end, we should not look forward to dying, but look upward to what lies beyond it, rejoicing with John Bunyan that 'Death is but a passage out of a prison into a palace.'[275]

Do you have the same vision—and longing? For many people death is 'the king of terrors' (Job 18:14), but Christians should have a very different perspective, as we know that in rising from the dead Jesus drew 'the sting of death' (1 Corinthians 15:56), abolishing its power so completely that in doing so God 'gives us the victory through our Lord Jesus Christ' (1 Corinthians 15:57). As the English preacher William Romaine (1714–1795) quaintly put it, 'Death stung himself to death when he stung Christ.'[276] Unless you are still living when Jesus returns to the earth, your path to heaven lies through the grave. Dying is not an attractive prospect, as the journey through 'the valley of the shadow of death' (Psalm 23:4) may be prolonged and painful, but as

Christians we can make it with the words of our Saviour ringing in our ears: 'I am the resurrection and the life. Whoever believes in me, though he die, *yet shall he live*' (John 11:25, emphasis added). It was this certainty that enabled Isobel Kuhn to say, shortly before her death from cancer, 'The platform of a dread disease becomes but a springboard for heaven.'[277]

Landing at a London airport after a preaching engagement in the United Kingdom or overseas, I find it difficult to obey the instructions to keep my seatbelt fastened until the plane has 'come to a complete stop'. Then I tend to get impatient if there is any delay in getting off the plane, collecting my luggage, or making contact with the driver who has been booked to meet me. *I want to get home!* Christians should have the same longing to get to heaven. J. I. Packer shrewdly asks, 'How many Christians live their lives packed up and ready to go?' and adds this excellent advice for every Christian hitch-hiker: 'Live in the present; gratefully enjoy its pleasures and work through its pains with God, knowing that both the pleasures and the pains are steps on the journey home. Open all your life to the Lord Jesus and spend time consciously in his company, basking in and responding to his love. Say to yourself that every day is one day nearer.'[278] It is never too soon to make friends with death, as it is the greatest fact of life and can come at any time.

It is easy to see why many people not only fear death but see it as the ultimate curse. Yet as we saw in a previous chapter, the death of Christians is 'precious in the sight of the LORD' (Psalm 116:15). It is not so much something that happens to them as something God brings about for their blessing. The believer's dying day is his best day, as death releases us from all the pressures, problems and pains of this life and brings us into the immediate presence of our Saviour, the one 'who loves us and has freed us from our sins by his blood' (Revelation 1:5). Jonathan Edwards puts this so well that I can do no better than quote him at length:

> We ought not to rest in the world and its enjoyments, but should desire heaven ... We ought above all things to desire a heavenly happiness; to be with God; and dwell with Jesus Christ. Though surrounded with outward enjoyments, and settled in families with desirable friends and relations; though we have companions whose society is delightful, and children in whom we see many promising qualifications; though we live by good neighbours and are generally beloved where known; yet we ought not to take our rest in these things as our portion ... We ought to possess, enjoy and use them *with no other view but readily to quit them, whenever we are called to it, and to change them willingly and cheerfully for heaven*' (emphasis added).[279]

This is great advice for Christian hitch-hikers of all ages, as it gets the whole of life into perspective.

John Wesley (1703–1791), one of the founders of Methodism, used to say of his followers, 'Our people die well.' Christians have every reason for doing so. In the seventeenth century, the Scottish Covenanters were viciously persecuted for their refusal to acknowledge that the nation's king was the spiritual head of the church of Christ. As the persecution reached its peak, Donald Cargill joined those who were sentenced to death for their godly principles, and on 27 July 1681 he was hanged in public in Edinburgh. As he mounted the scaffold he said, 'The Lord knows I go up this ladder with less fear, confusion or perturbation of mind than I ever entered a pulpit to preach'. When he reached the platform he added this: 'Farewell, all created enjoyments, pleasures and delights; farewell, sinning and suffering; farewell praying and believing, and welcome, heaven and singing. Welcome, joy in the Holy Ghost; welcome, Father, Son and Holy Ghost; into thy hands I commend my spirit.'[280]

Shortly before he died, John Newton told a friend, 'I am packed and sealed and waiting for the post'; it came on 21 December 1807. In December 2008 Mark Ashton, Vicar of St Andrew's, Cambridge, was diagnosed with incurable cancer. Reflecting on his position he wrote, 'Once you have been told that you are going to die, the months that follow are a very good time spiritually.[281] Later, he added, 'My death may be the event with which my physical life on earth ends, but it will also be the moment at which my relationship with Jesus becomes complete. That relationship is the only thing that has made sense of my physical life, and at my death it will be everything.[282]

Onwards and upwards!

Peter urges his readers to 'make every effort to supplement your faith with virtue, and virtue with knowledge, and knowledge with self-control, and self-control with steadfastness, and steadfastness with godliness, and godliness with brotherly affection, and brotherly affection with love' (2 Peter 1:5–7). He then adds, 'Be all the more diligent to make your calling and election sure, for if you practise these qualities you will never fall. For in this way there will be richly provided for you an entrance into the eternal kingdom of our Lord and Saviour Jesus Christ' (2 Peter 1:10–11).

The 'travel directions' in these two final chapters have been written in the same spirit. They are not meant to be hurdles, but helps in making you increasingly sure of two things.

The first is that you 'will never fall'. This does not mean that you will never put a foot wrong, but although it is possible to fall *in* grace, it is not possible to fall *from* grace. You may fall *within* God's family, but you can never fall *out* of it: 'The steps of a man are established by the LORD, when he delights in his way; though he fall, he shall not be cast headlong' (Psalm 37:23–24).

The second is that you will have 'an entrance into the eternal kingdom of our Lord and Saviour Jesus Christ'. Christian assurance of heaven is not based on emotions, hopes, longings, visions, dreams or special revelations. Instead, it is a conviction exercised by faith and based on certainties. Jesus died in your place and rose again from the dead, dynamic proof that the penalty for your sins has been paid in full. The more you see the fruit of the Holy Spirit developing in your life, the greater confidence you will have that 'he who began a good work in you will bring it to completion at the day of Jesus Christ' (Philippians 1:6). I once read, 'The best way to make a tired horse move more quickly is not to use the whip, but to turn his head towards home.' I would not dare to press that analogy too far, but I trust that reading this book has helped to turn your head and your heart in the right direction.

In *The Last Battle*, the final book in *The Chronicles of Narnia*, C. S. Lewis sees heaven as being centred on the great lion Aslan, which Lewis wanted to be seen as a picture of Jesus, who is described in the Bible as 'the Lion of the tribe of Judah' (Revelation 5:5). In the story, the Narnians leave Shadowlands (death) behind and as they move into Aslan's country things begin to happen that, in Lewis' words, 'were so great and beautiful that I cannot write them'. He then adds, 'And for us this is the end of all the stories, and we can most truly say that they all lived happily ever after. But for them it was only the beginning of the real story. All their life in this world and all their adventures in Narnia had only been the cover and the title page. Now at last they were beginning Chapter One of the Great Story which no one on earth has read; which goes on for ever; in which every chapter is better than the one before.'[283]

That sounds remarkably like heaven to me!

Notes

1 Salon.com, 15 September 2011.
2 Walt Whitman, *Song of Myself*, Part 52.
3 Alan Groves, cited in Sinclair Ferguson, *In Christ Alone* (Reformation Trust), p.144.
4 Richard Baxter, in the hymn 'Lord, it belongs not to my care'.
5 Richard Dawkins, *The God Delusion* (Bantam Books), p.117.
6 As above, p.5.
7 *Oxford Dictionary of English* (Oxford University Press), p.379.
8 John Blanchard, *Anyone for Heaven* (EP Books).
9 See Judges 15:14-17.
10 Cited in John Blanchard, *The Complete Gathered Gold* (Evangelical Press), p.379.
11 Cited in George Sweeting, *Great Quotes and Illustrations* (Word Books), p.217.
12 http://www.antiochan.org.
13 *Oxford Dictionary of English*, p.312.
14 R. L. Dabney, *Systematic Theology* (Banner of Truth), p.849.
15 Louis Berkhof, *Systematic Theology*, (Banner of Truth), p.737.
16 *Christian Hymns* (Evangelical Movement of Wales).
17 *Praise!* (Praise Trust).
18 *Oxford Dictionary of English*, p.803.
19 Wilbur Smith, *The Biblical Doctrine of Heaven* (Moody Press), p.27.
20 Berkhof, *Systematic Theology*, pp.60-61.
21 John Calvin, *Institutes of the Christian Religion*, trans. Ford Lewis Battles (Westminster), 2:16:15, p.524.
22 BBC Television, 20 October 2012.

23   J. B. Phillips, *Letters to Young Churches* (Geoffrey Bles), p.18.

24   Philip Graham, Ryken, *What is the Christian Worldview?* (P & R), p.41.

25   William Hendriksen, *New Testament Commentary: The Gospel of Matthew* (Banner of Truth), p.729.

26   Ryken, *What is the Christian Worldview?*, p.35.

27   Stuart Olyott, *The Gospel As It Really is* (Evangelical Press), p.78.

28   Edward Hitchcock, *The Religion of Geology and its Connected Sciences* (Phillips, Sampson and Company), pp.371, 375, 497.

29   F. F. Bruce, "The Bible and the environment", in Morris Inch & Ronald Youngblood (eds.), *Living and Active Word of God: Essays in Honor of Samuel J. Schultz*, (Eisenbrauns), p.30.

30   Derek Kidner, *Genesis: An Introduction and Commentary* (Tyndale Press), p.70.

31   Edgar Andrews, *A Glorious High Throne* (Evangelical Press), p.307.

32   As above, p.456.

33   Spiros Zodhiates, *The Complete Word Study Dictionary: New Testament* (AMG Publishers), p.804.

34   John F. MacArthur, *The Glory of Heaven* (Christian Focus), p 60.

35   J. B. Phillips, *The Book of Revelation* (Collins), p.9.

36   C. H. Spurgeon, *Metropolitan Tabernacle Pulpit*, vol. 26, sermon 1516, 'Salvation by knowing the truth' (1 Timothy 2:3-4).

37   The 1522 'Preface to the Revelation of St. John' in Luther's translation of the New Testament. E. Theodore Bachmann (ed.), *Luther's Works Volume 35: Word and Sacrament I* (Fortress), pp.398-99.

38   R. C. Sproul, *Unseen Realities* (Christian Focus), p.13.

39   J. Philip Arthur, *Strength in Weakness* (Evangelical Press), p.220.

40   Alister E. McGrath, *A Brief History of Heaven* (Blackwell), p.5.

41   Leon Morris, *The Book of Revelation: An Introduction and Commentary* (IVP), p.17.

42   C. H. Spurgeon, *Sword and Trowel*, 1:470, October 1867.

43   J. C. Ryle, *Expository Thoughts of the Gospels: Matthew* (Baker), p.312.

44   Gary Benfold, *Revelation Revealed* (Day One), pp.6-7.

45   Kim Riddlebarger, *Tabletalk*, January 2012 (Ligonier Ministries), p.7.

46   Alister E. McGrath, *NIV Bible Commentary* (Hodder & Stoughton), p.392.

47   Martin Franzmann, *The Word of the Lord Grows* (Concordia), p 270.

48   Thomas N. Smith, *Reformation & Revival*, vol. 6, no. 2, Spring 1997 (Reformation & Revival Ministries), p.1349.

49   Smith, *The Biblical Doctrine of Heaven*, p.249.

50   Benfold, *Revelation Revealed*, p.175.

51   Herman Hoeksema, *Behold He Cometh* (Reformed Free Publishing Association), p.134.

52   As above, p.492.

53   Albert Barnes, *Barnes' Notes on the New Testament* (Kregel), p.1568.

54   John Gilmore, *Probing Heaven* (Baker), p.114.

55   As above, p.116.

56   Morris, *The Book of Revelation*, p.244.

57   John R. W. Stott, *The Message of Ephesians* (IVP), p.107.

58   Luther Poellot, *Revelation* (Concordia), p.285.

59   Matthew Henry, *Matthew Henry's Commentary* (Marshall, Morgan & Scott), p.625.

60   Charles Wesley, in the hymn, ''Tis finished! the Messiah dies', as amended in *Praise!*.

61   *Evangelicals Now,* April 1998.

62   Richard Brooks, *The Lamb is all the Glory* (Evangelical Press), p.185.

63   Henry, *Matthew Henry's Commentary*, p.989.

64   Martyn Lloyd-Jones, *Romans 8:17-39: The Final Perseverance of the Saints* (Banner of Truth), p.80.

65   As above, p.89.

66   Paul Marshall with Lela Gilbert, *Heaven Is Not My Home* (IVP), p.11.

67   Jessie Duplantis, *Heaven, Close Encounters of the God Kind* (Harrison House), p.1.

68   As above, p.21.

69   Paul D. Wolfe, *Setting our Sights on Heaven* (Banner of Truth), p.34.

70   See A. T. Robertson, *Grammar of the Greek New Testament in the Light of Historical Research* (Broadman), p.787.

71   Sproul, *Unseen Realities*, p.81.

72   As above.

73   MacArthur, *The Glory of Heaven*, p.125.

74   C. G. Berkouwer, *De Wederkomst van Christus*, vol. 1 (Kok), p.79, as translated by A. A. Hoekema (*The Bible and the Future* [Eerdmans], p.94).

75   Zodhiates, *The Complete Word Study Dictionary: New Testament*, p.1373.

76   John Murray, *Collected Writings of John Murray* (Banner of Truth), vol. 2, p.403.

77   *TIME,* 24 March 1997, p.75.

78   Randy Alcorn, *Heaven* (Tyndale House), p.112.

79   A. A. Hodge, *The Confession of Faith: A Handbook of Christian Doctrine Expounding the Westminster Confession* (Banner of Truth), p.386.

80   Thomas Watson, *A Body of Divinity* (Banner of Truth), p.305.

81 Calvin, *Institutes of the Christian Religion*, 3:25:8, p.1003.

82 John R. W. Stott, *Men Made New* (IVP), p.97.

83 A. A. Hodge, *Evangelical Theology* (Banner of Truth), p 371.

84 John Flavel, *Works* (Banner of Truth), vol. 3, p.29.

85 Arthur, *Strength in Weakness*, p.136.

86 Murray, *Collected Writings of John Murray*, vol. 2, pp.411-412.

87 Bill Bryson, *At Home* (Doubleday), pp.155, 156.

88 Hendriksen, *The Gospel of Matthew*, p.869.

89 Cited in Blanchard, *The Complete Gathered Gold*, p.565.

90 Cited in James Montgomery Boice, *Philippians* (Zondervan), p.248.

91 C. S. Lewis, *The World's Last Night and Other Essays* (Harcourt, Brace and Company), p.107.

92 William Hendriksen, *New Testament Commentary: 1 & 2 Thessalonians* (Banner of Truth), p.117.

93 As above.

94 Wayne Grudem, *Systematic Theology* (IVP), pp.1158-1159.

95 Anthony Hoekema, *The Bible and The Future* (Eerdmans), p.274.

96 Sproul, *Unseen Realities*, p.39.

97 C. H. Spurgeon, *Metropolitan Tabernacle Pulpit*, vol. 18, sermon 1043, 'Glorious Predestination' (Romans 8:29).

98 Herman Bavinck, *The Doctrine of God* (Banner of Truth), p.343.

99 For an excellent explanation of 'foreknew', see David Steel and Curtis Thomas, *Romans: An Interpretive Outline* (P & R).

100 J. I. Packer, *God's Words* (IVP), p.160.

101 Martin Luther, *Commentary on Romans* (Kregel), p.130.

102 Wolfe, *Setting our Sights on Heaven*, p.31.

103 Bruce Hunt, *For a Testimony* (Banner of Truth), pp.104-105.

104 Stott, *Men Made New*, p.101.

105 Herman Bavinck, *Our Reasonable Faith* (Baker), p.553.

106 Geoffrey Thomas, *Evangelical Times*, September 2012.

107 Thomas Brooks, *The Complete Works of Thomas Brooks* (Banner of Truth), vol. 2, p.317.

108 Fanny Crosby, in the hymn, 'Blessed Assurance'.

109 Simon J. Kistemaker, *New Testament Commentary: Peter and Jude* (Baker), p.45.

110 Augustus M. Toplady, in the hymn 'A debtor to mercy alone'.

111 R. V. G. Tasker, *The Gospel According to Matthew* (Tyndale Press), p.122.

112 Loraine Boettner, *Roman Catholicism* (Banner of Truth), p.377.

113   Alec Motyer, *After Death* (Christian Focus), p.76.

114   Augustine, *Confessions, Book 1.*

115   D. Martyn Lloyd-Jones, *The Christian Warfare* (Banner of Truth), p.155.

116   Zodhiates, *The Complete Word Study Dictionary: New Testament*, p.474.

117   Richard Baxter, *The Saints' Everlasting Rest* (Baker), p.73.

118   K. Scott Oliphint and Sinclair B. Ferguson, *If I Should Die Before I Wake* (Baker), p.81.

119   Thomas Boston, *Human Nature in its Fourfold State,* cited in MacArthur, *The Glory of Heaven*, p.204.

120   Augustine, *The City of God*, Book 22.

121   Alcorn, *Heaven*, p.72.

122   Cited by Lois Hoadley Dick, *Isobel* Kuhn (Bethany House), p.157.

123   Richard Brooks, *The Lamb is all the Glory* (Evangelical Press), p.74.

124   Alec Motyer, *The Prophecy of Isaiah* (IVP), p.529.

125   *Oxford Dictionary of English*, p.1483.

126   Edward Donnelly, *Biblical Teaching on the Doctrines of Heaven and Hell* (Banner of Truth), p.117.

127   As above, p.82.

128   Cited in P. B. Coombs, *Life After Death* (Church Pastoral-Aid Society), p.9.

129   Sigmund Freud, *The Complete Psychological Works,* Vol.14, cited in Eryl Davies, *Condemned for Ever!* (Evangelical Press), p.13.

130   *Daily Telegraph, Seven* magazine, 16 November 2011, p.11.

131   As above, p.13.

132   *Daily Telegraph,* 7 June 2012.

133   Woody Allen, 'Death' (a play) in *Without Feathers.*

134   *Oxford Dictionary of English*, p.1947.

135   Andrews, *A Glorious High Throne*, p.423.

136   C. S. Lewis, *Mere Christianity* (Collins), p.119.

137   Alec Motyer, *The Richness of Christ* (IVP), p.131.

138   John Calvin, *Institutes of the Christian Religion*, 4:17:2, p.1362.

139   Jonathan Edwards, *Heaven: A World of Love* (Calvary Press), p.16.

140   Cited in Dick, *Isobel Kuhn*, p.157.

141   See Zodhiates, *The Complete Word Study Dictionary: New Testament*, p.478.

142   Steven J. Lawson, *Heaven Help Us!*, NavPress, p.142.

143   *Times,* 21 November 2009.

144   Jonathan Edwards, 'The End for which God created the world,' cited in John Piper, *God's Passion for His Glory* (Baker), p.24.

145   Roland Bainton, *Here I Stand* (Lion Publishing), p.296.

146 George Bernard Shaw, *Misalliance, the Dark lady of the Sonnets, and Fanny's First Play* (Wildside Press), p.xlv.

147 Mark Twain, 'Capt. Stormfield's visit to heaven' in Damon Knight (ed.), *The Golden Road* (Simon and Schuster), p.131.

148 John Mortimer, *Character Parts* (Viking), p.182.

149 Henry, *Matthew Henry's Commentary*, p.683.

150 Alcorn, *Heaven*, p.114.

151 As above, p.366.

152 As above, p.259.

153 As above, p.448.

154 As above, p.404.

155 As above, p.388.

156 As above, p.388.

157 As above, p.395.

158 As above, p.399.

159 As above, p.363.

160 As above, p.326.

161 As above, p.275.

162 As above, p.307.

163 As above, p.299.

164 As above, p.188.

165 As above, p.428.

166 As above, p.484.

167 Oliphint and Ferguson, *If I Should Die Before I Wake*, p.94.

168 Cited in Alcorn, *Heaven*, p.104.

169 Leslie S. M'Caw, *The New Bible Commentary* (IVP), p.431.

170 Jonathan Edwards, *The Works of Jonathan Edwards* (Banner of Truth), vol. 2, p.210.

171 Peter Lewis, *The Message of the Living God* (IVP), p.47.

172 C. H. Spurgeon, *The Treasury of David* (Passmore & Alabaster), vol. 1, p.305.

173 C. S. Lewis, *Letters to Malcolm: Chiefly on Prayer* (Harcourt Brace Jovanovich), p.92.

174 Sheldon Vanauken, *A Severe Mercy* (Harper Collins), p.203.

175 Joni Eareckson Tada, *Heaven—Your Real Home* (Zondervan), p.61.

176 Hendrikus Berkhof, *Christ the Meaning of History* (Wipf & Stock), p.188.

177 Augustus H. Strong, *Systematic Theology* (Pickering & Inglis), p.1031.

178 Zodhiates, *The Complete Word Study Dictionary: New Testament*, p.482.

179 John Calvin, *The Epistles of Paul the Apostle to the Romans and to the Thessalonians,* trans. Ross MacKenzie (Eerdmans), p.264.

180 Hodge, *Evangelical Theology*, p.400.

181 Wolfe, *Setting our Sights on Heaven*, p.111.

182 Jamieson, Fausset and Brown, *Commentary on the Whole Bible* (Oliphants), p.1589.

183 Morris, *The Book of Revelation*, pp.177-178.

184 Barnes, *Barnes' Notes on the New Testament*, p.89.

185 Henry, *Matthew Henry's Commentary*, p.585.

186 Morris, *The Book of Revelation*, p.84.

187 David Gooding, *According to Luke: a new exposition of the third Gospel* (IVP), p.333.

188 See Luke 19:11-27.

189 For a very readable discussion of this see Eryl Davies, *Heaven is a Far Better Place* (Evangelical Press), pp.213-233.

190 Craig L. Blomberg, *Journal of the Evangelical Theological Society*, 35/2, June 1992, p.165.

191 Gilmore, *Probing Heaven*, p.277.

192 Davies, *Heaven is a Far Better Place*, p.219.

193 Paul Helm, *The Last Things* (Banner of Truth), p.104.

194 Used in the hymn, 'The sands of time are sinking', by Anne Ross Cousin.

195 Grudem, *Systematic Theology,* p.1145.

196 William B. Barcley, *A Study Commentary on 1 and 2 Timothy* (Evangelical Press), p.251.

197 Henry, *Matthew Henry's Commentary*, p.585.

198 Keith Getty & Kristyn Lennox: © 2003 Thankyou Music/MCPS.

199 Motyer, *After Death*, p.117.

200 William Shakespeare, *As You Like It*, Act 2, Scene 7.

201 Bertrand Russell, *Why I am not a Christian* (Simon and Schuster), p.111.

202 *Oxford Dictionary of English*, p.576.

203 R. L. Dabney, *Systematic Theology* (Banner of Truth), p.849.

204 D. Martyn Lloyd-Jones, *Studies in the Sermon on the Mount* (IVP), vol. 1, p.114.

205 Charles Wesley, in the hymn 'Hark! the herald angels sing'.

206 Lloyd-Jones, *Studies in the Sermon on the Mount*, vol. 1, p.113.

207 Smith, *The Biblical Doctrine of Heaven,* p.254.

208 Thomas Boston, *Human Nature in its Fourfold State,* cited in MacArthur, *The Glory of Heaven*, p.218.

209 Peter Jackson, *Heaven in Sight* (Ambassador Publications), p.156.

210 Donnelly, *Biblical Teaching on the Doctrines of Heaven and Hell,* p.96.

211 Cited in McGrath, *A Brief History of Heaven*, p.36.

212 Tada, *Heaven: Your Real Home,* p.53.

213 Thomas Aquinas, *Summa Theologica*, supplement, q.81, art.1.

214 MacArthur, *The Glory of Heaven*, p.133.

215 Grudem, *Systematic Theology,* p.832.

216 William Hendricksen, *New Testament Commentary: Romans 1-8* (Banner of Truth), p.234.

217 Gerhardt Tersteegen, in the hymn "Midst the darkness, storm, and sorrow".

218 Charles Wesley, from a modern revision of his hymn 'Love divine, all loves excelling'.

219 Millard J. Erickson, *Christian Theology* (Baker), p.1129.

220 Brian Edwards, *Grace – Amazing Grace* (Day One), p.281.

221 As above, p.283.

222 Jonathan Edwards, 'The Christian Pilgrim,' sermon preached in 1733, cited in McGrath, *A Brief History of Heaven*, p.115.

223 Sproul, *Unseen Realities*, p.42.

224 Grudem, *Systematic Theology*, p.1164.

225 Bruce Milne, *Know the Truth* (IVP), p.278.

226 Chris Gray, *Bible Basics* (Chris Gray), p.287.

227 Leon Morris, *The Epistles of Paul to the Thessalonians* (Tyndale Press), p.89.

228 Zodhiates, *The Complete Word Study Dictionary: New Testament*, p.959.

229 Gordon Keddie, *Study Commentary on John* (Evangelical Press), p.75.

230 Stuart Townend/Mark Edwards, 'There is a hope that burns within my heart', © Thankyou Music.

231 Tada, *Heaven: Your Real Home,* p.39.

232 Dan Barber and Robert Peterson, *Life Everlasting* (P & R), p.117.

233 Baxter, *The Saints' Everlasting Rest,* p.62.

234 Donnelly, *Biblical Teaching on the Doctrines of Heaven and Hell,* p.119.

235 Ryken, *What is the Christian Wordview?,* pp.42-43.

236 C. S. Lewis, *The Problem of Pain* (Macmillan), p.147.

237 Edwards, *Heaven: A World of Love*, pp.27-29.

238 Paul Davies, *The Mind of God* (Touchstone Books), p.232.

239 John Gill, *A Body of Doctrinal Divinity* (Christian Classics Ethereal Library), pp.638-639.

240 Alfred Lord Tennyson, *In Memoriam A.H.H.*, Canto 56.

241 Motyer, *The Prophecy of Isaiah,* p.124.

242 *The UK Clean Air Act 1956: An Empirical Investigation*, by Veronica Giussani, C SERGE Working Paper GEC 94–20, p.50.

243 Milne, *Know the Truth*, p.68.

244 Helm, *The Last Things*, p.92.

245 Motyer, *The Prophecy of Isaiah*, p.530.

246 David Dickson, *A Commentary on the Psalms* (Banner of Truth), p.278.

247 Boston, *Human Nature in its Fourfold State*, cited in MacArthur, *The Glory of Heaven*, pp.226-227.

248 Zodhiates, *The Complete Word Study Dictionary: New Testament*, p.475.

249 C. S. Lewis, *Theology*, November 1941 (S.P.C.K.).

250 Zodhiates, *The Complete Word Study Dictionary: New Testament*, p.1454.

251 Arthur, *Strength in Weakness*, p.184.

252 John R. W. Stott, *The Message of Galatians* (IVP), p.148.

253 Voddie Baucham, *Tabletalk*, August 2012 (Ligonier Ministries), p.83.

254 Martin Luther, *Bondage of the Will*, ed. H. Cole (Fleming H. Revell), p.26.

255 Cited in Sidney Greidanus, *Preaching Christ from the Old Testament* (Eerdmans), p.120.

256 Cited in McGrath, *A Brief History of Heaven*, pp.174-175.

257 C. S. Lewis, *Surprised by Joy* (Collins), p.182.

258 *Evangelical Times*, November 2012.

259 Don Fortner, *The Church of God* (Evangelical Press), p.3.

260 Olyott, *The Gospel As It Really Is*, p.136.

261 J. C. Ryle, *Expository Thoughts on the Gospels* (Baker), vol. 2, pp.115–116.

262 C. H. Spurgeon, *Metropolitan Tabernacle Pulpit*, vol. 37, sermon 2234, 'The Best Donation' (2 Corinthians 8:5).

263 Wolfe, *Setting our Sights on Heaven*, p.151.

264 Erickson, *Christian Theology*, p.1229.

265 C. H. Spurgeon, *The Treasury of David*, vol. 6, pp.428-29.

266 Tom Ascol, 'One Family under God', *Tabletalk*, March 2013 (Ligonier Ministries), p.27.

267 Lewis, *The Message of the Living God*, p.327.

268 Lewis, *Mere Christianity*, p.118.

269 Cited in George R. Knight, *Exploring Hebrews: A Devotional Commentary* (Pacific Press), p.183.

270 John Gillespie, *Beware of living too long!* (Day Three Editions), p.161.

271 John Blanchard, *Major Points from the Minor Prophets* (EP Books) , pp.267-274.

272 Jim Elliot, *The Journals of Jim Elliot*, ed. Elisabeth Elliot (Fleming H. Revell), p.174.

273 Cited in Eric Metaxes, *Bonhoeffer: Pastor, Martyr, Prophet, Spy* (Thomas Nelson), p.531.

274 Eberhard Bethge, *Dietrich Bonhoeffer: A Biography* (Fortress Press), p.927.

275 Cited in Blanchard, *The Complete Gathered Gold*, p.136.

276 As above, p.141.

277 Isobel Kuhn, *In the Arena* (OMF Books), p.232.

278 Packer, *God's Words*, p.104.

279 Jonathan Edwards, *The Works of Jonathan Edwards* (Banner of Truth), vol. 2, p.243.

280 Cited in Jock Purves, *Fair Sunshine* (Banner of Truth), pp.191–192.

281 *Evangelicals Now*, April 2012, p.17.

282 *Evangelicals Now*, May 2012, p.17.

283 C. S. Lewis, *The Last Battle* (Harper Collins), p.228.